ADAM SMITH'S SOCIOLOGICAL ECONOMICS

Adam Smith's Sociological Economics

D.A. REISMAN

CROOM HELM LONDON

BARNES & NOBLE BOOKS · NEW YORK

(a division of Harper & Row Publishers, Inc.)

Published in Great Britain 1976
© 1976 by D.A. Reisman

Croom Helm Ltd, 2-10 St. John's Road, London SW11

ISBN 0-85664-284-3

Published in the U.S.A. 1976 by
Harper & Row Publishers, Inc.
Barnes & Noble Import Division
ISBN 0-06-495830-2

Printed in Great Britain
by Redwood Burn Ltd, Trowbridge and Esher

CONTENTS

1 INTRODUCTION

John Stuart Mill warned that the definition of a science, like the walls of a city, is usually constructed 'not to be a receptacle for such edifices as might afterwards spring up, but to circumscribe an aggregation already in existence'.[1] Aggregations change, and there is no reason to suppose that the scope and method of economics in the eighteenth century were the same as they are today, after making allowance for the fact that its techniques were less sophisticated and its scholars less enlightened. In particular, the attempt to interpret Adam Smith as a primitive forebear of Paul Samuelson (*homo sapiens*) rather than as a thinker in his own right, unique but equal, has led to a considerable misapprehension of Smith's theories of economics and sociology. It is the aim of the present study to show how synthesis and human society formed the basis of Smith's multidisciplinary model of man and to point out that it is precisely in these respects that his approach most differed from that of the present day.

Lord Robbins defines economics as the science which expresses one thing in terms of another, a state of mind which can be applied to the precise subjective valuation of any trade-off between two objects or activities, where indulging one desire means foregoing the other: 'Economics is the science which studies human behaviour as a relationship between ends and scarce means which have alternative uses.'[2] If Robinson Crusoe talks to his parrot, this is as much economic activity as if he were to dig potatoes; and the cost of allocating time to a discussion with his parrot is an opportunity cost, the number of potatoes foregone. Unfortunately, there are an infinite number of economic relationships of the form: 'The cost of reading *The Wealth of Nations* is the opportunity sacrificed of practising the tuba.' No economist, however dedicated and talented, can cope with an infinite number of relationships. A choice must be made; and an empirical study would almost certainly reveal that economists today are more concerned with the production, distribution and exchange of what Marshall referred to as 'the material requisites of wellbeing'[3] than with the production, distribution and exchange of, say, philosophical ideas.

Economics, in the last analysis, is what economists do; and a science which defines itself in terms of a subjective perception, scarcity, cannot logically be faulted for concerning itself with improved allocation and expanded production. Adam Smith too was concerned with these problems, with allocation (for example, by the unfettered and invisible hand of perfect competition in markets unregulated either by the state

9

or by private monopolies) and with production (for example, through the division of labour and the accumulation of capital). His approach to these questions, however, differed in three fundamental respects from that of the modern economist: First, he saw economic actions as forming only one strand in a massive interdisciplinary pattern, and stressed interconnection (of individuals and of academic disciplines) rather than intellectual isolation. Second, he believed his massive social aggregate to be in the process of change, and sought to predict the direction in which it was evolving. Third, he was an economic determinist, convinced that social and institutional phenomena are principally emanations of a country's habitual manner of working and earning a living. It will perhaps clarify the argument to examine each of these points in more detail.

First, Adam Smith saw society as an aggregate of Robinson Crusoes, living together and not in isolation, and interacting with one another in institutions and according to norms accepted by all participants as proper. He was particularly interested in those ideas which Nisbet identifies as the 'nucleus of the sociological tradition', namely 'community, authority, status, the sacred, and alienation'.[4] Thus he believed that, in a stable community, people are led by the love of sympathy from the spectator to conform to socially sanctioned standards of propriety and patterns of behaviour; and that these social instincts rather than mere individual self-interest or the pursuit of a utilitarian goal were essential to ensure predictability in role-playing and thus to preserve social cohesion and solidarity. As for authority, he studied the redistribution of power between social groups (such as aristocracy, clergy, monarchy, capitalist entrepreneurs, salaried managers, family) that resulted from economic upheaval, and welcomed the resultant balance of political power for the same reason that he had welcomed the balance of countervailing power in the economy: the inability of any individual or group to impose his will on all others. He recognised that traditional status positions would be modified once they were confronted with the new three-class structure based on the factor-incomes of rent, profit and wages; but welcomed the continuance of the older orders as a source of continuity. As for the sacred, he was aware that monolithic established churches were threatened by the process of economic growth, and that science would destroy superstition; but he felt that small sects, more suitable and sensitive to the needs of the common people, would develop instead. Finally, concerning alienation, he felt that the division of labour and resultant concentration on one small task would mean the intellectual starvation of the lower classes; while anomie or normlessness might result from the concentration of population in the impersonal anonymity of new urban agglomerations, and from the rapid changes in norms of propriety that rapid economic growth would create. All of this was to be perceived subjectively: like Max Weber, Smith was passionately concerned with the subjective meaning that human interaction had for the individuals involved.

Such an approach is broader than that usually taken by the economist, and is easiest to describe in terms of what Emile Durkheim called 'sociology'. Aware of the need to reunite the parts to form a whole, anxious lest excessive abstraction cause people to 'create a mental construction out of nothing', Durkheim says: 'At all times, economic phenomena, the state, law, morality and religion have been studied scientifically, thus giving birth to five sciences which can rightly be called sociological . . . Political economy loses its autonomy, because one cannot study one social function wholly in isolation from others.'[5] Smith avoided the temptation to reify economic activity, to study the economy as if it were an empirical entity and not merely a fictitious theoretical construct, by situating economic activity in a complex matrix that included all other functions and sub-systems of the social organism or machine. As Parsons has pointed out, neither Pareto nor Weber was successful in this task of constructing a multi-disciplinary model of man, although both realised that synthesis rather than decomposition and reduction was a precondition for total explanation, whether or not it was useful for the simple prediction of habitual associations.[6] To some extent Parsons himself has remedied the defect by constructing holistic, totalitarian models of empirical phenomena rather than trying to isolate some unidisciplinary aspect of them.[7]

Adam Smith shared this distrust of idealised and partial models; and would probably have dismissed much of contemporary economic theory as an alienated approach where things and symbols representing things take on a fictitious identity of their own. Because of his anthropocentrism, he would have sought to integrate economic activity into the broad science of humanity which he (like Comte later) was trying to create, independent of theology and metaphysics. Lines of demarcation between the disciplines that constitute that science of humanity may exist today, but they were meaningless and non-existent in the eighteenth century. As Burrow warns us, 'The intellectual historian should not allow today's conceptual maps to obliterate or distort those of the past, which it is his job to recover and explain . . . There seems no *prima facie* reason for supposing that everyone, or indeed anyone, in the past might have been like us.'[8] The problem with Adam Smith is not simply where to locate a cosmopolitan intellectual of the eighteenth century in terms of the boundaries laid down by our more modern maps, but also where he would have located himself. Here his view is clear: since academic overspecialisation can so easily lead to confusion, intellectual anomie, and the emergence of the Fachidiot, it is best not to locate oneself at all. As Montesquieu says, 'tout est extrèmement lié', and for this reason the scholar ought to do nothing but observe everything.

Smith, a sometime (1752-1763) Professor of Moral Philosophy in the University of Glasgow and perennial intellectual in an age which, as Hampson puts it, 'would have regarded the conception of "two cultures" as equivalent to no culture at all',[9] would be a bit of an embarrassment nowadays, and most of all to the brotherhood of economists. It is unfortunately all too often the case in today's rigid academic environment that an economist who rejects or questions the positivist and utilitarian Geist that has become compulsory in his subject finds himself defined out of economics altogether, as has been the case with Sombart, Weber and Veblen. Were Adam Smith alive today, his contempt for our own conventional wisdom, as Professor Galbraith has said, 'could probably have cost him any chance for tenure in any modern department of economics that is decently beholden to the accepted view'.[10] The need to survive professionally in a free labour market, the desire for 'sympathy' from one's colleagues, the love of a quiet existence free from controversy, the imperative of a hungry mortgage to support, all effectively prevent a new Adam Smith from arising. The true wealth of nations may be its youth;[11] but each generation of economists, by passing on the same unidisciplinary methodological tradition it inherited, by concentrating on techniques to the exclusion of ideas, by always asking 'how' and never 'why', is only creating its successors in its own image.

As well as cutting across disciplines to study phenomena, there is a second aspect of Smith's thought that is worth noting: his view that a purely empirical approach to economy and society must be supplemented by historicism, since what human institutions are today is only part of a great chain extending from what they were to what they will become.[12] No man steps more than once into the same river, matter is in motion, and it is of the utmost importance not just to study what is but what is about to be. The social sciences are dynamic, and a new environment is evolving before our very eyes.

Smith believed that economic progress would bring considerable benefits. It would create jobs for the unemployed, raise the living standards of the lower classes, weaken the despotic authority of aristocracy, clergy and state, and reverse the managerial revolution. It would foster freedom of speech, security of contract, security of property rights, the rule of law. It would lead to the establishment of rational religion, founded on the commercial principle of free competition (a power so strong that it could even force the universities to abandon the teaching of antiquated and outdated systems of ideas). In the course of economic progress, moral empiricism would replace casuistry of all sorts and science would vanquish superstition. Meanwhile, the very process of economic advance itself would mean increased resources and greater leisure for scientific investigation and artistic activity. All these social benefits were of more importance to Smith than the obvious, intended, manifest objectives of economic activity, i.e. commodity-utility for the consumer and profit-making for the producer.

Alongside its benefits, however, Smith was aware that economic advance had its disadvantages as well. Work (seldom enjoyable and creative at the best of times, and almost always performed so as to be able to buy consumer goods with one's pay) comes to have an adverse intellectual effect on the masses once the division of labour proceeds beyond a certain point. Martial virtues and education are neglected, the family decays, moral standards become muddled because rapid change destabilises accepted standards of propriety and because reduced opportunities for human contact in industrial towns means there is no impartial spectator of man's behaviour. Social conflict can result from the antagonism of labour to capital, an antagonism arising either for objective reasons (in a market economy, factor-shares depend on market power, not justice or productivity, and may reflect exploitation) or purely subjectively (men desire independence, and resent and envy their bosses). In a dynamic commercial society, utility comes to supplant propriety as the basis for decision-making, and solidarity comes to depend more and more on the complementarity of self-love, the exchange of equivalents, and the commercial mentality. Commodity consumption and the status that expensive symbols confer make men excessively ambitious, thus causing them to lose their tranquility and peace of mind. Scarcity is a social perception of which we may be far more aware than any savage is; and in that sense possibly civilisation breeds its own discontents.

Thirdly, the new environment which is evolving before our very eyes is, to an economic determinist like Adam Smith, evolving principally because of economic causes: a unique set of wants, a unique set of patterns of conduct and character, a unique set of institutions, all constitute the social superstructure which must arise and does arise from a unique economic basis. Economics cannot be about scarcity if the very perception of scarcity is social, a desire to acquire those tokens which in a particular society are properly and habitually associated with prestige and power. Nor can it be about the universal expression of pecuniary self-interest, since Smith insists that a man's character is the result, not the cause, of the way he earns a living; and that, similarly, a nation's character is the product of the most common form of economic activity practised within it (not a reflection of climate or geography save in so far as they influence economic activity; nor of religion or government save in so far as they are influenced by it). Furthermore, economic activity cannot be seen as imprisoned within the narrow confines of institutional constraint, since those very institutions are the product of the economic basis and change with it: thus commerce and the market mechanism helped destroy feudalism, introduce the rule of law and the balance of powers, and strengthen the House of Commons.

Man makes his own history and is in turn made by it. The empirical method means the observation of habitual associations; but those associations, rather than being static, are productive of changes which transcend them and establish a new economic basis generating a new set of habitual associations. There is a natural equilibrium in a given situation, but that very equilibrium is productive of its own transcendence. The conservative who identifies aesthetic beauty with habitual association must be made to grasp that the proper pursuit by the businessman of proper ends with proper means will lead to a negation of both ends and means and the establishment of a new convention of habitual associations, in a quite different institutional environment. It is impossible to escape from the Existentialist concept of the absurd: what we consume, what we do, even who we are, is only meaningful in a particular situation, which indeed our action may help to destroy. To an economic determinist such as Adam Smith, the institutional and normative framework of society cannot simply be dismissed with a 'ceteris paribus' assumption: economic activity itself is alone enough to prevent *ceteris* from remaining *paribus*.

It is impossible, once the interdependence of phenomena has been posited, once social science has been defined dynamically as the science of 'becoming', once the social and intellectual superstructure have been identified as the product of the economic basis, to deny the responsibility of the scientist. Galbraith wryly notes 'the sharp cleavage which exists in our attitude towards technological and social change. If a man seeks to design a better mousetrap he is the soul of enterprise; if he seeks to design a better society he is a crackpot.'[13] Yet for Adam Smith this classical dichotomy did not exist: Firstly, the sovereign consumer who votes for a mousetrap is not expressing his individuality so much as the reflexes conditioned in him by life in a particular society which resulted from a particular economic basis; and, secondly, economic change, whether to produce a better mousetrap or a better colour television, inevitably has the latent function of bringing about social change. In short, the mousetrap and the social whole are inevitably and inextricably linked. Whereas, however, the scientist can find objective criteria for deciding which is the better of the two mouse-traps, he is bound to have more difficulty in finding objective criteria for deciding between two social systems.

Naturally, there is an alternative course of action open to him, namely to flee altogether from the choice and concentrate simply on the correct formulation of verifiable or falsifiable hypotheses. Here discovery of 'what is' replaces discussion of 'what ought to be'. Kolakowski criticises such positivism for being 'the escapist's design for living . . . an act of escape from commitments, an escape masked as a definition of knowledge'.[14] But Adam Smith was no escapist: because of his economic determinism and his belief that 'what is' is productive of 'what is about to be', he was unable to avoid commitment. Try as he might to remain the impartial spectator of other people's habitual associations, he was nonetheless ultimately forced to ask himself if 'what is' is actually producing 'what ought to be' and not generating 'what ought not to be' by an act of deplorable perversity. Dispassionate observation cannot but be joined by passionate commitment once the scholar reaches the conclusion that means are productive of ends.

Manipulation of symbols is no excuse for avoiding concepts them-selves. Smith's view of the intimate and reciprocal relationship between sociology and philosophy resembles that of C. Wright Mills who, like many thinkers, related freedom to the constraint of engagement:

> That men have lived in certain kinds of society in the past does not set exact or absolute limits to the kinds of society they may create in the future. We study history to discern the alternatives within which human reason and human freedom can now make history . . . Freedom is, first of all, the chance to formulate the available choices, to argue over them − and then, the opportunity to choose.[15]

Smith chose. A narrow constructionist tends to see the role of the economist in terms of making an existing machine work more efficiently; while a broad constructionist like Adam Smith tries to compare the existing machine in its situational context with the machine and the situation that will take its place. Economics to Smith was about creating facts: if he advocated the market-mechanism and laissez-faire, if his ideology depends so much on self-interest, this must be seen as part of an attempt at social engineering, an attempt to produce an ideal society, adequately affluent but not excessively individualist. Smith persevered in his advocacy of mercantile and industrial means to attain this desirable end, but neglected to say what would happen once the goal was reached. The mighty djinn might refuse to return to the bottle, the master might become the slave, and *ceteris* might go on becoming progressively less *paribus* until finally even the ideal situation so desired by the philosopher becomes itself transcended. History teaches us that it was impossible to turn off the tap of revolutionary change in 1851. Smith did not foresee the general commodity-hedonism of the affluent society, the universality of the commercial mentality, the rise of the large corporation with its economies of scale, or of the large trade union and strong state to provide countervailing power. Nor did he anticipate political democracy and the enfranchisement of the masses. His dynamism did not extend from the negation of the negation to the negation of the negation's negation, and his guarded optimism about the future of civil society may not have been borne out by events. Were Adam Smith to converse over coffee or a pot of ale after a meeting of the Edinburgh Poker Club with one of our contemporary economists, he would probably emerge shattered from the encounter and dismiss the man as a sort of Captain Ahab, blinded by his obsession, compulsively searching for an elusive white whale. Ahab, at least, could himself admit what the contemporary economist would not even care to discuss: 'All my means are sane: my motives and object mad.'

Adam Smith was born in Kirkcaldy on the 5th of June, 1723, and died in Edinburgh on the 17th of July, 1790, aged 67. Educated at the University of Glasgow and at Oxford, the highest academic post he held was as Professor of Moral Philosophy in Glasgow; and he also spent just under three years in Paris, Geneva and Toulouse as tutor to the Duke of Buccleuch (from whom he later received an annuity that permitted him to spend much time in Kirkcaldy reading, writing and thinking) and thirteen years as Commissioner of Customs in Edinburgh. He was an intellectual in an era when intellectuals enjoyed meeting together to discuss virtually everything (from speculative philosophy to astronomy, aesthetics, political economy, ethics, politics); and was a leading member of that remarkable group of thinkers sometimes referred to as the Scottish Enlightenment. He was bookish, academic, absent-minded, and at times a trifle eccentric. He was unmarried.

His main works are five in number: *The Theory of Moral Sentiments* (1759), *The Wealth of Nations* (1776), two sets of students' lecture notes, *Lectures on Rhetoric and Belles Lettres* (given in 1762-3) and *Lectures on Justice, Police, Revenue and Arms* (given in 1763), and a collection of essays published posthumously under the title *Essays on Philosophical Subjects* (1975). Virtually all other manuscripts were destroyed at his death by his faithful friends, Hutton and Black.[16]

Lukács regards Smith as a pioneer of bourgeois ideology, a man responsible for some of the 'great scientific pronouncements of the bourgeois class'.[17] In this he is following Marx who was convinced that Smith, like Balzac, mirrored the fanatical utilitarian money-worship characteristic of the new world the commercial and industrial middle classes were in the process of creating: 'According to Adam Smith, *society* is a *commercial enterprise*. Every one of its members is a *salesman*.'[18] Certainly it is possible that Smith's attitude to life was influenced by the material environment in which he lived and worked, since it posed the questions he was trying to answer, and that environment was clearly one of economic advance: rapid expansion of overseas trade, the enclosure movement in agriculture, capital accumulation, the beginnings of the factory system, the improvements in transport, the use of steam power, the birth of the urban working class (raising in turn problems of idleness and unemployment), were all characteristic of the increasingly commercial and industrial world that was evolving. Moreover, Smith was particularly concerned with laws (e.g. of primogeniture), institutions (e.g. apprenticeship) and ideas (e.g. mercantilism) which had clearly become fetters on the expansion of the bourgeois mode of production. It is perhaps symbolic that, of his two great books, the first was published in the same year as the opening of the Carron ironworks, and the second in the year of the American Revolution. In the background to Smith's work lurks the spectre of continental absolutism, of Prussian and Hapsburg bureaucracy, of the extravagance of Versailles and Sans Souci, as well as the doubling of the British national debt in the Seven Years War (1756-63) and the outdated restraints on commerce in France which were clearly making many a good French burgess distinctively restive.

Naturally, Smith was not alone in discussing the economic and social problems of his times. As part of a cosmopolitan republic of letters stretching from St Petersburg (where there was no significant bourgeoisie) to St Andrews by way of Paris, it is no surprise that he shared many beliefs, attitudes and ideas common to Enlightenment intellectuals. The same year as the opening of the Carron ironworks also saw the publication of Voltaire's *Candide* and Johnson's *Rasselas*, while the year of the American Revolution witnessed Bentham's *Fragment on Government*. It could even be argued that Smith's ideals had little directly to do with the material basis of his society, and were hammered out in general philosophical debates in the taverns of Edinburgh and the salons of Paris. Smith may have seen the bourgeoisie as playing some great historical role of which it was unaware, and may himself have been unaware of the great need felt by shopkeepers and manufacturers for an articulate and enlightened spokesman. In other words, similarity of ideas need not mean congruence of ideology. Certain it is that Smith, a serious-minded academic rather than an entrepreneur or a gambler, did not personally share that love of hedonistic commodity-utility or aggressive profit-maximisation that one would expect from the ideologue of a society comprised of salesmen.

In this book we will not attempt to answer the difficult question of how far Smith's own *Weltanschauung* was itself the product of the economic basis of his society, of how far he enunciated the new ideas generated by that new basis rather than by his own personality or through the abstract philosophical discussions in which he participated with friends. In any case, it is important not to oversimplify the complexity and organic solidarity of Smith's writings into a neo-Benthamite utilitarian ideology which it most assuredly was not. Smith is a difficult author whose name has often been invoked by men he would instantaneously have disliked to support causes he would have viewed with extreme suspicion. The fact that he elected to write the economic sociology of a period of intense commercial and industrial activity does not mean he was forced to surrender his academic detachment. The fact that he chose to be a philosopher of the business life does not mean he was any the less a philosopher.

Indeed, had Adam Smith been less of a philosopher, he would probably have been a happier man. The theme of this book is his fundamental moral dilemma: convinced that there is massive interdependence between the parts of the social whole; convinced that the totality is in the process of 'becoming'; convinced that the social superstructure results from the economic basis, Smith felt unable to stop himself from looking into the distance and wondering if what is 'about to be' is what 'ought to be'. His sense of the absurd forced him to eat from the forbidden tree of the knowledge of good and evil. Because the empirical choices expressed in the market-place and the behaviour patterns of economic actors are no more than the results of social conditioning, the economic factor must be studied in its social context. And if wants and character patterns are dynamic, not static, then the economist becomes a sort of futurologist. He cannot help wondering what the symmetrical barbed-wire fences, the pleasant if austere barracks, the gently curving concrete ovens will be used for, and whether or not the future will be productive of more happiness than the present. Here a 'mass flight from reality into statistics'[19] is not enough. The economist is forced to compare one situation with another. But such thoughts are dangerous: when the little men in white coats come for him, they will find nothing more than a babbling social philosopher.

So it was with Adam Smith, whose humanism caused him to leave the paradise of positive science and dwell East of Eden with those who, as Albion Small put it, saw the human process as

the tribunal of last resort for verdict upon the economic process . . . The apostolic succession in social philosophy from Adam Smith is through the sociologists rather than the economists. The sociologists have kept alive the vital spark of Smith's moral philosophy. They have contended for a view of life in terms of persons rather than in terms of technology. That is, they have put *persons* in the center of their picture of life, and have assigned a subordinate place to the theory of those technical activities which deal with the material products of persons.[20]

2 METHODOLOGY

Introduction

Adam Smith sought to construct a closed system from proper association, beauty and utility. Men derive aesthetic pleasure from the
contemplation of means ideally suited to ends, from observing behaviour
in conformity and harmony with the social norm rather than deviating
from it, from a scientific system which demonstrates unity amidst the
variety of diverse phenomena and makes quantitative prediction
possible. Beauty consists in balance, arrangement, connection, correct-
ness, continuity, tranquillity, and hence scientific inquiry is the essential
means of combating aesthetic discomfort, of pacifying that psychological unrest which arises when the observer notices something out of the
ordinary which he cannot classify or fit into his established frame of
reference.

A rusty machine is 'naturally offensive' quite apart from the
utilitarian product it produces; but, since beauty consists in the optimal
adjustment of means to ends, that product results too, as an unintended
outcome. Society is just such a machine: its smooth functioning is only
possible if each person plays his assigned role with propriety, and such
proper and habitual associations are beautiful and agreeable in themselves, independent of their utilitarian implications.

Society is desirable for its own sake, and is far more than a mere
contractual arrangement for the preservation of life and property.
There is no conflict of interest between the individual and the group
precisely because the group mind is internalised in the individual: man
is born in society and to break away from it is to alienate part of himself from the other part in the interests of some ephemeral and probably
fictitious 'individual' freedom. Yet a life in society presupposes propriety of sentiments, which in turn depends on a high degree of
sensitivity to the reactions of our fellow men and a strong desire to
accommodate ourselves to the social norm. In short, a life in society
presupposes that each man becomes, in some measure, a philosopher.
There is a strong pragmatic streak in positivism, epitomised by Comte's
dictum 'Savoir pour prévoir, prévoir pour pouvoir'; and to a man in
society this inevitably refers to the need to discover proper convections
of sentiments (so as to win the approval of the 'impartial spectator' of
his actions). It does not refer to the pursuit of utility or the practicality
of results. Thus, whereas John Stuart Mill believed that the development of a science of ethics along the lines of experimental physics
would replace evaluation based on intention by evaluation based on
outcome, Adam Smith took the view that social propriety is social duty

regardless of actual consequences. Propriety of sentiments remains the immediate guideline of action. Nonetheless, the 'beauty of order'[1] and the utility of the smoothly functioning social whole do result, and are unintended outcomes. Such beneficent consequences suggest that perhaps the rational 'why' can after all be deduced from the instinctual 'how': '(Nature) has . . . not only endowed mankind with an appetite for the end which she proposes, but likewise with an appetite for the means by which alone this end can be brought about, for their own sakes, and independent of their tendency to produce it.'[2]

Man in society attempts to act as a scientist, isolating and identifying the proper mode of function of each element in the social matrix, and also (in the absence of any other standard) infers propriety from probability. Moreover, man applies the same method to the study of natural phenomena, once they arouse his curiosity and as soon as he discovers that metaphysics yields poor predictions: he orders and systematises the raw data of experience and induces laws from it which tell him what to expect in a particular situation. Naturally, no law can systematise the totality of experience, which must remain in the shadows. Absolute Truth cannot be discovered, and certainly should not be sought for its own sake: even an incorrect or partially correct theory is acceptable to an epistemological sceptic (so long as it is comprehensive yet simple, uses familiar concepts, and is aesthetically satisfying) provided that it yields good predictions and thereby stills the unrest of the senses.

Different societies generate different sets of habitual associations, and in that sense much of science is social science. Moreover, there is a two-way relationship between science and society: scientific knowledge raises the national income (providing leisure, opulence, and more opportunity to create knowledge), helps to alter the material infrastructure (encouraging civil society, the market, and especially law and order, the preconditions for inquiry, growth, and more inquiry), and thus participates in the creation of a new set of habitual associations demanding investigation. Like Heraclitus and Bergson, Smith saw social reality as existing in a state of flux. This being the case, the work of the scientist is never done.

Aesthetics too, like the sciences, both exists in a social context and is to be concerned with prediction and propriety (rather than with trivial qualitative relationships of shape and colour). There may or may not be an ideal standard of perfect beauty: but if the beauty arising from customary association should conflict with the absolute, it is the latter that must give way. Human communication is approximate at the best of times, and relies on the stimulation of a predictable response by a conventionally specified symbol. Only if such social standards of propriety are clear and respected will society be like an orchestra, playing in unison because each instrument accepts its function as proper.

In this Chapter we shall examine four aspects of the 'beauty of order'. In Section I we will discuss Smith's epistemological scepticism and his stress on the passionate source of knowledge (in contrast to the Puritan doctrine of the mortification of the flesh, to casuistry, to idealism of all kinds), in Section II, the features of a good theory in the sciences (natural or social); in Section III, the importance of aesthetics; and in Section IV, the relationship between the sciences and the arts on the one hand, and economy and society on the other.

I. Epistemology

Adam Smith believed that sense perception is the only dependable means of acquiring knowledge about external phenomena. Like Locke he rejected the Platonic notion of innate ideas (emphasised in the seventeenth century by Descartes and in the eighteenth by Leibniz), according to which basic truths reside automatically in the intellect, since there is nothing in the mind that was not first in the senses. Like Locke, he believed that the mind is initially 'white paper, void of all character, without any ideas',[1] which subsequently obtains knowledge by observation and induction from experience: as Locke wrote, 'since there appear not to be any ideas in the mind before the senses have conveyed any in, I conceive that the ideas in the understanding are coeval with *sensation*'.[2] In short, knowledge is *a posteriori*, not *a priori*: it follows experience and does not precede it, and depends very much on the link with reality provided by the passions. Smith would have accepted Hume's view that 'it is impossible for us to *think* of any thing, which we have not antecedently *felt*'.[3] After all, Smith believed Hume to be 'by far the most illustrious philosopher and historian of the present age',[4] and actively participated with him in the Enlightenment's struggle against metaphysics, superstition, the unquestioning acceptance of outmoded traditions and values, against mere 'sophistry and illusion'.[5] In that struggle the watchword might well have been Hume's dictum: 'A wise man . . . proportions his belief to the evidence.'[6]

In his essay 'Of the External Senses', Smith expounds his view of the sources and the limitations of our knowledge of external phenomena, and demonstrates his debt to Locke and Hume. This is particularly clear in his example of the table. Suppose I lay my hand upon the table. I am bound to discover that, despite the force of gravity, the movement of my hand is impeded by some external resistance; and by this means I become aware of the existence of the table, and of the fact that it is both external to me and independent of my hand. In this sense each of us is like a man born blind who learns about the nature of external phenomena by touching and groping: 'Pressure or resistance necessarily supposes externality in the thing which presses or resists. The table could not press upon, or resist the further motion of my hand, if it was not external to my hand.'[7]

Unfortunately, however, such certainty does not extend from touching to feeling. My perception that an object feels warm only means that it arouses this sensation to me; and my perception that I feel cold tells me more about myself than it does about the weather. Whereas I can be reasonably confident about the existence and nature of my sense-perception, I can never be at all sure how well it captures or reproduces all the objective features of the external object:

> What we feel while we stand in the sunshine during a hot, or in the shade during a frosty, day, is evidently felt, not as pressing upon the body, but as in the body. It does not necessarily suggest the presence of any external object, nor could we from thence alone infer the existence of any such object. It is a sensation which neither does nor can exist any where but either in the organ which feels it, or in the unknown principle of perception, whatever that may be, which feels in that organ, or by means of that organ . . . The sensations of heat and cold do not necessarily suggest the presence of any external object. [8]

Three observations may be made about this example:

First, Smith (unlike Berkeley and Hume) appears to have accepted Locke's distinction between the primary and the secondary qualities of an object, and thus to have believed that we can perceive more than merely our perceptions, sense more than simply our sensations. Locke argued that primary qualities (such as solidity, size and shape of an object) are not only quantitative and measureable, but can be said to exist objectively, independent of the percipient. The existence of such 'originals' cannot but lead to a philosophy which is a form of materialism. Secondary qualities, on the other hand (such as colour, sound and taste), being qualitative stimuli and no more, are as liable to be in the mind of the observer as in the object perceived. Locke expresses the distinction as follows: 'The ideas of primary qualities of bodies are resemblances of them, and their patterns do really exist in the bodies themselves, but the ideas produced in us by these secondary qualities have no resemblance of them at all. There is nothing like our ideas, existing in the bodies themselves.'[9]

Consider the example of 'a piece of manna of a sensible bulk'. This object, Locke says,

> is able to produce in us the idea of a round or square figure and by being removed from one place to another, the idea of motion. The idea of motion represents it as it really is in manna moving: a circle or square are the same, whether in idea or existence, in the mind or in the manna. And thus, both motion and figure, are really in the manna, whether we take notice of them or no.[10]

The sensations of sweetness and whiteness, however, unlike motion and figure, are not really in the manna, even if we do take notice of them: such secondary qualities 'are but the effects of the operations of manna, by the motion, size, and figure of its particles, on the eyes and palate'.[11] Clearly, what is in the mind of the observer should not be attributed to the object observed.

Smith's example of the table, and his distinction between touching (of primary qualities which are inherent in and inseparable from the object) and feeling (of secondary qualities which may only exist in the intellect of the percipient subject), shows he followed the Lockean dualism between mind and matter. In doing so, of course, he laid himself open to the usual criticisms of such dualism: from materialists (that the philosopher underestimates the importance of 'noumena', of objective reality, of 'things as they really are') and from idealists (that 'to be' is the same as 'to be perceived', and that all we can know is the content of our own minds). Smith was certainly guilty of what A.N. Whitehead calls the 'fallacy of misplaced concreteness' in that he did believe it was meaningful to distinguish between touching and feeling, two kinds of experiental sensations which a mentalist would find it hard to distinguish. Smith believed that the material object to which we give the name 'table' actually exists independently of the perceptions of the sensing agent, and that man cannot create nature simply by thinking; but it is hard to defend him against the quasi-Berkeleyean argument that shape and size may be no less immaterial, no less mental, than are colour and sound.

Secondly, Smith's example of the table, because it shows his scepticism about the extent to which we can ever get at the essence of things, helps to explain the importance he assigned to the regular recurrence of sense impressions and empirically ascertained habitual associations as a source of knowledge. Descartes and Leibniz had believed that innate ideas had been implanted by God in the mind of

each individual, which made logical deduction of further truths from
these initial axioms a reasonable method of building up a picture of
reality. Smith, because he could not accept the existence or validity of
these first principles (which are in fact more likely than not the result
of unconscious environmental conditioning at some stage in the past),
felt that there is no substitute for induction from observed experience.
In this sense Smith, like many other Positivists, was an anti-philosopher:
he advises us to include in our *Weltbild* only those observations which
actual experience compels us to include (following Ockham's Razor,
the well-known nominalist principle that entities are not to be multiplied
unnecessarily).

Man's problem is that, despite his experiencing a multitude of
sensations, he is frustrated and confused, depressed by his inability to
know what external objects are really like. The niggardliness of nature
is an epistemological as well as an economic problem, and empiricist
science cannot help man to know the world around him in its totality
and richness. Science can, however, soothe the mind by making
prediction possible. Words are tools which help us to classify the raw
data of experience; mathematics provides schemata for ordering our
sense-impressions. Thus, however little can be known about the true
and universal nature of phenomena, man can, by the classification and
ordering of observations and experiences, construct as a matter of
convenience theories of causality based on the habitual succession of
sensations. Such knowledge is of pragmatic interest: it is, after all,
psychologically comforting to know that B will probably follow A.
Consider the following instance:

> Though the sensations of heat and cold do not necessarily suggest
> the presence of any external object, we soon learn from experience
> that they are commonly excited by some such object . . . By the
> frequency and uniformity of this experience, by the custom and
> habit of thought which that frequency and uniformity necessarily
> occasion, the Internal Sensation, and the External Cause of that
> Sensation, come in our conception to be so strictly connected, that
> in our ordinary and careless way of thinking, we are apt to consider
> them as almost one and the same thing.[12]

From experience we discover that a given external stimulus (e.g. a
certain type of food) excites in us a predictable sense-reaction (e.g. a
pleasant taste or smell). But the stimulus does not *contain the reaction*
('Nobody ever fancies that our food feels its own agreeable or disagreeable taste'[13]), it simply *leads to it*: 'When we say that the smell is in the

flower, we do not thereby mean that the flower itself has any feeling of the sensation which we feel; but that it has the power of exciting this sensation in our nostrils, or in the principle of perception which feels in our nostrils.'[14] Of course, we never perceive the same object twice in exactly the same way; but approximate prediction of perceptions and sensations can still be of considerable use in governing our conduct. Even though we cannot know the true nature of things, at least we know what sensations to expect from a given stimulus: such associations are customary and habitual, and we can thus from observed regularities infer the future from the past without recourse to metaphysical fictions such as revelation, innate ideas, or natural law. As David Hume put it:

> In all single instances of the operation of bodies or minds, there is nothing that produces any impression, nor consequently can suggest any idea of power or necessary connexion. But when many uniform instances appear, and the same object is always followed by the same event; we then begin to entertain the notion of cause and connexion. We then *feel* a new sentiment or impression, to wit, a customary connexion in the thought or imagination between one object and its usual attendant; and this sentiment is the original of that idea which we seek for. [15]

Thirdly, since sensory perception is highly individual, human communication can only be approximate. Every situation has such a multitude of characteristics as to render any description incomplete and selective,[16] and what is important to me may not be important to you. Even the words we use take on a separate identity of their own depending on their propriety and the beauty of their sound. Their very elasticity is an impediment to communication.[17] Most important, 'we have no immediate experience of what other men feel':[18] what I see, taste or smell when influenced by a particular stimulus may be quite different from what you see, taste or smell, since no two experiences are exactly alike.[19] For want of a better solution, however, we are compelled to act on the null hypothesis that we can comprehend the feelings of another man 'by conceiving what we ourselves should feel in the like situation ... Whatever is the passion which arises from any object in the person principally concerned, an analogous emotion springs up, at the thought of his situation, in the breast of every attentive spectator.'[20] This is very much a second-best solution: 'Every faculty in one man is the measure by which he judges of the like faculty in another. I judge of your sight by my sight, of your ear by my ear, of your reason by my reason, of your resentment by my resentment, of your love by my love.

I neither have, nor can have, any other way of judging about them.'[21]

Smith's concern with the communication of sense-perceptions helps to explain his interest in aesthetics: whereas the natural sciences can but describe the 'primary qualities' of an object, the arts, recognising that size and shape are but a small part of our total sensory experience, can help us to convey to others our subjective perceptions of 'secondary qualities'. Hence, although each person has a tendency to perceive the nature of a particular phenomenon in a different way, aesthetic tools can still help men to share each other's impressions with some degree of precision.

Literature cannot portray the reality and totality of external objects, since indeed this cannot be known. It can, however, appeal to the sympathy of the reader; and since by definition the reader can only sympathise with the feelings of other passionate creatures, a writer's perception of an external object is brought home most forcefully where the object is not described at all save through its effect on human beings, as refracted through the five senses. For example: 'The humming of a swarm of bees and the cooing of a turtle give us ideas agreeable and soothing, but this is greatly heightened when Virgil describes Meliboeus lulled asleep by their soothing sound.'[22] And again: 'Pindar, Homer, and Milton never attempt to describe music directly; they always do it by describing the effects it produced on some other creatures.'[23] In short: 'That way of expressing any quality of an object which does it by describing the several parts that constitute the quality we want to express, may be called the direct method. When, again, we do it by describing the effects this quality produces on those who behold it, (this) may be called the indirect method. The latter in most cases is by far the best.'[24]

The problem of communication of perceptions, serious though it may be, should not be seen out of perspective. Men do, after all, reach consensus on the 'primary qualities' of an object, and on many of its 'secondary qualities' (both peasant and professor are likely to respond in the same way if they hold their finger over a lighted candle, regardless of the epistemological justification for doing so). As for the moral sentiments, life in society does tend to concentrate reflexes around the mean, so that the sentiments and motivations of men in like situations do tend to become alike. Nonetheless, to Adam Smith, subjective sensory perception is in the first instance individual, primary and absolute: 'Every sense is supreme over its own objects. There is no appeal from the eye with regard to the beauty of colours, nor from the ear with regard to the harmony of sounds, nor from the taste with regard to the agreeableness of flavours . . . Whatever gratifies the taste is sweet, whatever pleases the eye is beautiful, whatever soothes the ear is harmonious.'[25]

Our argument so far in this section has been that Adam Smith stressed the importance to epistemological inquiry of the habitual association of sense perceptions, a relationship gleaned directly from experience. It would, however, be wrong to overstate Smith's anti-intellectualism. He recognised that there are numerous occasions when an effort of the mind is indispensable, simply because sensory impressions can be misleading. If I hold my finger in front of my eye, I could be given the false idea that it is almost as big as the room in which I am sitting and which it has almost completely blotted out.[26] If I look in the mirror, I could be led by my sense of sight to think that I am continually being observed by an ugly little man who seems to have nothing else to do but to watch me.[27] In the case of such optical illusions, judgement corrects the verdict of the senses, and explanation proves as necessary as simple observation. Consider the following illustration:

> To the eye of the body, objects appear great or small, not so much according to their real dimensions as according to the nearness or distance of their situation . . . In my present situation, an immense landscape of lawns and woods, and distant mountains, seems to do no more than cover the little window which I write by, and to be out of all proportion less than the chamber in which I am sitting. I can form a just comparison between those great objects and the little objects around me, in no other way than by transporting myself, at least in fancy, to a different station, from whence I can survey both at nearly equal distances, and thereby form some judgement of their real proportions. Habit and experience have taught me to do this so easily and so readily, that I am scarce sensible that I do it; and a man must be, in some measure, acquainted with the philosophy of vision, before he can be thoroughly convinced how little those distant objects would appear to the eye, if the imagination, from a knowledge of their real magnitudes, did not swell and dilate them.[28]

In other words, our minds are not virgin territory. We select and order new sense-perceptions according to our established habits of thought and form new impressions in the imposing and inhibiting shadow of existing ideas. Our minds become more and more closed as we become more and more accustomed to seeing certain things in particular ways. We may, for example, have in our memory the stored-up image of a particular tree as seen from a particular perspective, and may continue to imagine it in that way, whether we in fact see it from a distance of a mile, half a mile, or a few yards.[29] The sameness is an illusion (albeit of the mind and not of the eye); but such countervailing delusions are essential if there is to be classification and prediction. The very desire to predict B on the basis of A implies some constancy in the phenomena over time. In every case, Smith says, 'Species, or Universals, and not Individuals, are the objects of Philosophy',[30] and goes on to praise physics for studying the 'specific Essence',[31] the 'Universal Nature',[32] the *Gattungswesen*, the ideal-typical form of each phenomenon. Yet no man can step twice into the same river or have exactly the same experience on more than one occasion; and hence an intellectual effort is necessary to reduce the sensory perceptions I have of, say, the glass of water standing in front of me to their lowest common denominator, those perceptions associated with water in general, with all water. I must, in short, by a conceptual experiment, abstract from the temperature of the water, the shape of my glass, and any other peculiarities which may be unique: 'These are all accidental circumstances, which are altogether extraneous to its general nature, and upon which none of its effects as Water depend.'[33]

It would thus be correct to speak of a second dualism in Smith's epistemology, between the senses and the intellect, where the intellect has the function of correcting the false perceptions of the untutored senses. Clearly Smith was not a 'sensationalist' in the sense of Rousseau, *Sturm und Drang*, or nascent Romanticism. Neither, however, should we underestimate the role of sense-perception in his theory of knowledge, or of passionate motivation in the theory of action: in both cases, a dialectical relationship exists between heart and head, and it is this relationship which ensures both perception of, and adaptation to, the environment.

Action to Smith means the reasoned response to a sensory and instinctual impulse. That impulse may be psychological in origin (such as the confusion or imbalance of the mind when it has been troubled by an unexpected or unknown influence), or it may be social (such as the desire to survive both physically and as an accepted member of the group). Accordingly we will divide our discussion of the theory of action into two parts.

Let us consider first the case of psychological upset as a cause of action. Adam Smith believed that the motivation for scientific inquiry was passionate, not rational. The imagination 'accompanies with ease and delight any regular and orderly motion',[34] but is troubled by uncertain, unpredictable motions, by an 'incoherent diversity of movements'.[35] Such psychological discomfort, such disruption of mental tranquillity, can occur in two ways:

Firstly, through 'Surprise'. This is a destabilising emotion, a shock resulting from the discovery of a known object in an unexpected context. Thus, 'we are surprised at the sudden appearance of a friend, whom we have seen a thousand times, but whom we did not imagine we were to see then'.[36] Such an unforeseen event is upsetting to the mind and can have disastrous consequences, ranging from an 'agony of extravagant fear',[37] through 'a frenzy or habitual lunacy',[38] to 'faintings, deliriums, and sometimes instant death'.[39] On the other hand, if a given association of ideas is known and thus an object or event expected (be the utilitarian consequences good or bad), we are psychologically prepared for it and 'Suprise' is avoided: 'The emotion or passion which it excites glides gradually and easily into the heart, without violence, pain, or difficulty.'[40]

Secondly, through 'Wonder'. This passion too is destabilising since we are here suddenly confronted with an object or succession of objects that is 'new and singular' and 'with which we have before been either little or not at all acquainted'.[41] The unknown is uncertain, possibly evil, and a cause for alarm. But, unlike 'Surprise', 'Wonder' contains active as well as passive elements; it contains the potential motion that leads to its own suppression, namely scientific curiosity. 'Wonder' is thus productive of its direct opposite, mental tranquillity. When we observe a new object (say, a new plant or animal), we are at first perplexed: 'We remain still uncertain and undetermined where to place it, or what to think of it . . . What sort of thing can that be? What is that like? are the questions which, upon such an occasion, we are all naturally disposed to ask.'[42] In other words, we attempt to classify the unknown object in terms of a common property it shares with some known group of objects: 'If we can recollect many such objects which exactly resemble this new appearance, and which present themselves to the imagination naturally, and as it were of their own accord, our Wonder is entirely at an end.'[43] Similarly, an unusual succession of objects or events is explained by finding some chain of intermediate events which successfully bridge the gap between two 'disjointed appearances'. A scientific theory attempts to 'allay this confusion, to connect together those disjointed appearances, and to introduce harmony and order into the mind's conception of the movements of those bodies'.[44] This relieves the mind's 'embarrassment'; it becomes capable again of predicting with regularity and uniformity.

Not all cases of Surprise and Wonder justify scientific treatment, however. Science must be selective, since it cannot investigate every aspect of every phenomenon; and even the selection of its subject-matter

is based on passion, in this case the sentiment of Admiration. Our
Admiration is aroused by 'whatever we see that is great or noble':[45]
the Supernatural,[46] the Heavenly Bodies ('the noblest works of
nature'[47]), military exploits,[48] and, of course, civil society ('As it is
mankind we are chiefly connected with, it must be their actions which
chiefly interest our attention'[49]).

The aim of scientific inquiry is thus passionate, not utilitarian or
practical. It is not to discover 'useful' facts or to give us control over
nature but to smooth the passage of the imagination.[50] Science is
productive of pleasure, not because it leads to the development of new
and better commodities, but because it restores tranquillity of mind.
Once an offending object or succession of objects has been assigned to a
suitable category, internal peace is restored and the observer can sleep
easily without being puzzled: 'Philosophy, by representing the invisible
chains which bind together all these disjointed objects, endeavours to
introduce order into this chaos of jarring and discordant appearances,
to allay this tumult of the imagination, and to restore it, when it
surveys the great revolutions of the universe, to . . . tranquillity and
composure.'[51]

The scientist studies the real world purely in order to satisfy his
curiosity:

> Wonder, therefore, and not any expectation of advantage from its
> discoveries, is the first principle which prompts mankind to the
> study of Philosophy, of that science which pretends to lay open the
> concealed connections that unite the various appearances of nature;
> and they pursue this study for its own sake, as an original pleasure
> or good in itself, without regarding its tendency to procure them the
> means of many other pleasures.[52]

Perhaps, however, Smith meant this to be an ideal-typical picture of the
scientist. He certainly admits that some scientists will go to any lengths for
'reputation'[53] or to further their career by pandering to the powers-
that-be; and that some inventions are made for highly utilitarian reasons
(e.g. those made by workers and slaves in an effort to abridge their
labour[54]). But Smith did believe that scientific inquiry was more and
more being centralised in the hands of philosophers, 'whose trade it is
not to do any thing, but to observe every thing'.[55] Such professionals
are not more devoted to truth than are other men, but they are less
tranquil. They are aware of more elaborate categories, classes and sub-
classes of things, and thus notice a gap where ordinary men see only a
smooth progression. Because they are experienced observers, their

Wonder is often awakened when untrained people are satisfied with existing explanations of connection and causation. Their superior perception in noticing that intermediate stages are missing is almost aesthetic in its nature:

> As in those sounds, which to the greater part of men seem perfectly agreeable to measure and harmony, the nicer ear of a musician will discover a want . . . so the more practised thought of a philosopher, who has spent his whole life in the study of the connecting principles of nature, will often feel an interval betwixt two objects, which, to more careless observers, seem very strictly conjoined.[56]

As industrialisation means the division of labour, and the division of labour means the professionalisation of science, it is probable that Smith thought his ideal type was in the process of becoming reality. It is ironical that to Smith the rationalisation of the economy appears to have brought with it the de-utilitarianisation of scientific inquiry.

Precisely because passion is the motive for scientific investigation, that passion must be transcended by empirical research. If observation clearly falsifies a theory, then a new theory must be developed, since a theory 'altogether wide of what was the real situation'[57] is useless in assuaging Wonder or in predicting B on the basis of A. There is a psychological necessity for a theory to 'correspond with exact precision to the phaenomena'[58] if the mind is to be at ease, it must be known what to expect. For this reason he praises Newton's system: 'It is every where the most precise and particular that can be imagined, and ascertains the time, the place, the quantity, the duration of each individual phaenomenon, to be exactly such as, by observation, they have been determined to be.'[59] It can even be used accurately to predict the return of a comet.[60] It is no wonder the Cartesian philosophy is 'almost universally exploded':[61] rather than inducing laws from empirical data, the Cartesians deduced motion from abstract principles and axioms. Descartes' theory of vortices seems 'very plausible' on the surface but in fact has

> no foundation in nature, nor any sort of resemblance to the truth . . . It has been demonstrated, to the conviction of all mankind, that these pretended causes of those wonderful effects, not only do not actually exist, but are utterly impossible, and, if they did exist, could produce no such effects as are ascribed to them.[62]

The laws uniting phenomena can only be found by observing nature, not by retreating into *a priori* axioms, mathematical deduction, and the philosophy of mind. Smith warned scientists against engaging 'chiefly in ethical, rhetorical, and dialectical questions.'[63] Such an approach confounds every thing and explains nothing'.[64] He disparaged the study of the 'cobweb science', metaphysics, since it offers nothing that can restore tranquillity to a confused mind. It is a 'subject in which, after a few very simple and almost obvious truths, the most careful attention can discover nothing but obscurity and uncertainty, and can consequently produce nothing but subtleties and sophisms'.[65] For the same reason he dismissed Plato's theory of ideas based on introspection as a 'fallacious experiment': it sought to show 'that a person might be led to discover himself, without any information, any general truth, of which he was before ignorant, merely by being asked a number of properly arranged and connected questions concerning it'.[66] In fact, however, knowledge is accessible only by observation of regularities in real world phenomena, not by contemplation. The Platonic methodology postulates an ideal essence of things, 'exemplars, according to which the Deity formed the world';[67] but Smith found such ideal universals excessively speculative. We have no way of knowing whether they are real or not. Such an abstract approach clearly has arisen 'more from the nature of language, than from the nature of things'.[68] Metaphysical essences cannot be known save as names or words.

The advantage of physics, on the other hand, is that it is 'the proper subject of experiment and observation'.[69] Its theories yield good predictions, and are open to verification by experiment. Consider the following law: 'Air . . . by the application of a very moderate force, is easily reducible within a much smaller portion of space than that which it usually occupies.'[70] An epistemological sceptic does not need to take this fact on trust: 'We may easily satisfy ourselves of the truth of it, by squeezing a full-blown bladder of which the neck is well tied.'[71] This is a vast improvement on contemplative philosophy: 'The reasonings of philosophy . . . though they may confound and perplex the understanding, can never break down the necessary connection which nature has established between causes and their effects.'[72] Man lives in the world of nature and must learn to predict the behaviour of natural occurences if his 'Wonder' is ever to be at an end.

It is important in doing so for a scientist to stand on the shoulders of giants in his subject. In astronomy, Tycho Brahe's system built on that of Ptolemy and Copernicus; Kepler's on Copernicus and Brahe; Cassini's on Kepler; Newton's on Kepler and Cassini. He must not, however, become enslaved dogmatically to the great thinkers of the past or perpetuate their doctrines unquestioningly. Once he loses his own curiosity to investigate reality, he becomes imprisoned by an intellectual system, a mere commentator on classics which cannot be improved upon:

> After the reign of Antoninus, and, indeed, after the age of Hipparchus, who lived almost three hundred years before Antoninus, the great reputation which the earlier philosophers had acquired, so imposed upon the imaginations of mankind, that they seem to have despaired of ever equalling their renown. All human wisdom, they supposed, was comprehended in the writings of those elder sages.[73]

As a result, scientific inquiry stagnated.

In the short run, a new theory, like anything new, arouses 'Suprise' and 'Wonder', more so even than the phenomena it seeks to explain. For example, it was once hard to imagine that the Earth revolved at all, let alone at 1,000 m.p.h. Such a theory does 'violence to the usual habits of the imagination'[74] and goes against 'the natural prejudices of sense, confirmed by education'.[75] Of course, in the long run the superior predictive power of a new theory causes the public to accept it; but in the short run it faces what Professor Galbraith calls 'the greatest of vested interests, those of the mind'.[76]

Let us now consider the second case in the theory of action, namely those actions resulting from the passions that link men to society. Here it is important to remember that, just as the scientist is motivated by 'Wonder' to discover general (and, incidentally, useful) laws, so the individual in society is motivated by similar passionate impulses to attain similarly desirable but unintended objectives. It is instinct and appetite, not reason and reflection, which guarantee the smooth working of the social machine. For example, the division of labour originates in an instinctual 'propensity to truck, barter, and exchange',[77] and in a 'principle to persuade which so much prevails in human nature'.[78] Such an appetite is 'known to no other animal. Nobody ever saw a dog, the most sagacious animal, exchange a bone with his companion for another.'[79] Again, the growth of population occurs not as a result of a rational desire to populate, strengthen and enrich the Kingdom, but because of the 'passion which unites the two sexes'.[80] And elsewhere he shows that, while reason teaches that kings are the servants of the people and may with no impropriety be overthrown if they infringe the rules of justice, the passions encourage sympathy with the rich and powerful, prevent revolution, and thus promote social stability and political continuity.[81]

In economic affairs, because men are made of 'coarse clay',[82] because they have a 'base and selfish disposition',[83] it is a relief to know that their passion of self-love can be enlisted to promote the material welfare of the community. While 'benevolence may, perhaps, be the sole principle of action in the Deity',[84] we must recognise that men are imperfect creatures: 'The brewer and the baker serve us not from benevolence, but from self-love',[85] but at least they do serve us. Unlike misguided idealists, who attempt to act in the economic sphere on the basis of instincts which are simply not normally found there: 'I have never known much good done by those who affected to trade for the public good.'[86] In important matters like self-preservation and the propagation of the species, ends which virtually every man would accept as desirable, it has nonetheless 'not been entrusted to the slow and uncertain determinations of our reason, to find out the proper means of bringing them about. Nature has directed us to the greater part of these by original and immediate instincts.[87] Specifically, we have, each of us, a 'desire of bettering our condition, a desire which, though generally calm and dispassionate, comes with us from the womb, and never leaves us till we go into the grave';[88] and it is on the socially beneficial outcome of this desire that the legislator ought to count. Self-love may, of course, be anything but enlightened. From the point of view of a philosopher such as Smith, commodity-utility is a 'deception',[89] since greater commodity-consumption need not bring greater satisfaction, and may even reduce it. What matters, however, is not the manifest function but the latent function; and clearly the economic, political and social improvement of the nation is the unintended outcome of the individual's lust for a fuller trough.

Social cohesion too results from sensation and passion. Man's love of company and of justified approbation causes him to conform to social pressures: 'Nature, when she formed man for society, endowed him with an original desire to please, and an original aversion to offend his brethren.'[90] Propriety is the basis of our concepts of virtue and morality; and it consists of habitual associations internalised since childhood in a given society. It is 'altogether absurd and unintelligible' to suppose that such norms can be constructed by logic and reason: 'Nothing can be agreeable or disagreeable for its own sake, which is not rendered such by immediate sense and feeling.'[91] Rather, our standards of right and wrong depend on what our fellow-men, whose friendship and sympathy we desperately need, choose to define as right and wrong. When we evaluate a particular series of actions, 'it satisfies us that we view them in the proper light, when we see other people view them in the same light'.[92]

Once again, because passion is the immediate cause of action, there is no substitute for empirical observation. Smith announced in *The Wealth of Nations* that his aim was simply to write a 'speculative work', [93] and that he in any case had 'no great faith in political arithmetic'.[94] In fact, however, his 'speculation' was not abstract reflection but generalisation based on experience; and, despite the absence of reliable statistics (something that had not discouraged Petty, King and Davenant), he did not hesitate to make quite sophisticated use of the data that he had. Hence in the *Lectures* he calculates that 72 per cent of the national product originates in agriculture,[95] and in *The Wealth of Nations* computes that some hundred thousand workmen were at that time 'employed in the greatest manufactures'.[96] Indicative of his methodology is the casual empiricism that 'decency no where requires that any man should eat butchers meat'.[97] This is, after all, both an inference from observation and a statement formulated in such a way as to be falsifiable if new data were to become available. Similarly, his proof of the beneficial effects of potatoes is not pure speculation since he attempts to give evidence based on a large sample of consumers:

> The chairmen, porters, and coal-heavers in London, and those unfortunate women who live by prostitution, the strongest men and the most beautiful women perhaps in the British dominions, are said to be, the greater part of them, from the lowest rank of people in Ireland, who are generally fed with this root. No food can afford a more decisive proof of its nourishing quality.[98]

His detailed account of the Scottish linen and Yorkshire woollens industry,[99] or even of the progress of the division of labour in the famous pin-factory,[100] show the influence of his own observation (e.g. of sailors, nailmakers, colliers in Kirkcaldy), reading (e.g. history, travellers' tales, or the article on 'Epingle' in the *Encyclopédie*) and conversation (e.g. with academics, inventors and businessmen in the Glasgow Literary Club, the Edinburgh Select Society, and other clubs).

The scientific method must also be applied to the normative constraint. Naturally, social norms cannot be quantified; but, by induction from actual practice, a sort of composite collective consciousness can nonetheless be codified. To Smith, unlike Rousseau, morality is not engraved in each individual heart: there is no inner voice, absolute, morally autonomous, independent of education and social conditioning. There is no Kantian spirit capable of distinguishing obligation and duty in the form of categorical imperatives. To Smith, normative constraint is social: the norms are clearest, their force greatest, the more man is integrated in the group, the less he is left in solitude. In this respect Smith appears more 'Catholic' than 'Protestant'.

Observation and experience of moral norms, not active reason, help us gradually to build up a stock of conditioned responses to various sorts of stimuli. If we are confronted with a new experience, we then can automatically consult the mental case-law that we have imperceptibly and unintentionally built up: 'Our continual observations upon the conduct of others insensibly leads us to form to ourselves certain general rules concerning what is fit and proper either to be done or to be avoided.'[101] On cannot impose an *a priori* ethical system on people and expect it to work. When he says that 'the two useful parts of moral philosophy . . . are Ethics and Jurisprudence',[102] he is really offering a defence of scientific method. After all, ethics and jurisprudence are the only parts of moral philosophy that can be formulated precisely and empirically, since in both cases the philosopher does no more than record existing patterns of behaviour. Smith's own investigation into morality is concerned with 'a matter of fact', not with 'a matter of right': 'We are not at present examining upon what principles a perfect being would approve of the punishment of bad actions, but upon what principles so weak and imperfect a creature as man *actually and in fact* approves of it.'[103] Morality is to be concerned with what is, not with what ought to be; and makes prediction possible.

An inability to distinguish between metaphysics and physics is thus particularly dangerous in the human sciences. Contemplation, meditation, 'abstract and speculative reasonings', probably 'tend very little to the bettering of our practice',[104] and in any case are not necessary: the instinctual mechanism of 'sympathy' is enough to generate the right consciousness and the correct motivation for action in any situation. Contemplation of the sublime 'can never be an excuse for . . . neglecting the most humble department': 'The most sublime speculation of the contemplative philosopher can scarce compensate the neglect of the smallest active duty.'[105]

II. Scientific Method

It has long been realised that one of Adam Smith's greatest contributions was in clarifying the methodology of the physical sciences and in trying to apply it to the science of society. As early as 1793 his friend Dugald Stewart suggested that the merit of *The Wealth of Nations* 'is to be estimated less from the novelty of the principles it contains, than from the reasonings employed to support these principles, and from the scientific manner in which they are unfolded in their proper order and connection . . . and followed . . . out to their remote consequences.'[1] And his student, John Millar, stated categorically: 'The great Montesquieu pointed out the road. He was the Lord Bacon in this branch of philosophy. Dr. Smith is the Newton.'[2]

Smith, in common with many other eighteenth-century intellectuals, used the words 'philosophy' and 'science' interchangeably. Thus he defined philosophy as 'the science of the connecting principles of nature',[3] described both physics[4] and metaphysics[5] as sciences, and called optics 'the philosophy of vision',[6] chemistry the 'chemical philosophy'.[7] It was very much as a methodologist that he approached the study of external phenomena. Hutton and Black, who prepared his 'History of Astronomy' for posthumous publication, advised that it 'be viewed, not as a History or Account of Sir Isaac Newton's Astronomy, but chiefly as an additional illustration of those Principles in the Human Mind which Mr. Smith has pointed out to be the universal motives of Philosophical Researches'.[8] Indeed, the full title of the essay is 'The Principles Which Lead and Direct Philosophical Enquiries: Illustrated By The History of Astronomy'; just as the full title of *The Wealth of Nations* reads *An Inquiry into the Nature and Causes of the Wealth of Nations*, indicating his interest in the method (inquiry) as well as the result (wealth).

It seems clear from his application of the empirical method to 'social facts' such as economy or morality that Smith saw little difference between theory construction in the physical and in the social sciences: after all, an epistemological sceptic is dependent on observation and experiment for any knowledge he can hope to gain, whether about the world of things or about the world of men. There is, however, one significant distinction: the world of men, unlike the world of things, involves subjective perceptions, and thus Smith's sociology, like that of Max Weber, is based on *Verstehen*. As Weber puts it: 'Sociology . . . is a science which attempts the interpretive understanding of social action in order thereby to arrive at a causal explanation of its course and effects. In "action" is included all human behaviour when and in so far as the acting individual attaches a subjective meaning to it.'[9] To Smith, this subjective factor poses no problem: norms and values (religious and secular) can be studied using the same experimental, observational method that the philosopher utilises when studying the natural sciences such as physics, chemistry or astronomy. If, therefore, we can deduce from his extensive writings on the physical sciences (and particularly astronomy) what Smith felt the features of a good theory to be, then we can feel reasonably confident that he would not have hesitated to apply the same method of approach to the social sciences as well.

In fact, the features of a good theory to Smith appear to have been the same as the four reasons he gives for the triumph of the Copernican system over that of Ptolemy:

(i)   it was 'more completely coherent';
(ii)   it was 'more simple and intelligible';
(iii)   it used familiar concepts;
(iv)   it had 'more beautiful machinery'.[10]

Let us now examine these four criteria more closely:

(i) Coherence

A good theory should unite a large number of apparently 'loose and incoherent' phenomena, bridging the gap between discrete observations in order to 'introduce order and coherence into the mind's conception of this seeming chaos of dissimilar and disjointed appearances'.[11] Such classification can be either static or dynamic.

In the case of static classification, dissimilitude is resolved into similitude and 'Wonder' is assuaged by the discovery of 'connecting principles': 'It is evident that the mind takes pleasure in observing the resemblances that are discoverable betwixt different objects. It is by means of such observations that it endeavours to arrange and methodize all its ideas, and to reduce them into proper classes and assortments.'[12] In its simplest form, this means that the heat of a stove and the heat of an open chimney can be conceived of in terms of a common quality, fire. The same tendency to organise phenomena into genera and species is observed in the development of language: mankind is tempted to give the name of one thing to another which resembles it, 'and thus to denominate a multitude, by what originally was intended to express an individual'.[13] Language is, after all, a classificatory system, grouping phenomena with considerable sophistication according to category ('a tree'), relation to other phenomena ('the tree in the meadow'), and peculiar features ('a green tree'). Nor was the 'beauty of a systematical arrangement of different observations connected by a few common principles' lost on the moral scientists:

> The maxims of common life were arranged in some methodical order, and connected together by a few common principles, in the same manner as they had attempted to arrange and connect the phenomena of nature. The science which pretends to investigate and explain those connecting principles, is what is properly called moral philosophy.[14]

Observation without arrangement cannot satisfy the imagination or be productive of mental tranquillity.

In the case of dynamic classification, dissimilar objects are related by habitual association of ideas, by some customary succession or sequence. The imagination, having noticed A (e.g. lightning) comes to anticipate or expect B (e.g. thunder). Since ideas move faster than things, prediction provides reassurance in the face of a succession of events:

> They come to be so connected together in the fancy, that the idea of the one seems, of its own accord, to call up and introduce that of the other. If the objects are still observed to succeed each other as before, this connection, or, as it has been called, this association of their ideas, becomes stricter and stricter, and the habit of the imagination to pass from the conception of the one to that of the other, grows more and more rivetted and confirmed . . . There is no break, no stop, no gap, no interval. The ideas excited by so coherent a chain of things seem, as it were, to float through the mind of their own accord, without obliging it to exert itself, or to make any effort in order to pass from one of them to another.[15]

Obviously, the more micro-classificatory models (both static and dynamic) that we accumulate, the more our model of society becomes a macro-classificatory functionalist system. This being the case, coherence of the model is likely to be improved by reference to the analogy of some other fully integrated system. In practice, although Smith does occasionally make comparisons between human society and the human body,[16] his functionalism tends to prefer a mechanistic to an organic analogy. Thus he in one place states that society is 'like a great, an immense machine';[17] elsewhere diagnoses that prosperity and order will cause 'the wheels of the political machine' to move 'with more harmony and ease';[18] and ultimately concludes that human action, however selfishly motivated, can still benefit the species, just as 'the wheels of the watch are all admirably adjusted to the end for which it was made, the pointing of the hour'.[19]

It is perhaps surprising that Smith turned away from the organic analogy. In the age of the Enlightenment, biology was very much 'in the air': Mandeville, Locke, La Mettrie and Quesnay were all physicians, and Smith himself attended William Hunter's lectures on anatomy in Glasgow (just as Voltaire attended those of Boerhaave in Leyden).[20] The analogy between the circular flow of income and the circulation of the blood is almost too obvious to remark upon. But in the Enlightenment mechanics too was 'in the air': Voltaire described Newton as 'the greatest

man who ever lived' and claimed to be the first poet to have used a
comparison based on the refraction of light, while in 1767 Smith's
friend, James Watt, invented the steam-engine. Naturally, the vagueness
of eighteenth-century philosophers with respect to organic evolution
reduced the opposition between the two analogies: they were not as
aware as was Spencer that an organism is a self-regulating structure
which must be left alone if it is to adapt properly to its environment,
whereas a machine (being no more than the sum of its parts) can be
redesigned by a skilled machine-maker. Nonetheless it is not impossible
that Smith prefered the mechanistic to the organic analogy because he
wanted to emphasise that laissez-faire need not mean human passivity.
A new social machine with a new centre of gravity *can* be designed,
albeit here the philosopher must demonstrate exemplary Newtonian
modesty and not attempt too much. A new social organism, however,
even in an era of the most modern technology, is never likely to go
beyond neo-gothic science fiction.

In any case, whether the analogy is organic or mechanistic, Smith is
insistent that it is just an analogy. Philosophical systems are *'mere
inventions of the imagination*, to connect together the otherwise
disjointed and discordant phaenomena of nature'; they should not be
taken as depicting the *'real* chains which Nature makes use of to bind
together her several operations',[22] as, indeed, these cannot be known.
Connecting principles do not have to be real principles: 'A system is an
imaginary machine invented to connect together *in the fancy* those
different movements and effects which are *already in reality
performed.*'[23] The machine is imaginary; but since reality is unknow-
able, at least it predicts 'as if'[24] natural mechanics were known. A
fictional system can be as useful as an actual one in restoring tranquillity
to a troubled spirit, provided that it yields accurate predictions.

(ii) Simplicity

As long as a system is 'intricate and complex', the imagination cannot
'rest in it with complete tranquillity and satisfaction'.[25] As science
progresses, however, theories become more simplified and the number
of connecting principles is reduced. Indeed, 'it often happens, that one
great connecting principle is afterwards found to be sufficient to bind
together all the discordant phaenomena that occur in a whole species of
things'.[26]

Consider the case of astronomy. The earliest theories were extremely
simple: casual empiricism suggested that the stars kept the same
distance with respect to one another, and this led astronomers to postulate that they were fixed to a concave solid which revolved round the

Earth. Later, however, more accurate observation revealed that the relative positions of certain Heavenly bodies altered with respect to the others. Clearly, all Heavenly bodies could no longer be assumed fixed to the same sphere, and separate spheres had to be assigned to those whose position changed. By the time of Aristotle there were thought to be fifty-six such spheres, further observation necessitated the addition of more and more, and there was a real danger that there would soon be one model per phenomenon. The system was becoming 'as intricate and complex as those appearances themselves, which it had been invented to render uniform and coherent'.[27] Nature and nature's laws lay hid in night; but then, as Pope put it, 'GOD said, *Let Newton Be*! and all was Light.'[28]

The Newtonian system has rendered present-day astronomy comprehensive, rigorous, and yet simple. The 'superior genius and sagacity of Sir Isaac Newton'[29] discovered 'an immense chain of the most important and sublime truths, all closely connected together, by one capital fact',[30] the principle of gravity, and capable of predicting the behaviour of the most diverse phenomena (the sun, moon, stars, planets, even the comets) with the most remarkable precision: 'Allow his principle, the universality of gravity, and that it decreases as the squares of the distance increase, and all the appearances, which he joins together by it, necessarily follow.'[31] The fact that the Newtonian system has 'introduced such complete coherence into the motions of all the Heavenly Bodies, has served not a little to recommend it to the imaginations of mankind':[32] the ordering of diversity and transcendence of complexity by reference to a single principle of motion cannot but be a great relief to the troubled mind.

Smith, in common with many other Enlightenment scholars, took Newton as his mentor. Indeed, his interest in the gravitation of bodies towards some natural equilibrium or state of physical inertia was at the root of his opposition to tariffs, settlement laws, and statutes of apprenticeship. Given that the 'natural price' of a commodity is 'as it were, the central price, to which the prices of all commodities are continually gravitating',[33] laissez-faire may be thought of as a means for freeing that motion from friction imposed by the repression exercised by corrupt politicians and misguided clerics. In the long run, economy and society would thereby come to rest in that state of affairs intended by nature 'if human institutions had never thwarted those natural inclinations'.[34] The rule is: 'All systems either of preference or of restraint, therefore, being thus completely taken away, the obvious and simple system of natural liberty establishes itself of its own accord.'[35]

As well as by the law of gravity itself, however, Smith was attracted by the very idea of accounting 'for all appearances from as few principles as possible.'[36] He much regretted that the English, with all their aptitude for invention, seem nonetheless to have neglected 'the more inglorious but not less useful labour of arranging and methodizing their discoveries',[37] but clearly was attempting himself to fill this gap by both collecting a mass of data on a variety of phenomena and systematising it in terms of a few central principles. Professor Schumpeter (hardly one of Smith's most ardent admirers) complains that 'the *Wealth of Nations* contained no really novel ideas', but then adds, significantly, about Smith, that 'his mental stature was up to mastering the unwieldy material that flowed from many sources and to subjecting it, with a strong hand, to the rule of a small number of coherent principles'.[38] Surely it is Smith's supreme debt to Newton that he was able to eliminate unnecessary explanatory factors to the extent of being left with only two key concepts. In his social statics, his connecting principle appears to have been the love of 'sympathy', which impels men to act with 'propriety' so as to deserve the approbation of the 'impartial spectator'. In his social dynamics, it appears to have been his guarded belief in the doctrine of progress, economic and social. These two concepts taken together (with the first the *primum mobile* behind the second) link up virtually all of Adam Smith's observations on the nature of economy and society.

(iii) Familiarity

Science plays on the imagination. It endeavours to 'render the theatre of nature a more coherent, and therefore a more magnificent spectacle, than otherwise it would have appeared to be'.[39] Precisely for this reason, because the 'repose and tranquillity of the imagination is the ultimate end of philosophy',[40] familiarity of concepts is virtually indispensable: 'No system, how well soever in other respects supported, has ever been able to gain any general credit on the world, whose connecting principles were not such as were familiar to all mankind.'[41]

It is comforting to find that the less familiar is explicable in terms of the more familiar. The success of ancient physics in satisfying the imagination lay in its ability to reduce all complex compounds to four elements, fire, water, earth and air;[42] just as one of the main reasons for the popularity of the Newtonian system is that it is based on the principle of gravity, a fact 'of the reality of which we have daily experience'.[43] Not only was the Newtonian system 'the greatest discovery that ever was made by man', but it won the 'general and complete approbation of mankind'[44] through its immediate accessibility. Smith himself is fond of familiar analogies. For example, he explains the revolutions of the planets around the sun in terms of two ships sailing in different directions or at different speeds.[45]

The appeal to common experience explains Galileo's success in rendering generally acceptable the Copernican view that the Earth revolved round the Sun. It was known that the Moon revolved round the Earth; and when Galileo used his telescope to observe mountains and seas on the Moon, 'rendering that Planet, in every respect, similar to the Earth', he 'made it less contrary to the analogy of nature, that, as the Moon revolved round the Earth, the Earth should revolve round the Sun'.[46] The demonstration that the singular is in fact classifiable with the familiar overcomes 'the prejudices of sense', and renders it acceptable, thereby satisfying 'the great end of Philosophy'.[47]

Not all scientists are so fortunate, however. Chemistry has 'crept along in obscurity', despite the fact that the chemist studies problems much more useful than is the case in some other disciplines. The reason for this obscurity is obvious:

> The connecting principles of the chemical philosophy are such as the generality of mankind know nothing about, have rarely seen, and have never been acquainted with; and which to them, therefore, are incapable of smoothing the passage of the imagination betwixt any two seemingly disjointed objects. Salts, sulphurs, and mercuries, acids, and alkalis, are principles which can smooth things to those only who live about the furnace.[48]

There is a habitual association, a predictable sequence of occurrences expressed with the greatest precision; but it is too technical to restore peace of mind to anyone but a chemist.

At times, therefore, there may be a contradiction between the need for science to make accurate predictions and the need for it to reassure the troubled mind. Many phenomena are simply too complex to be explained in terms comprehensible to the layman, as Kepler discovered to his cost. Kepler found that the Heavenly bodies do not move in a perfect circle but in an ellipse; and not with constant velocity but with velocity varying according to a formula which he specified. His system 'was better supported by observations than any system had ever been before',[49] and could more precisely predict the behaviour of the Heavenly bodies; yet it was universally neglected, even by philosophers and astronomers, because it depended on 'an analogy too difficult to be followed, or comprehended'.[50] It was perfectly accurate but unfortunately 'of too intricate a nature to facilitate very much the effort of the imagination in conceiving it'.[51] In brief, it was not 'agreeable to the natural taste of mankind'.[52]

It is not always possible to explain an unknown object in terms of a familiar one or to fit it into a familiar sequence; and in the last analysis it may be that 'a philosopher is company to a philosopher only'.[53]

(iv) Aesthetically satisfying

A scientific system, like a painting or statue, is a model of reality, an analogy. The model should be designed not just to fit the empirical facts one wishes to unify, but to do so as artistically as possible.

Thus, one of the advantages of the theory of the spheres was 'the beauty of the system . . . like an harmonic proportion';[54] and mathematics itself was originally studied, not because it was useful, but because of the beauty of its method.[55] One of the disadvantages of Kepler's discovery of elliptical orbits and variable velocities of Heavenly bodies was that it was aesthetically disappointing. After all, the general imagination had previously 'determined that a circular motion was the most perfect of all motions, and that none but the most perfect motion could be worthy of such beautiful and divine objects';[56] while inconstancy of motion was felt to be 'unworthy of those bodies which revolved in the celestial regions, and to be fit only for inferior and sublunary things'.[57] It was felt that, since the movement of the stars is beautiful, and since regularity is beautiful, therefore the movement of the stars must be regular. Of course, the desire for beauty has to make way for the facts. It is striking, however, that Smith still casts around to find an aesthetic justification for Kepler's system, and decides finally that the ellipse is undeniably, 'of all curve lines after a circle, the simplest and most easily conceived'.[58]

III. Aesthetics

Adam Smith came very close to identifying truth with beauty, and scientific method with aesthetics. Partly this was the natural consequence of his conviction that the sciences and the arts both appeal more directly to the sensations than to the reason; and partly it resulted from Smith's tendency to follow Hutcheson in relating beauty to order, making science itself as much a source of aesthetic pleasure as of useful knowledge. It is therefore no surprise to learn that the preconditions for a good model in the arts are the same as those in the sciences: coherence, simplicity and familiarity of concepts. All three are subject to the test of propriety which, since it is a social conception, provides a link between aesthetics and sociology.

(i) Coherence

Like any other model, a work of art unites a mass of data by a
connecting chain. In the arts as in the sciences, the Newtonian method
is 'the most philosophical' approach: 'It gives us a pleasure to see the
phenomena which we reckoned the most unaccountable, all deduced
from some principle (commonly, a well-known one) and all united in
one chain, far superior to what we feel from the unconnected method,
where everything is accounted for by itself, without any reference to
the others.'[1]

Thus, the events narrated by a historian should be connected by
some link: 'Every part of the story should tend to some one end,
whatever that be.'[2] Herodotus, for example, recounted events in
several countries and over a period of two hundred and forty years,
but he still was successful in focusing the reader's attention: knowing
that it was impossible to include every event in every country, he
selected only those events which were not only 'fabulous' and
'marvellous', but also 'agreeable' and 'amusing', and connected them
together 'in such an easy and natural manner as to leave no gap nor
chasm in his narration'.[3] And for a similar reason Smith admired those
French classical dramatists such as Racine who observed the unities —
of time, because if four years or so elapse between the acts of a play we
will feel uneasy at 'being kept in the dark with regard to what happened
in so long a time';[4] of place, because if the distance between places is
great 'we are anxious to know what has happened in the interval'.[5] An
audience in the theatre may be willing to suspend its disbelief and
forget that Richard III is only an actor playing Richard III; it will,
however, never be willing to suspend its curiosity, and will never forgive
a playwright for not providing it with adequate information. Clearly
Smith would have had little patience with the *nouveau roman* or the
theatre of the absurd. As Dugald Stewart points out, 'the general
character of his taste . . . delighted more to remark that pliancy of
genius which accomodates itself to established rules, than to wonder at
the bolder flights of an undisciplined imagination'.[6] Order, to Adam
Smith, was preferable to novelty.

Indeed, the very order produced by a model (in belles lettres as in
astronomy) seems to have appeared to Smith a thing of beauty and
source of pleasure in its own right. There is beauty in a 'systematical
arrangement of different observations'[7] by means of a connecting
principle. On the one hand, 'easy connexion . . . renders objects
agreeable'; while on the other, 'when we see no reason for the contiguity
of the parts, when they are without any natural connexion, when they

have neither a proper resemblance nor contrast, they never fail of being disagreeable'.[8] Consider the history of language and you will find that the 'love of analogy' is 'the foundation of by far the greater part of the rules of grammar'.[9] This accounts for the agreement of adjectival and noun endings: the aim was not clarity alone but love of the connecting principle represented by 'similarity of sound'.[10] Again, in painting and sculpture, pleasure results from seeing one object resemble another, from seeing disparity transcended by unity, and in such a way that we can comprehend how the effect was produced.[11]

Similarly, the musician links a number of instruments and a variety of sounds by a 'key note' and rhythm. No one wants his tranquillity to be disturbed by surprising disharmonies and unexpected discordances: the enjoyment of music is only possible where the succession of sounds is regular and anticipated. The mind is soothed by predictable patterns in music (a pleasure 'not unlike that which it derives from the contemplation of a great system in any other science'[12]), and for this reason, virtuous passions are more suitable for musical presentation than anti-social sentiments:

> The voice of furious anger, for example, is harsh and discordant; its periods are all irregular, sometimes very long and sometimes very short, and distinguished by no regular pauses. The obscure and almost inarticulate grumblings of black malice and envy, the screaming outcries of dastardly fear, the hideous growlings of brutal and implacable revenge, are all equally discordant. It is with difficulty that Music can imitate any of those passions, and the Music which does imitate them is not the most agreeable.[13]

It so happens, moreover, that the virtuous passions are those very passions which 'bind men together in society'. Thus, social harmony and aesthetic harmony are inseparable, and the love of regularity makes art fulfil for Smith the same function that socialist realism did for Stalin. In the case of Smith, however, social harmony was merely the latent function of the arts, the unintended outcome of the quest for coherence, aesthetic harmony and intellectual tranquillity.

An artist enjoys more freedom than a scientist since he can first select a connecting principle and then create a situation to illustrate it. He can select and juxtapose a number of objects arousing the same emotion, in order to emphasise a point via the association of their ideas. Milton, for example,

often places a philosopher meditating under the shade of the mountain, a magician at the mouth of a cavern, and a hermit amidst the desert and torrents . . . These objects are connected together and excite the same emotion . . . The philosopher adds to the awful, majestic appearance of the mountain, the magician to the gloomy horror of the cavern. The hermit tends to excite in a strong degree the emotions we are apt to conceive at the sight of a desert.[14]

In Milton's poems, 'almost every word tends to convey some idea suited to the subject'.[15] Pope tends to be more careless in his choice of expressions. He speaks of a 'brown horror', but in fact ' "brown" joined to "horror" conveys no idea at all'.[16] And Shakespeare could have ruined *Hamlet* by improper associations: the grave-digger scenes 'had better been away' as they have 'no share in bringing about the main design of the piece' and are 'somewhat contrary to the temper of the rest of the scenes'.[17] Given his connecting principle, the artist should not confuse the audience by creating subsidiary centres of attention provoking contradictory emotions. This would go against the sense of order that Smith inherited from the 'never-to-be-forgotten' Francis Hutcheson, who defined beauty as existing where 'unity amidst variety is observed'.[18]

(ii) Simplicity

As a rule, 'we may observe that the most beautiful passages are generally the most simple'.[19] Smith feels that form is subservient to content, and that the writer should use words to express his ideas with precision rather than aiming at elegance of expression for its own sake. Literature is an appeal for 'sympathy' from the reader, and thus a literary model may be deemed successful if it convinces the reader to think and feel what the writer thought and felt: 'The perfection of style consists in expressing in the most concise, proper, and precise manner the thought of the author, and that in the manner which best conveys the sentiment, passion, or affection with which it affects − or he pretends it does affect − him, and which he designs to communicate to his reader.'[20] Such expression would have 'all the beauty language was capable of bestowing on it'.[21]

Thus Moses should be called Moses, not 'the Jewish lawgiver',[22] and Plato should be called Plato, not 'the philosopher of noble birth'.[23] Pope should have spoken of the 'ocean', not 'the watery waste'.[24] Machines, scientific systems, languages, all have a natural tendency to move from the complex to the more simplified,[25] and there is a good case for style to do likewise. Superfluous words have a tendency to make an author's style 'dark and perplexed': Shaftesbury can only be censured for leading his readers 'into a dungeon of metaphorical obscurity'.[26]

At the same time, however, one should not forget one is constructing a model: 'The most perfect imitation of an object of any kind must in all cases, it is evident, be another object of the same kind.'[27] Yet a copy, the simplest representation of all, would yield *less* pleasure than the original, not more. A work of art should be inventive and creative, a commentary on the object. A dance may resemble and represent a social event or action, but it is still distinct from it and has an identity of its own. In sculpture, our pleasure results from 'the disparity between the object imitating, and the object imitated',[28] and a statue should hence be left uncoloured precisely to underline its differences with (and transcendence of) the original. It is also in the interests of a writer trying to influence others not to be excessively simple. If he is, his readers may not take him seriously. Thus Swift, 'who is the plainest as well as the most proper and precise of all the English writers, is despised as nothing out of the common road: each of us thinks he would have wrote as well'.[29] Such is the price for trying to imitate the language of ordinary people!

Here, as in so many other things, Smith was arguing for moderation and a middle way. There should neither be too much embellishment nor too little: 'Nothing without variety pleases us: a long uniform wall is a disagreeable object. Too much variety, such as the crowded objects of a parterre, is also disagreeable. Uniformity tires the mind; too much variety, too far increased, occasions an over-great dissipation of it.'[30]

(iii) Familiarity

The familiar is beautiful because we are used to it. Smith quotes with some approval the highly conservative aesthetic views of 'a learned Jesuit, Father Buffier', that 'in each species of creatures, what is most beautiful bears the strongest characters of the general fabric of the species, and has the strongest resemblance to the greater part of the individuals with which it is classed . . . The most customary form therefore is, in each species of things . . . the most beautiful.'[31] Our perception of beauty is thus dependent on time and place, since what is normal in one culture is unusual and pathological in another: 'What different ideas are formed in different nations concerning the beauty of the human shape and countenance! A fair complexion is a shocking deformity upon the coast of Guinea. Thick lips and a flat nose are a beauty. In some nations long ears that hang down upon the shoulders are the objects of universal admiration.'[32] A monster is only perceived as ugly because it bears the least resemblance to the norm of the species to which it belongs.

Familiarity of phenomena and their relationships, while not 'the sole principle of beauty', was to Smith an important one: 'There is scarce any one external form so beautiful as to please', he cautioned, 'if quite contrary to custom, and unlike whatever we have been used to in that particular species of things.'[33] Hence Ovid's descriptions of men with the heads and paws of bears can never be aesthetically satisfying: they are 'so very much out of the common course of nature as to shock us by their incredibility',[34] and thus upset our tranquillity by arousing our Surprise and Wonder. On the other hand, the familiar is reassuring, comforting, and thus a treat to our aesthetic sentiments: 'There is, perhaps, no form of external objects, how absurd and fantastical soever, to which custom will not reconcile us, or which fashion will not render even agreeable.'[35]

In the choice of words, too, the more familiar should be preferred to the less familiar. A selection of expressions must be made in any case, and it is easier to know the exact connotations of English words than of foreign ones. Thus, in the interests of perspicuity, the expressions we use should not only 'be free from all ambiguity proceeding from synonymous words', but they should be 'natives . . . of the language we speak in'.[36]

(iv) Propriety

The suitability of a symbol to a particular object is beautiful in itself, just as the perfect adjustment of inputs to outputs in a 'well-oiled machine' is admired for its own sake, irrespective of what the machine produces. In short, aesthetic satisfactions are independent of utilitarian consequences (pleasant or painful):

> That this fitness, this happy contrivance of any production of art, should often be more valued than the very end for which it was intended; and that the exact adjustment of the means for attaining any conveniency or pleasure should frequently be more regarded than that very conveniency or pleasure . . . has not, so far as I know, been yet taken notice of by any body. That this, however, is very frequently the case, may be observed in a thousand instances, both in the most frivolous and in the most important concerns of human life.[37]

Smith on occasion compares the 'great machine of the Universe' (designed by the 'Superintendent of the Universe') to a watch designed by a watchmaker. In both cases, the smooth functioning of all the parts

of the machine yields satisfaction because of its beauty, independent of
any other service the machine may render:

> Human society, when we contemplate it in a certain abstract and
> philosophical light, appears like a great, an immense machine, whose
> regular and harmonious movements produce a thousand agreeable
> effects. As in any other beautiful and noble machine that was the
> production of human art, whatever tended to render its movements
> more smooth and easy, would derive a beauty from this effect.[38]

Indeed, the legislature may pass laws to make the social machine work
more smoothly, not necessarily because it is interested in the product
of the machine (say, economic growth through laissez-faire), but simply
because the regular and orderly functioning of the machine is a joy in
itself to the beholder:

> The perfection of police, the extension of trade and manufactures,
> are noble and magnificent objects. The contemplation of them
> pleases us, and we are interested in whatever can tend to advance
> them. They make part of the great system of government, and the
> wheels of the political machine seem to move with more harmony
> and ease by means of them. We take pleasure in beholding the
> perfection of so beautiful and so grand a system, and we are uneasy
> till we remove any obstruction that can in the least disturb or
> encumber the regularity of its motions.[39]

It thus appears that, to Smith, utility is the unintended outcome of the
pursuit of beauty, and that ends are aesthetically indifferent so long as
means are optimally suited to their attainment. It appears that the
logico-experimental method is used in economics simply because the
proper adjustment of inputs to outputs is a pleasure to behold, and that
commodity-utility is a residual by-product, an almost unintended result.
Such a conclusion would, however, be misleading. Smith is in fact
arguing a far more utilitarian case than his language would lead us to
suppose. It may be true that 'the fitness of any system or machine to
produce the end for which it was intended, bestows a certain propriety
and beauty upon the whole';[40] but the reference to the 'end' which is
determined before the machine is designed shows that, when all is said
and done, it is impossible to escape teleology. The propriety of means
chosen is beautiful precisely because of their purposeful and optimal
satisfaction of a utilitarian goal-function. If propriety is beautiful, this
must be because utility itself is a source of beauty: 'When we consider

... actions, as making a part of a system of behaviour which tends to promote the happiness either of the individual or of the society, they appear to derive a beauty from this utility, not unlike that which we ascribe to any well-contrived machine.'[41] In certain circumstances a well-designed and efficiently-run concentration camp can be as beautiful as the Parthenon, provided that it promotes social utility, the aim of the Architect of Nature.[42]

Smith's attempt to construct a closed system from propriety, utility and beauty was not completely successful. He failed to explain possible contradictions between propriety and utility (as when, for example, our admiration for the rich and great causes us to overlook their crimes), or to integrate his aesthetic theories with his theory of social conflict (however beautifully the invisible hand allocates resources, there may still be resentment between labour and capital). He failed to explain why, although congruence of your perception of beauty with mine is the test of propriety of sentiments, we must nonetheless on occasion both bow to 'the acute and delicate discernment of the man of taste, who distinguishes the minute, and scarce perceptible differences of beauty and deformity';[43] and to say what aesthetic standards such an omniscient critic would apply. He failed adequately to link up his doctrine of propriety of an artifact in a situation with his doctrine of natural association of ideas, and thus was forced to conclude that the depiction of objects of surgery in a painting would be 'absurd and shocking';[44] they may be symmetrical and well-shaped in their design, and they are certainly useful to the health of the human organism, but unfortunately 'as the immediate effect of them is pain and suffering, the sight of them always displeases us'.[45]

Finally, his association of beauty with propriety and propriety with social utility may be criticised as an attempt to disguise a rather conservative social philosophy in the garb of a theory of aesthetics. Smith seems to be saying that, if each part of the social machine functions with propriety, then the utilitarian product will be social order; and that the beautiful sight of men working together in harmony to produce this order is a thrill to the philosopher. He seems to be arguing that if each actor plays the role assigned to him with propriety, wears the usual costumes and repeats the usual lines in response to the usual cues, then the outcome cannot but be continuity, tranquillity and cohesion. In short, he seems to have believed that there was nothing more beautiful than a functionalist model of society acted out by real actors on the stage of life.

It is from life, then, that the creative (or, more accurately, the re-creative) artist is to derive his perception of propriety. In particular,

there are four aspects of propriety which Smith considers of relevance
to aesthetic theory:

1. Propriety of the subject to its situation. Ridicule results when a
thing is out of harmony with its surroundings, when there is an improper
association of ideas. For example, 'a tall man is no object of laughter,
neither is a little; but a very tall man amongst a number of dwarfs, like
Gulliver amongst the Lilliputians . . . appears very ridiculous. There is
no real foundation for laughter here, but the odd association of grand
and mean or little ideas.'[46] Laughter is not caused by the object itself
but by the inappropriateness of the object in a particular context: 'A
sow wallowing in the mire is certainly a loathsome object, but no one
would laugh at it, as it is agreeable to the nature of the beast. But if he
saw the sow afterwards in a drawing-room, the case would be
altered.'[47]

Propriety is a social concept, since people in different cultures are
habituated to different things. Thus the height of pillars with Ionic,
Doric and Corinthian capitals is determined not by absolute, immutable
laws of aesthetics, but by customary association in a given place at a
given time: 'The propriety of each of those appropriations can be
founded upon nothing but habit and custom. The eye having been used
to see a particular proportion connected with a particular ornament,
would be offended if they were not joined together.'[48]

Social norms prescribe particular patterns of conduct and character,
and these are beautiful to behold because of their propriety. Thus the
behaviour of those who, 'walking in the humble paths of life', demonstrate the virtues usually deemed proper for their class (temperance,
decency, modesty, moderation, industry, self-command, frugality) has
'beauty and grace' quite independent of the utilitarian results thereby
produced. Indeed, it would be unjustifiable to praise a man simply for
the consequences of his actions, since this would mean we were
regarding him as a tool, a means to an end, and not as a man: 'It seems
impossible . . . that we should have no other reason for praising a man
than that for which we commend a chest of drawers.'[49] Virtuous
behaviour adds 'the fine polish to the wheels of society',[50] and the
smooth functioning of the social machine (proof of the proper co-ordi-
nation and co-operation of the parts) is a source of aesthetic pleasure
'independent of the advantages it yields'. Nonetheless, the advantages
yielded do exist and are considerable: for the individual, the approbation
of his conscience and his fellow men, and for society, the guarantee of
social continuity and tranquillity.

Our sense of propriety helps to repress social conflict: rather than being envied, the rich are admired, and the reason is aesthetic — not simply because they possess more wealth and power than the poor, but because they have the most suitable means to attain those desirable ends. Whether happiness is in fact the result is of secondary importance to the spectator: 'It is the ingenious and artful adjustment of those means to the end for which they were intended, that is the principal source of his admiration.'[51] Social stability is thus a special topic in aesthetics: no one would want to disturb such 'conveniency and arrangement', such harmony, such perfection, such order. The creative writer should remember that 'there is in human nature a servility which inclines us to adore our superiors'; and thus, while 'kings and nobles are what make the best characters in a tragedy', these same 'persons of high rank make very bad actors in a comedy. Dukes and princes and men of high rank, though they be never so ridiculous in themselves, never appear the subject of laughter.'[52]

Our sense of propriety helps too to determine our patterns of commodity-consumption. Social norms determine the proper decoration of the home: 'There seems to be an absurdity . . . in ornamenting a house after a quite different manner from that which custom and fashion have prescribed; though the new ornaments should in themselves be somewhat superior to the common ones.'[53] Social norms also dictate standards of dress: 'A man would be ridiculous who should appear in public with a suit of clothes quite different from those which are commonly worn, though the new dress should in itself be ever so graceful or convenient.'[54] We would, after all, miss what we are used to seeing: 'The modes of furniture and dress which seem ridiculous to strangers, give no offence to the people who are used to them.'[55] In short, social norms determine standards of propriety in commodity-consumption: we expect to see a given commodity associated with a particular kind of consumer, and find it aesthetically satisfying to discover the habitual association repeated yet again. A coxcomb like Monsieur Jourdain whose consumption-patterns are inappropriate to his social status arouses our ridicule; and because this perception that the contemptible has been juxtaposed to the admirable is no more than a socially conditioned reflex, we can truly say, with Bergson, that laughter is a group activity. Wild Peter of Hanover would not have had much of a sense of humour: 'Il n'y a pas de comique en dehors de ce qui est proprement *humain* . . . On ne goûterait pas le comique si l'on se sentait isolé.'[56]

So anxious is Smith to protect the social integration that results from the structured observance of these norms that he does not trouble to explain how he knows that some ornaments are 'superior', some

modes of dress 'graceful or convenient', where the actual spectator
dismisses them as ridiculous. Possibly Smith did have an absolute
standard of beauty in the back of his mind which he chose to keep to
himself lest true beauty conflict with the functionally necessary beauty
of habitual association. Certainly it is difficult to avoid this suspicion
when confronted with his repeated assertion that, when two objects are
usually associated, it is generally felt to be improper to separate them,
'though, independent of custom, there should be no *real* beauty in their
union'.[57] If the beauty of habitual association should conflict with any
other standard of beauty, it is evidently the latter which must give way.

    2. Propriety of language. Different styles are proper, depending on
whether the aim of the writer or speaker is to inform (didactic) or to
persuade (rhetoric); and style is beautiful precisely because of its
suitability. If proper symbols are used, the spectator will have no
difficulty in entering into and sharing the experience of the creator:
'When the sentiment of the speaker is expressed in a neat, clear, plain
and clever manner, and the passion or affection he is possessed of and
intends, *by sympathy,* to communicate to his hearer, is plainly and
cleverly hit off, then and then only the expression has all the force and
beauty that language can give it.'[58]
    Style is intimately related to content and should reinforce it, not
detract from it. Shaftesbury was aware of this: 'Polite dignity is the
character he aimed at, and as this seems to be best supported by a grand
and pompous diction, that was the style he made choice of.'[59] If an
orator wishes to be convincing, he should take care to be moderate of
expression, neither too 'refined' nor too 'blustering': 'The Philippics of
Demosthenes, the Catilinarians of Cicero, derive their whole beauty
from the noble propriety with which this passion is expressed.'[60]
Smith's own *Wealth of Nations* was itself written to influence public
opinion, which may account for its readable style, its practical approach,
its humour, and especially its occasional deliberate exaggeration ('If the
rod be bent too much one way, says the proverb, in order to make it
straight you must bend it as much the other'[61]). In this Smith was
unfortunately too successful. Possibly overestimating the strength of
the mercantilist opposition and underestimating the propitiousness of
economic and social conditions for a book of this sort, he overshot the
mark. Not only did he vanquish mercantilist economics for good, but
he was quickly made into the guru of liberal bourgeois capitalism, a role
which he filled as incongruously as a sow in a drawing-room.
    Language must be proper to the character depicted in a work of
fiction. Clearly, in a stratified society the speech of 'men of rank and

breeding' is different from that of the 'vulgar', and the writer should be careful to use words that are 'agreeable . . . to the custom of some particular part of the nation' he is portraying: 'Hence it is that words equally expressive and more commonly used would appear very absurd if used in common conversation by one in the character of a gentleman. Thus perhaps nine-tenths of the people of England say "I'se do it" instead of "I will do it", but no gentleman would use that expression without the imputation of vulgarity.'[62] Indeed, such language, by being habitually associated with the common people, appears to have something mean and low about it; while the best English is that English habitually associated with the best people, the aristocracy and Court. Once again, aesthetics reflects social standards of what is fitting and proper.

What is proper in one culture, of course, need not be proper in another: 'What in English appears to be the verse of the greatest gravity and dignity, appears in Italian to be the most burlesque and ludicrous; for no other reason, I apprehend, but because in the one language it is the ordinary verse, whereas in the other it departs the most from the movement of the ordinary verse.'[63] In France, the alexandrine is customarily associated with tragedy, while in England it is judged most suitable for comedy.[64] The difference reflects the different practices of the two countries, not the structure of the verse itself: 'What shocks at first will soon become easy from custom, which sanctifies everything.'[65] A psychological upheaval would be necessary before the English accepted the alexandrine as suitable for tragedy, and revolutions should be avoided wherever possible.

On the other hand, Smith does once again speak at times as if he believed there was an absolute standard of beauty independent of habitual associations. He argues, for example, that the English language has over time become more melodious:

> The harsh and uncouth gutterals which so much prevailed have been almost entirely laid aside: *thought, wrought, taught,* are now pronounced as if there were no gutteral in them . . . The final syllable —ed, which has a sound nearly as harsh as —eth, is now laid aside as often as possible . . . The English have been led into all these practices, without thinking of them, to remedy the natural harshness of their language.[66]

It seems that words can have an intrinsic beauty of their own, based on some abstract rules of aesthetics independent of habitual association. But this Smith elsewhere denies: the beauty of an expression 'flows

from the sentiment and the method of expressing it being suitable to
the passion, and not from the figure in which delivered'.[67]

3. Propriety with respect to the author himself. A writer should suit
his style to his 'genius and temper', not to some abstract standard of
beauty:

> One of grace cast of mind will describe an object in a very different
> way from one of more lively; a plain man will have a style very
> different from that of a simple man . . . These characters, though
> all good and agreeable, must nevertheless, as they are different, be
> expressed in very different styles, all of which may be very agreeable.
> And here likewise the rule may be applied, that one should stick to
> his natural character. A gay man should not endeavour to be grave,
> nor the grave man to be gay, but each should regulate that character
> and manner that is natural to him.[68]

Consider the case of Shaftesbury, who was 'of a very puny and weakly
constitution, always either under some disorder or in dread of falling
into one'.[69] Such a 'weakly state of body' is not usually found associated
with 'abstract reasoning', 'deep searches' or 'the violence of the passions'.
Such approaches would be 'too fatiguing for persons of this delicate
frame',[70] who ought to select a pompous and ornate rather than a profound or emotional style. Shaftesbury is admirable because he recognised the existence of a double constraint on his work, that the mind is
the prisoner of the body and the body the prisoner of society.

4. Propriety with respect to the audience. A work of art must be
comprehensible to the viewer or auditor, and acceptable to him. Thus,
although Shaftesbury modelled his character of Theocles on Socrates,
he had to make some modifications. The 'time and circumstances'[71]
of ancient Greece were different from those of eighteenth-century
England, and an eighteenth-century audience would simply not have
believed that an actual philosopher could behave as Socrates actually
did: 'As Socrates' humour is often too coarse and his sarcasms too
biting for this age, he has softened him in this respect and made his
Theocles altogether polite, and his wit such as suits the character of a
gentleman.'[72] All art is an appeal for 'sympathy' from a *particular*
audience. Savages, being ignorant and superstitious, are delighted with
tales of 'elves and fairies, dragons, griffins, and other monsters',[73] with
fables 'that would not be relished by a people of more knowledge'.[74]
As Sartre says, 'il paraît que les bananes ont meilleur goût quand on

vient de les cueillir: les ouvrages de l'esprit, pareillement, doivent se consommer sur place.'[75]

An artist who insists on supplying a product for which there is no demand must reconcile himself to the fact that he is doomed to failure. Swift's more serious works, for example, are almost never read. His religious views 'are not at all suitable to those which have for some time past prevailed in this country',[76] while his philosophy was pragmatic at a time when the intelligensia preferred the contemplative: 'Such confined thoughts do not suit the present taste, which delights only in general and abstract speculations.'[77] An artist who is willing to flatter his audience stands a better chance of success. Thus modesty and deference would be desirable when addressing a work of art to one's superiors: 'The orator often lays aside the dictatorial style and barely offers his arguments in a plain modest manner, especially when his discourse is directed to those of greater judgement and higher rank than himself.'[78] Similarly, the much-maligned Machiavelli was not writing in a 'party spirit'. He was only describing 'the politics then in fashion' and appealing to an audience, in a given place at a given time, by describing to them that with which they were familiar: 'The different courts of Italy at that time piqued themselves greatly on a refined and subtle politics. Nothing could be a greater reproach to a man of genius than that he was of an open and undesigning character.'[79]

Tacitus wrote of sentiment, emotion, the mind, not of external events and causality, and he did so because he was the product of his own society. Under Trajan, Rome enjoyed a period of security, stability and prosperity, the populace became introspective, and Tacitus had to appeal to the tastes of his audience:

> They who live in a great city where they have the free liberty of disposing of their wealth in all the luxuries and refinements of life, who are not called to any public enjoyment but what they inclined and obtained from the favour and indulgence of the prince — such a people, I say, having nothing to engage them in the hurry of life, would naturally turn their attention to the motions of the human mind, and those events that were accounted for by the different internal affections that influenced the persons concerned would be what most suited their taste.[80]

It is interesting that Sartre, like Smith, explains literary introspection in terms of social conditions rather than simply the personality of the individual writer. Thus he insists that, if 'l'art du XVII siècle est un processus strictement interne . . . un cogito perpétuel',[81] the reason must be sought in the nature of a stratified society lacking change of any sort, a 'société hierarchisée' which 'confond le présent avec l'éternel'.[82]

Another example of the social origins of literature is Smith's comparison of the Athenian, Demosthenes, and the Roman, Cicero. In Athens there was less inequality of fortunes than in Rome, and one citizen was considered the equal of another. Moreover, 'commerce gave the lowest of the people an opportunity of raising themselves fortunes, and by that means power'.[83] In Rome, on the other hand, there was a great gap between rich and poor, powerful and weak; no middle class; and no chance of social mobility since politics (not commerce) was the only means to wealth and power, and the plebeians were excluded from it. Thus Demosthenes, writing for a society where people spoke to one another as equals and where 'difference of fortune or employment did not hinder the ease and familiarity of behaviour',[84] avoided pomposity, used familiar analogies, and could afford to be careless with grammar. Cicero, however, writing for the upper classes of a highly stratified society, used more grave and formal language, the language most in keeping with the superior dignity of an established aristocracy. In short, the difference in style between the two men 'may probably arise from the different condition of the countries in which they lived',[85] not simply from differences in their individual temperament. Each adapted his style to the country where he lived and to the clientele for which he worked.

IV. Science and Social Science

David Hume believed that scientific inquiry ought to 'have a direct reference to action and society', and preached to the scholar the Enlightenment gospel of anthropocentrism: 'Be a philosopher; but, amidst all your philosophy, be still a man.'[1] Indeed, he found it impossible to imagine a science that was not in the last analysis human-orientated:

> 'Tis evident, that all the sciences have a relation, greater or less, to human nature; and that however wide any of them may seem to run from it, they still return back by one passage or another. Even *Mathematics, Natural Philosophy,* and *Natural Religion,* are in some measure dependent on the science of MAN; since they lie under the cognizance of men, and are judged of by their powers and faculties.[2]

Smith, like Hume, was of the opinion that the proper study of mankind is man; and in this section we shall investigate his views on the reciprocal relationship enjoyed by science and art with economy and society. There are three points to note: Firstly, law and order, leisure and opulence, are the preconditions for scientific and artistic activity. Secondly, the habitual associations that are the basis of both science and art are contingent since they are perceived in a particular situational context. Thirdly, science and art can play an active role in helping to bring about substantial changes in that context, and can thus contribute to the creation of a new situation, with a new set of habitual associations, which may indeed be precisely those which are the preconditions for scientific and artistic activity.

1. The preconditions for scientific and artistic activity are, first, law, order and security; and second, leisure, tranquillity, opulence and freedom from want. It is understandable that

mankind, in the first ages of society, before the establishment of law, order, and security, have little curiosity to find out those hidden chains of events which bind together the seemingly disjointed appearances of nature. A savage, whose subsistence is precarious, whose life is every day exposed to the rudest dangers, has no inclination to amuse himself with searching out what, when discovered, seems to serve no other purpose than to render the theatre of nature a more connected spectacle to his imagination.[3]

In the absence of scientific inquiry, primitive man despairs of discovering any regular system in nature.[4] When Wonder is inescapable (for example, when occasioned by comets, eclipses or thunder), it is assuaged by 'pusillanimous superstition', by the construction of fictitious models with no empirical content and no predictive power whatsoever. This is the origin of polytheism, 'which ascribes all the irregular events of nature to the favour or displeasure of intelligent, though invisible beings, to gods, daemons, witches, genii, fairies'.[5] In short, primitive man seeks to explain the less familiar in terms of the more familiar by creating gods in his own image: hence a calm sea is attributed to Neptune, a good vintage to Bacchus, an abundant harvest to Ceres.

Fortunately, economic growth puts paid to such ignorance. It institutes the market mechanism, which in turn leads to the political balance of powers and the rule of law. It raises the national income, and thus ensures both opulence and leisure. It guarantees differentiation of function and differentiation of wealth, so important for political security: in poor countries where there is 'no room for any evident distinction of ranks', there is of necessity 'the confusion and misrule which flows from a want of all regular subordination'.[6] And in all these ways economic growth fosters an environment conducive to scientific inquiry:

> When law has established order and security, and subsistence ceases to be precarious, the curiosity of mankind is increased, and their fears are diminished. The leisure which they then enjoy renders them more attentive to the appearances of nature, more observant of her smallest irregularities, and more desirous to know what is the chain which links them all together. That some such chain subsists betwixt all her seemingly disjointed phaenomena, they are necessarily led to conceive; and that magnanimity, and cheerfulness, which all generous natures acquire who are bred in civilized societies, where they have so few occasions to feel their weakness, and so many to be conscious of their strength and security, renders them less disposed to employ, for this connecting chain, those invisible beings whom the fear and ignorance of their rude forefathers had engendered.[7]

Hence, a commercial society, as it guarantees security, opulence and leisure, is the enemy of superstition and ignorance and the ally of thought, inquiry and reasoned argument. It is no less a friend to the fine arts: 'Wherever the inhabitants of a city are rich and opulent, where they enjoy the necessaries and conveniences of life in ease and security, there the arts will be cultivated, and refinement of manners a never-failing attendant.'[8] Once again, social stratification has an active role to play, since it is, after all, the leisured classes that patronise and encourage the arts: 'In all such states it must necessarily happen that there are many who are not obliged to labour for their livelihood, and have nothing to do but display themselves in what most suits their taste, and seek out for pleasure in all its shapes.'[9] Smith would have found no grounds to disagree with Hume's view that 'industry, knowledge, and humanity, are linked together by an indissoluble chain, and are found, from experience as well as reason, to be peculiar to the more polished, and, what are commonly denominated, the more luxurious ages'.[10] To the members of the Scottish Enlightenment, commerce and culture were inseparable: 'The same age, which produces great philosophers and politicians, renowned generals and poets, usually abounds with skilful weavers, and ship-carpenters', Hume announced:

> We cannot reasonably expect, that a piece of woollen cloth will be brought to perfection in a nation, which is ignorant of astronomy,

or where ethics are neglected. The spirit of the age affects all the arts; and the minds of men, being once roused from their lethargy, and put into a fermentation, turn themselves on all sides, and carry improvements into every art and science.[11]

2. Smith's reliance on the Lockean formulation of the empirical method in science means he believed an external phenomenon had to exist before it could be perceived; and his aesthetics was founded on the beauty that results from the propriety of habitual associations. Thus both science and aesthetics are dependent on the pre-existence of a situational context.

Moreover, each situational context is different. What one accepts, what one questions, depends on what one is used to, and not all men are familiar with the same objects:

> The same orders of succession, which to one set of men seem quite according to the natural course of things, and such as require no intermediate events to join them, shall to another appear altogether incoherent and disjointed, unless some such events be supposed: and this for no other reason, but because such orders of succession are familiar to the one, and strange to the other.[12]

The best the scientist can do is to approach a given situation in the real world as he would an unknown card-game, by observing how the game is played and trying in that way to infer its rules. Empirical investigation only discovers those norms functionally necessary to keep the game in progress; and such standards of propriety (the 'done thing', whether in conduct and character patterns, or in commodity consumption) are beautiful precisely because such habitual associations ensure that the game will continue to be played in an orderly fashion. Literature too is empirical in nature, since it reflects social mores and values: the writer mirrors his society and different societies, different groups and sub-groups within a society, being placed in different material circumstances, play different games and have different sets of beliefs. In short, the scientist and the writer alike ought to be an observer of 'social things', and not a merchant of his own ideas: the student of action, like the actor himself, would be well advised to do society's thing rather than his own.

Smith's apparent identification of 'what is' with 'what ought to be' leaves him open to the charge of excessive conservatism. In his defence, however, it is important to recall the terrible burden of epistemological scepticism on a social philosopher, which must not be underestimated.

On the one hand, his perception of reality in terms of experience implies a critical challenge to the authority of untested assumptions, beliefs, traditions, and thus to the established order (especially where that order is founded on metaphysical ideas such as religious dogma, the divine right of kings, mysticism, or other doctrines for which there is no experimental evidence). Yet on the other hand there is the fear of intellectual chaos resulting from chaos in the world around us, since that chaos means the breakdown of habitual associations. As Hume puts it: 'Without the influence of custom, we should be entirely ignorant of every matter of fact beyond what is immediately present to the memory and senses. We should never know how to adjust means to ends, or to employ our natural powers in the production of any effect. There would be an end at once of all action, as well as of the chief part of speculation.'[13] Smith was obsessed with the problem of order for a very logical reason indeed: once customary, familiar successions are interrupted, once the tranquillity of the existing order is destroyed, then there is no further guarantee either of the regularity in observable phenomena so necessary for empirical knowledge, or of predictability in human behaviour, the basis of social cohesion and unity. Habitual association in the last analysis is the precondition for sanity:

> Could we conceive a person of the soundest judgement, who had grown up to maturity, and whose imagination had acquired those habits, and that mold, which the constitution of things in this world necessarily impress upon it, to be all at once transported alive to some other planet, where nature was governed by laws quite different from those which take place here; as he would be continually obliged to attend to events, which must to him appear in the highest degree jarring, irregular, and discordant, he would soon feel . . . confusion and giddiness begin to come upon him, which would at last end . . . in lunacy and distraction.[14]

Nonetheless, some sets of habitual associations might to a sensitive thinker be more attractive than others. Smith admits that many a great artist is aware of 'that ideal perfection of which he has formed some conception, which he imitates as well as he can, but which he despairs of ever equalling'.[15] Such an artist strives to reproduce some abstract idea independent of existing worldly images and 'imitates the work of a divine artist, which can never be equalled'.[16] An absolute standard of 'real beauty'[17] might exist quite apart from what we are used to: 'A man, and in the same manner a horse, is handsome or ugly, each of them, on account of his own intrinsic beauty or deformity, without

regard to their resembling or not resembling, the one, another man, or
the other, another horse.'[18] And if there can be an absolute standard
of beauty, there might also be an absolute standard of truth and an
absolute standard of morality.

Clearly, a theoretical system founded on empiricism, materialism,
the propriety of the customary and the guarded identification of 'is'
with 'ought' appears beset with contradictions once the possibility of a
non-empirical absolute is admitted. Possibly Adam Smith was secretly
an idealist, but one who recognised the tremendous disorder that a
move towards the ideal might cost (particularly since the politician and
civil servant are sure to make mincemeat of the philosopher's dreams).
Possibly he felt that a second-rate set of habitual associations in a
second-best situation was the price that must be paid for stability and
order. Possibly, however, he felt that his ideal was in the process of
becoming reality. Each situation has its own centre of gravity, but no
two situations are alike; and in the course of progress a situation could
emerge which generates a new set of habitual associations such that the
viable and the ideal coincide. Philosophers have been able to interpret
the world in diverse ways because of the diversity of material situations
which have arisen and cried out to be observed. The point for Smith,
however, was to select that situation which realised his philosophy on
earth; and then encourage gradual (but in the long run major) changes
such that the ideal was approached. Because the revolution was to be
gradual rather than sudden, moreover, the actor need not lose his
equilibrium: tradition is challenged, and yet social upheaval is avoided
and continuity with the past maintained.

3. If economic and social progress is the precondition for science and
the arts to flourish, it is no less true that the flourishing state of science
and the arts is the precondition for economic and social progress.
Indeed, a philosopher might himself harness science and the arts to
bring about the gradual social revolution he so much desires.

Smith defines reason as 'the faculty which determines not only what
are the proper means for attaining any end, but also what ends are fit
to be pursued, and what degree of relative value we ought to put upon
each'.[19] In other words, science has a double role: it helps the actor
determine what goals he ought to seek in a given society at a given time
(since these goals are firmly embedded in the structure of society and
can be established by induction) and advises him on how best to attain
those goals. Smith reproaches Rousseau for being 'more capable of
feeling strongly than of analysing accurately':[20] in a modern
commercial, technological society there is no excuse for not being able

to think clearly. A businessman must be in the habit of noticing that B usually follows A, so that, desiring B, he can perform A, or, observing A, he can with a certain degree of probability expect B. Of course, the resultant change in the economic basis is bound to bring about derivative changes in the institutional superstructure, so that in the long run we may be left with an equation which predicts, not B on the basis of A, but D on the basis of C. Such a new set of habitual associations may to a sensitive philosopher even yield more pleasure than the old set; and for this reason the rational businessman takes on for Smith the dimensions of a Hegelian world-historical individual, the unwitting contributor to the realisation of philosophy on earth.[21]

The arts too are useful. Commercial society makes prose necessary for the first time: 'Prose is naturally the language of business, as poetry is of pleasure and amusement. Prose is the style in which all the common affairs of life, all business and agreements, are made. No one ever made a bargain in verse: pleasure is not what he there aims at.'[22] Poetry antedates prose: the savage composes words to go with his rhythms but has no need of prose literature, since the subjects of his creative arts are Wonder and Admiration, not utility.

Moreover, the arts are a welcome antidote to the poison of religious fanaticism: 'public diversions' should be encouraged, since they can easily dissipate 'that melancholy and gloomy humour which is almost always the nurse of popular superstition and enthusiasm' and expose 'to public ridicule, and sometimes even to public execration'[23] the artifices and manipulations of religious bigots. Indeed, the arts can go still further: not only can they combat false doctrines, but they can teach proper behavioural norms by example and help thereby to consolidate our social consciousness. Their aim is not just to entertain but to instruct, to 'assist us in our future conduct, by pointing out the means to avoid or produce any event'.[24] Historical writing teaches posterity 'how to produce the like events or shun others, and know what is to be expected from such and such circumstances';[25] while true satire, by making deviancy into an object of ridicule, 'tends to the reformation of manners and the benefit of mankind'.[26]

Unfortunately, however, for the philosopher who desires social change, the arts are basically conservative: a work of art, whether depicting propriety or causality, is only believable so long as it portrays the accepted norms of a given situation, and for this reason its pragmatic value falls short of altering men's consciousness or persuading them to alter the material conditions of their existence. Propaganda of this sort would be as ridiculous as a sow in a drawing-room. Only writers who are in touch with the *Zeitgeist* have any chance of being believed. The arts are the products of a particular situation and cannot be expected to impose spurious idealistic solutions on adverse material conditions. Thus the Greeks were instructed in music in order to overcome the 'rudeness and ferocity' of their manners,[27] to 'humanize the mind, to soften the temper, and to dispose it for performing all the social and moral duties both of public and private life';[28] while the Romans, on the other hand, were trained solely in the arts of war. Yet paradoxically 'the morals of the Romans . . . seem to have been, not only equal, but, upon the whole, a good deal superior to those of the Greeks'.[29] The character of a people has its own centre of gravity, and this cannot be altered simply by offering new 'amusements'. To Smith as to Durkheim, art is in the last analysis little more than 'a noble form of play'.[30]

3 CONDUCT AND CHARACTER

Introduction

Adam Smith believed that the 'selfish and confined' system of Thomas Hobbes[1] overestimated men's utilitarian motivation (the desire to win assistance and protection) and underestimated their fundamental social needs (the love of company and of proper approbation). Naturally man is aware that 'his own interest is connected with the prosperity of society, and that the happiness, perhaps the preservation of his existence, depends upon its preservation'.[2] But man is aware too of the natural love he has for society, and hence 'desires that the union of mankind should be preserved for its own sake, and though he himself was to derive no benefit from it'.[3] There is no historical evidence of a *bellum omnium contra omnes*, nor for a social contract, past or present,[4] and a wealth of evidence that man is a social animal, able to 'subsist only in society'[5] and taking pleasure in its 'orderly and flourishing state'.[6] Indeed, as we have already seen, this pleasure has a powerful aesthetic dimension, since propriety of conduct and conformity to society's customary and traditional standards appear beautiful to the lover of any 'well-contrived machine'.[7] In this Chapter we shall examine how love of community rather than mere association (as represented by the economic exchange of equivalents or the political balance of powers) causes the individual in society to observe those norms of propriety in conduct and character which the group prescribes for him, and makes himself thereby fit for society.

In Section I, we shall argue that, to Adam Smith, the main source of social integration is the desire to be accepted by one's fellow men: 'The chief part of human happiness arises from the consciousness of being beloved',[8] and this consciousness to a sensitive man 'is of more importance to happiness than all the advantage which he can expect to derive from it'.[9] For this reason, he must mentally record the reactions of the spectators present in a multitude of situations to the sentiments there expressed: a man's ideas of propriety are 'gradually formed from his observations upon the character and conduct both of himself and of other people'.[10] There is no absolute, universal, eternal standard of right and wrong; and a savage might be able to approve of sentiments which a Scotsman would find repulsive, ridiculous, deviant or contemptible.

Moral norms are always relative to the society in which they are observed, but this does not mean they are any the less imperative. Consider the case of a child entering school (and thus society): its class-mates are neither as indulgent nor as partial as its parents were, and yet it 'naturally wishes to gain their favour, and to avoid their hatred or contempt . . . It soon finds that it can do so in no other way than by moderating, not only its anger, but all its other passions, to the degree which its playfellows and companions are likely to be pleased with.'[11] In other words, moral standards are first to be discovered empirically (by common sense rather than Kantian *Vernunft*) and then respected because of the authority of the group. Man does not think in solitude: Alter as well as Ego (say, Robinson Crusoe) is necessary to determine propriety of sentiments through coincidence of perceptions (what Smith called 'sympathy'). The absence of sympathy, the perception that there is no coincidence of sentiments, is the sanction for impropriety; and it is the fear of this sanction that causes a man to practice self-control, avoid extremes of passion, and moderate his self-love. Thus, social cohesion results from shared values and shared sentiments, and sympathy is the cement of society.

Approbation is based on propriety of motivation, not utility of results. Smith is adamant that

> the utility of all qualities . . . is plainly an afterthought, and not
> what first recommends them to our approbation . . . Originally,
> however, we approve of another man's judgement, not as something
> useful, but as right, as accurate, as agreeable to truth and reality; and
> it is evident we attribute those qualities to it for no other reason but
> because we find that it agrees with our own. [12]

Our sympathy is aroused by the propriety or impropriety of the passions motivating an action, not by its actual results (which come under the heading of merit and demerit, sanctioned by reward and punishment); but, of course, we optimistically hope that good intentions will produce good results, and must (since we cannot see inside the mind of another actor) often deduce intention from outcome.

In doing so, however, we may be mistaken. We might praise a man for an action he never intended to perform, and in such a case he would find it difficult to derive any pleasure from our ignorance so long as 'the man within the breast', his conscience, knew the truth. In general, man wishes not just to be approved of, but to be that which is worthy of approbation. Whereas 'peevish individuals' and 'splenetic philosophers' had argued that man is motivated purely by a love of praise (and some economists that man is motivated mainly by pecuniary self-interest), Smith believed that men are governed principally by a love of praiseworthiness. To obtain knowledge of society's true standards of propriety, however, we cannot depend on the judgement of the real spectator, who might be biased or ill-informed. Instead we must decide in each situation that faces us how an impartial spectator, having exemplary powers of good judgement and so well informed that he attends 'to many things which we had overlooked',[14] would view our reaction. Suppose, for example, that we wished to determine the propriety of the grief shown by a man who had just lost his father: 'We know that if we took time to consider his situation fully, and in all its parts, we should without doubt most sincerely sympathize with him.'[15] We sympathise, in other words, not with an emotion alone (in this case, grief) but with an emotion proper in its context; and thus, before we sympathise there is a complex if automatic process of reason and thought[16] to determine how the (non-existent) impartial spectator, the sounding-board of all moral judgements, would react.

The parallels between Smith's theory of morality and that of Emile Durkheim are striking. Both men believed that it was possible to create an empiricist science of ethics 'according to the method of the positive sciences':[17] if social facts are to be treated as external things, then the sociologist cannot deal with what ought to be, only with what is observed to be. Both men defined the function of morality in terms of social solidarity: as Durkheim says, 'Man is a moral being only because he lives in society, since morality consists in being solidary with a group and varying with this solidarity. Let all social life disappear, and moral life will disappear with it, since it would no longer have any objective.'[18] Both men accepted that morality is based on a sense of duty, not on utility; and thus both emphasised (subjective) motivation and played down the relevance of (objective) results.[19] Both men believed that the exact content of moral codes varies from society to society, not because of imperfect comprehension of immutable moral principles, but because of variations in social structures: a moral system is built up by a society, helps it adapt naturally to the external physical and social world, and gives it cohesion sufficient to ensure its survival. Hence both accepted that there can be no division between 'the necessary' and 'the good':[20] norms must be derived inductively, not through Cartesian deduction, and in any case a society automatically gravitates to those norms 'found to be most in accord with the nature of things'.[21] Durkheim comments about society: 'Tell me the marriage patterns, the morals dominating family life, and I will tell you the principal characteristics of its organization.'[22] Moreover, as functionalists, both were pleased to see each part in the social whole playing its proper role with regularity and consistency.

Both men stressed the need for community and emotional attachment to the collectivity (Man 'is not truly himself', Durkheim says, 'except on the condition that he is involved in society'[23]), and thus both believed that moral constraint can only be social constraint (often reflected in one's own conscience[24]). Morality means the pursuit of supra-individual aims: 'To act morally is to act in terms of the collective interest.'[25]   Both rejected atomism and the cult of the individual, and emphasised that man lives in, and is part of, society. Finally, both Smith and Durkheim held that collective beliefs and practices are found in each individual precisely because they exist in the group, and that the process of socialisation internalises such beliefs and practices in the form of rules. As Durkheim puts it:

> All education is a continuous effort to impose on the child ways of seeing, feeling, and acting which he could not have arrived at spontaneously. From the very first hours of his life, we compel him to eat, drink, and sleep at regular hours; we constrain him to cleanliness, calmness, and obedience; later we exert pressure upon him in order that he may learn proper consideration for others, respect for customs and conventions, the need for work, etc . . . This unremitting pressure to which the child is subjected is the very pressure of the social milieu which tends to fashion him in its own image.[26]

In Section II we shall continue our discussion of 'sympathy' by showing how it is responsible for determining the balance between self-love and benevolence to other men; and by arguing that, despite the existence of this powerful social mechanism, common sense nonetheless tells us that concord of sentiments often is not enough to prevent misery and injustice.

It is universally agreed that every man should show proper benevolence to himself (he is, after all, his own best friend), and in so doing he wins the approbation of the spectator. If, however, his self-interest is judged excessive, then his individual pleasure (say, the pecuniary gains of the shopkeeper who indulges in sharp practices) will be more than spoiled by the displeasure of mankind in general: 'Compared with the contempt of mankind, all other external evils are easily supported.'[27] The 'correct' amount of self-love varies from society to society, but may in each case be determined empirically: 'As to love our neighbour as we love ourselves is the great law of Christianity, so it is the great precept of nature to love ourselves only as we love our neighbour, or, what comes to the same thing, as our neighbour is capable of loving us.'[28] Because of Smith's economic determinism, it is not unreasonable to suppose he felt self-love to be particularly proper in a mercantile environment. The fact that self-love is the predominant motive in the

economic sphere, however, does not mean that man is not simultaneously involved in other spheres, each with its corresponding mixture
of benevolence to oneself and benevolence to others.

It is useful to think of benevolence in terms of four concentric
circles. The innermost circle is oneself, and then come one's family and
friends, one's country, and finally humanity as a whole. Men are made
of 'coarse clay'[29] and as they move out from the nucleus their passions
become less intense. Nonetheless they behave with the proper degree of
benevolence in each of the four circles. Such propriety is not exchanged
for the applause of others (although that may be an unintended outcome), and the supreme source of satisfaction (to Smith as to
Shaftesbury) remains self-approbation.

The cause of conformity to moral sentiments is the desire of the
individual to win 'sympathy' (from his fellow-men and from his own
conscience). Their function, however, is clearly social solidarity: upon
the observance of norms and duties, Smith says, 'depends the very
existence of human society', which would otherwise 'crumble into
nothing'.[30] No Great Legislator on earth could have designed so
complex and perfect a network of relationships and interrelationships;
and thus Smith, in common with other Enlightenment philosophers,
brought in the concept of Providence. God is seen as a Great Designer
who designed the social machine with the aim of promoting men's
terrestrial happiness, and whose function it is to assuage men's *Angst*
about their personal future and about the teleology of things in general.
As Thomas Reid, Smith's successor to the Chair of Moral Philosophy
in Glasgow (and, like Frances Hutcheson and Adam Ferguson, an
ordained minister of religion), put it, human beings are like bees, who,
in constructing their honeycombs, behave *as if* they had a knowledge of
geometry. They do not, which causes the observer to believe in 'that
great Geometrician who made the bee'.[31]

Yet even Smith admits that the social machine does not always
function smoothly: witness the distress of the widow and the orphan
who are left with no redress of grievances on this earth and must
console themselves with thoughts of Heaven. Clearly, the belief in God
plays the dubious sociological role of completing a defective circuit,
and that this should be necessary is suprising in view of Smith's *ex
post*, conservative approach to morality. Norms tried and tested by
society are said to be the only acceptable moral standards (to avoid
spurious, irrelevant rules and a flight into idealism), and God's will is
derived from man's practice (since man's practice is said to be an index
of man's need); but then Smith requires of God not only to sanctify
existing social standards (which arose naturally in a given material

situation) but also to repair the evil they do. Apparently the seamless
web of sympathy does not after all generate the correct values, so that
a God in Heaven must be called in to correct the mistakes of the God of
Nature. As Professor Hampson has so eloquently put it, the philosopher
is faced with a terrible choice between the 'inscrutable' and the
'intolerable'.[32]

The contradiction can perhaps be resolved, however, by recalling
that Smith (unlike many Deists, such as Voltaire) had a qualified theory
of progressive social evolution. Nature being dynamic as well as static,
possibly Smith believed that many present-day abuses would be automatically corrected by historical change in the form of improved
administration of justice, more checks and balances in government,
restraints on the power of nobility and clergy, and a growing sense of
humanity. In short, perhaps Smith felt harmony would be established
by successive approximations in the course of Progress. Man can, moreover, help to remedy the evils of the existing situation by helping to
create a new situation with a new centre of gravity. After all, 'man was
made for action, and to promote by the exertion of his faculties such
changes in the external circumstances both of himself and others, as
may seem most favourable to the happiness of all'.[33]

In Section III we shall argue that customary standards of propriety
are not accidental, and that habitual association in a social context is
very often the product of that society's material basis. Matter has a
motion of its own, which the spectator can identify but not alter.
Specifically, Smith believed a man's character to be principally determined by his profession and work-function: 'The understandings of
the greater part of men are necessarily formed by their ordinary
employments.'[34] Thus, the virtues of frugality and honesty are
habitually associated with the merchant and he observes them in order
to win the approbation of his fellow men; but they are also uniquely
appropriate to his economic function, since if he were generous,
indolent, stupid or dissolute, he would ruin himself and go out of
business. A merchant is frugal and honest because he is a merchant; he
does not become a merchant because he has an inborn propensity to
be frugal and honest. The cult of the individual is spurious since men do
not have much of an essence independent of the conditions of their
material existence. If, instead of becoming a merchant, the same man
had become a clergyman, then he would have been grave (due both to
what one expects clergymen to be, and to the effects of spending his
office-hours reflecting on Heaven and Hell). If he had been a soldier,
then he would have been dissolute (as most soldiers are, in an attempt
to forget the ever-present threat of death). And if he had chosen to be a

bureaucrat, then he would have gravitated to apathy (since bureaucrats lack challenge). The norms in each case are those appropriate to his economic status; but his conformity to them results from a desire to be accepted in his chosen role.

In this sense Smith might have agreed with Professor Berger that 'it is not correct to say that each society gets the men it deserves. Rather, each society produces the men it needs.'[35] There is, however, a fundamental difference between Smith and Berger: whereas Berger favours individual self-expression, Smith both predicts and glorifies conformity of behaviour-patterns to the empirically determined mean type appropriate in each case. Such conformity has the function of ensuring the unity of the organism, a particularly valuable property in a modern society characterised by a great variety of job-functions and character-patterns. Men are disapproved of in proportion to their divergence from the mean type they are expected to resemble, and this sanction stimulates each actor to play his assigned role with the utmost propriety.[36] As a result, if we know a man's job, we are able to predict his character-pattern.

National character is formed in the same way: the manner in which the majority of the citizens earn their living determines the character-patterns that are habitual and proper in the situation. Behaviour that is fitting in one set of material conditions might not be suitable at all in another. It is no accident that citizens of an agricultural country are noted for their 'liberality, frankness, and good fellowship', while citizens of a mercantile country are notorious for their 'narrowness, meanness, and selfish disposition'.[37] Clearly, economic growth means more than rising standards of living or institutional change; it also creates new patterns of conduct and character, which a philosopher must accept as appropriate. Indeed, a philosopher may even want to use economic change as the means to produce a new material basis which in turn will produce a particular set of behaviour-patterns. To Adam Smith, the production of 'trinkets and baubles' is never more than the means. The end is the production of man himself.

I. Conduct

Man in society derives pleasure from discovering that his motives and sentiments are identical to, or congruent with, the motives and sentiments of his fellow men. He 'longs for that relief which nothing can afford him but the entire concord of the affections of the spectators with his own',[1] and this correspondence or sharing of sentiments creates a warm sense of fellow-feeling. 'the best and most comfortable of all social enjoyments'.[2] Smith calls this tendency to exchange places 'in fancy'[3] with other men and to try and feel as they do by the name of 'sympathy'.

This process of instinctive identification is unselfish. Thus a man can sympathise with a woman in childbirth and share her feelings even though he can never share her experience. He can sympathise with a madman insensible to his condition by reflecting on what 'he himself would feel if he was reduced to the same unhappy situation, and, what perhaps is impossible, was at the same time able to regard it with his present reason and judgement'.[4] Indeed, he can even sympathise with the dead, by putting himself in his imagination in the position of the dead man, although his sympathy is with shadow-feelings which the dead person might properly feel if he could but in fact does not. In none of these three cases is he personally involved. He stands neither to gain nor to lose. He can say with absolute truthfulness: 'My grief . . . is entirely upon your account, and not in the least upon my own.'[5]

We extend sympathy to others (by putting ourselves in our imagination in their situation) and receive it from them (when they put themselves in our situation). Men do not, however, sympathise purely with the raw passions themselves, but with the propriety of those passions in a particular situation: 'Sympathy . . . does not arise so much from the view of the passion, as from that of the situation which excites it.'[6] Man is a social animal, desperately craving the acceptance of his fellows and aware that the only way he can secure this concord of their sentiments with his own is 'by lowering his passion to that pitch, in which the spectators are capable of going along with him. He must flatten . . . the sharpness of its natural tone, in order to reduce it to harmony and concord with the emotions of those who are about him.'[7] A man who challenges the 'group mind' and puts individual preferences before social norms will find himself an outsider, properly rejected by a society whose standards of propriety he has rejected. A man, on the other hand, who exercises self-command and disciplines his passions by reference to what his fellow men expect in a given situation will be rewarded with their fellowship: 'What is it that makes a man agreeable company? Is it not, when his sentiments appear to be agreeably expressed, when the passion or affection is properly conveyed, and when their thoughts are so agreeable and natural that we find ourselves inclined to give our assent to them?'[8]

Self-command does not mean self-abnegation; it only means an attempt to see things in their proper perspective. No spectator can ever feel as strongly as the original actor himself (especially in the case of bodily passions such as hunger or sex), and thus a sensitive actor will avoid extremes of passion (such as 'clamorous grief'[9] or excessive anger) if he knows from past experience that these reactions are too exaggerated relative to the stimulus to attract sympathy. Similarly, the presence of disinterested spectators moderates aggression. If a person has been injured, feels resentment, and seeks revenge, the spectator sympathises with his proper resentment, but also with the fears of the offender; as a result, the resentment of the injured party will have to be moderate to be proper, since the spectator sympathises with the sentiments of both parties in the dispute. In general, behaviour-patterns in society do in fact cluster around an empirically ascertainable Golden Mean as men strive to become 'the natural object of the joyous congratulations and sympathetic attentions of mankind'.[10]

Men want, however, not only to receive applause, but to 'deserve applause'. They want not only to be loved but to be worthy of love, and desire 'not only praise, but praise-worthiness; or to be that thing which, though it should be praised by nobody, is, however, the natural and proper object of praise'.[11] In other words, men orientate themselves not to what the spectator does in fact applaud but to what he ought to applaud. The real spectator, after all, might be ignorant of the facts of the case (as when he thinks he is praising a woman's complexion when in truth he is praising her make-up; or when he allows himself to be deceived by the lies of a braggart), temporarily blinded by excessive passions of his own (as when he jealously plays down the achievements of a rival), partial (as when he has a vested interest), or simply insensitive to society's actual standards. Smith argues, therefore, that if a man wants confirmation of the propriety of his conduct, the only dependable sounding-board is 'the sympathetic feelings of the impartial and well-informed spectator'.[12]

A man who has behaved properly 'applauds himself by sympathy with the approbation of this supposed impartial judge',[13] even if the real spectator showers him with disapprobation: 'Misery and wretchedness can never enter the breast in which dwells complete self-satisfaction.'[14] His mind is serene and composed, since he has won the approval of the impartial spectator, as reflected in his own conscience, the distillate of social norms. A man who has behaved improperly, on the other hand, will be reprimanded by the 'man within the breast':

> When the happiness or misery of others depends in any respect upon our conduct, we dare not, as self-love might suggest to us, prefer the interest of one to that of many. The man within immediately calls to us, that we value ourselves too much and other people too little, and that, by doing so, we render ourselves the proper object of the

contempt and indignation of our brethren.[15]

No matter how great our success, it will bring us little joy if we know it is undeserved. For example, 'a woman who paints could derive, one should imagine, but little vanity from the compliments that are paid to her complexion'.[16]

Consider the case of a criminal who alone knows of his own guilt. Aware that the impartial spectator disapproves of his excessive self-love, and that the real spectators would disapprove if only the crime were known, the criminal feels cut off from all fellow-feeling. He can neither live in society (which he 'dares no longer look . . . in the face') nor outside of it ('solitude is still more dreadful'). He knows he is the natural and proper object of society's resentment, and 'it gives him little pleasure to look upon himself in the light in which other people actually look upon him, when he is conscious that, if they knew the truth, they would look upon him in a very different light'.[17] Ultimately he is even forced by remorse to confess his crime and seek punishment (clearly less of a deterrent than a bad conscience) since, as a member of society, he shares that resentment which society would feel if only it knew of his crime: 'By sympathizing with the hatred and abhorrence which other men must entertain for him, he becomes in some measure the object of his own hatred and abhorrence.'[18]

Propriety of sentiments is thus an end in itself. Our goal is not to win the esteem of the real spectator (this would be mere 'vanity') but to satisfy the impartial spectator (this is 'true glory'): 'The love of just fame, of true glory, even for its own sake, and independent of any advantage which he can derive from it, is not unworthy even of a wise man.'[19] Of course, men are particularly gratified when the propriety of their sentiments wins them the approval of their peers as well as of their conscience: 'What so great happiness as to be beloved, and to know that we deserve to be beloved?'[20] Yet such applause is an unintended outcome. Thus a soldier marches to certain death in a battle 'with shouts of the most joyful exultation',[21] not because he hopes to be remembered posthumously as a hero (and knows that if he refused to go he would be a coward and 'the scorn of his companions'[22]), but simply because he appreciates the propriety of the few sacrificing their lives for the sake of the many.[23] And Brutus sacrificed his sons, not because he sought the admiration of his fellow citizens, but because he felt it was proper to regard his children through the eyes of a Roman, not of a father.[24]

Propriety is relative to time and place, and thus a code of norms cannot be obtained from idealistic systems of philosophy, revelation or casuistry. Nor is there any reason to believe in an intrinsic Moral Sense of the kind postulated by Hutcheson. Knowledge of right and wrong can only be obtained by observation of the sentiments with which our fellow men, in a given society at a given time, are able to sympathise: 'The general maxims of morality are formed, like all other general maxims, from experience and induction.'[25] If there were no social looking-glass, there would be no way of knowing what we ought to do:

> Were it possible that a human creature could grow up to manhood in some solitary place, without any communication with his own species, he could no more think of his own character, of the propriety or demerit of his own sentiments and conduct, of the beauty or deformity of his own mind, than of the beauty or deformity of his own face . . . Bring him into society, and he is immediately provided with the mirror which he wanted before. It is placed in the countenance and behaviour of those he lives with, which always mark when they enter into, and when they disapprove of his sentiments; and it is here that he first views the propriety and impropriety of his own passions, the beauty and deformity of his own mind.[26]

Yet if the propriety of sentiments is to be measured by the reaction of those we live with, and if the basis of morality is to be induction from experience, why then does Smith so often advise us to reject the view of the real spectator and have recourse to the verdict of a non-empirical impartial spectator? Adam Ferguson was not the last to reproach Smith for contradicting his view that propriety is relative (dependent on the individual's sentiments in a given situation, as evaluated by his peers) and for bringing in a 'previous standard of estimation'[27] against which we must evaluate the real reactions of real spectators. It is clear, however, that there is no contradiction and that Smith's conception of morality was fully empirical.

Suppose that in, say, 95 cases out of 100 we have observed the real spectator (our friends, relatives, associates) praise a man willing to sacrifice his life for his country. We will, if we are at all sensitive, conclude that such an action is customarily praised and therefore praiseworthy, and that failure to perform it is improper. When entering society the individual is a *tabula rasa* in matters of propriety, but he then builds up a stock of behavioural norms in his mind as result of the continuous process of judging and being judged; and this set of habitual associations of action and reaction, distilled instinctually from the attitude of the real spectator in a multitude of cases, is the impartial spectator mechanism. Praiseworthiness is just as relative as praise, and society's rules are derived neither from considerations of utility nor *a priori* axioms, but through the gradual conditioning of men's reflexes:

> Our continual observations upon the conduct of others insensibly lead us to form to ourselves certain general rules concerning what is fit and proper either to be done or to be avoided . . . We do not originally approve or condemn particular actions, because, upon examination, they appear to be agreeable or inconsistent with a certain general rule. The general rule, on the contrary, is formed by finding from experience that all actions of a certain kind, or circumstances in a certain manner, are approved or disapproved of.[28]

Our sense of 'what ought to be' is the product of 'what is', and this is perfectly justifiable from a philosophical as well as a sociological point of view: empirically ascertained norms *cannot* be wrong since they are generally approved of, and hence demonstrably capable of uniting men in society.

Suppose now that we express sentiments we know to be proper (because in 95 cases out of 100 already observed they won the sympathy of the real spectator), and that nonetheless a long-haired young man refuses his approbation for our willingness to sacrifice our lives for our country (saying we should 'make love, not war'). In such a case we can properly ignore his criticism. Perhaps he is partial, reacting in the heat of passion, not well informed about the facts of the case, or simply a refugee from society rather than an active (and normal) participant in it. What matters is not how one person sees us but how most other persons would see us. To obtain this knowledge, we need to divide ourselves into two parts, and to make one part the judge of the other.[29] To see ourselves as others see us, we need to put ourselves in the position of the impartial spectator and 'view ourselves with his eyes and as he views us'.[30] Then, 'if in this view it pleases us, we are tolerably satisfied. We can be more indifferent about the applause, and, in some measure, despise the censure of the world; secure that, however misunderstood or misrepresented, we are the natural and proper objects of approbation.'[31]

If, however, in our next 100 experiences with the same affections, 95 of the real spectators condemn us in the same way, we will have no choice but to conclude that conditions have changed. What once was proper and praiseworthy is now out of date. A new set of proper action/

reaction relationships must be defined as the norms with which the impartial spectator will sympathise. There are no moral absolutes, but in their absence there is the empirical concept of statistical probability; and thus in the long run our behaviour must be orientated towards the approval of our peers, the only infallible index of right and wrong. The short run is particularly short in the case of artists, poets and the young, as they are the most uncertain of what is proper, and hence the most dependent on the opinion of the real spectator.[32] The short run is particularly long, on the other hand, in the case of mathematicians: such men are very little in need of encouragement from the public as they are more certain of the accuracy and importance of their work, more confident that they are praiseworthy even when not praised,[33] than is the creative artist.

The man of the 'most perfect virtue' is he who has 'the most exquisite sensibility both to the original and sympathetic feelings of others' and accompanies it with 'the most perfect command of his own original and selfish feelings'.[34] But how far does the average man have such 'delicacy or sensibility of character',[35] such 'acuteness of . . . sensibility',[36] that he is able and willing to put propriety of motivation before utility of results? Whereas Shaftesbury had argued that virtue could only be perceived by a small minority of highly-educated 'virtuosi', with time and skill for contemplation, Smith believed that knowledge of right and wrong was accessible even to the 'most injudicious and inexperienced'[37] person through personal experience. It does not require any great intellectual effort to guess what sort of reaction the 'impartial spectator' is likely to sympathise with: 'Habit and experience have taught us to do this so easily and so readily, that we are scarce sensible that we do it.'[38] The guarantee of social cohesion is the fact that reason is the slave of the passions. Perhaps the philosopher is best equipped to discover laws in the physical sciences, but this cannot be the case in discussions of morality: every man living in a society has personal experience of its norms.[39]

At times, however, Smith appears to contradict his view that all men have adequate sensitivity and self-command to make the social machine function smoothly. He gives the example of 'profligate criminals' who 'have frequently little sense of the baseness of their own conduct'[40] and whose hearts have 'grown callous by the habit of crimes'.[41] A man brought up 'amidst violence, licentiousness, falsehood, and injustice'[42] may come to regard impropriety as a necessary evil, the way of the world. And even non-criminal groups may suffer from 'stupid insensibility'.[43] A factory operative in the anonymity of a new industrial town may feel confused and disorientated once he loses the mirror of propriety he had enjoyed in the intimate social contacts of a stable, small-scale village community;[44] and his ability to think clearly may suffer once a repetitive work function has made him 'stupid and ignorant'.[45]   Again, the mercantile classes are characterised by 'narrowness, meanness, and a selfish disposition',[46] since a profit-orientated, market-orientated way of life places a premium on utilitarian results (and a willingness to see one's neighbours as one's customers) rather than on the 'perfect concord'[47] of moral sentiments. In any case, standards of propriety depend on the situation, and in a changing economy and society the situation itself is in a state of flux. It may be difficult to get a clear picture of what the impartial spectator regards as fitting and proper where the reactions of the real spectator are confused and random, not falling into any orderly distribution.

Thus consensus and sympathy could in certain circumstances prove inadequate to guarantee social cohesion, which might have to depend on law and order (a return to the impersonal strait-jacket of casuistry) or on the exchange of equivalents (the 'trinkets and baubles' of the affluent society). Lacking the ability to sympathise, confused and disorientated men could still act 'merely from a regard to what they saw were the established rules of behaviour'.[48] Such motivation is utilitarian: to avoid disapproval and punishment, to win approval and reward. Many a 'weak man'[49] comes to love praise more than praise-worthiness, consequences more than motivation; and neglects propriety save in so far as it is the means to advantage. Yet not only does this make society into a desert where hearts are never open to one another, but it makes moral standards themselves less precise: whereas the laws of justice can be codified like the rules of grammar, moral rules are analogous to literary style, 'loose, vague, and indeterminate',[50] capable only of accurate definition through sympathy in a particular situation, and it is this very sensitivity that many men may come to lack. Of course, as long as there is adequate justice to prevent one man from actually injuring another, society can continue to function. Society may 'be upheld by a mercenary exchange of good offices according to an agreed valuation';[51] but for it to flourish and be truly happy, the necessary assistance must be 'reciprocally afforded from love, from gratitude, from friendship, and esteem'.[53] This is inconceivable without sensitivity and a high degree of sympathy.

II. Benevolence and the Sacred

Smith used the mechanism of sympathy and the 'correspondent affection of the spectator'[1] to provide a psychological explanation for the most diverse of phenomena, including property rights, incest, divorce, the distinction of ranks and political stability. Of particular interest is his discussion, in terms of convergence of sentiments, of the proper balance between the virtues of prudence (the promotion of one's own happiness), justice (the abstention from hurting others) and benevolence (the promotion of the happiness of others without expecting a utilitarian equivalent in return). Unlike Hutcheson, he refused to define virtue solely in terms of benevolence; while, unlike Mandeville, he did not regard self-love as a vice (the message of the *Fable of the Bees* is 'Private Vices, Publick Benefits'). To Smith, virtue was a bundle of three qualities, not one quality alone, and even benevolence could be a vice if excessive: 'Every affection is useful when it is confined to a certain degree of moderation; and every affection is disadvantageous when it exceeds the proper bounds.'[2] Those bounds are specified by society; and the desire for sympathy from the spectator (both real and impartial) leads to a convergence of behaviour-patterns on conventional standards. Nothing in society is invariant or universal, not even pecuniary self-love.

In society, some self-love is regarded as completely proper and its absence would even be treated as a 'failing'.[3] Nature has left 'the care of the health, of the fortune, of the rank and reputation of the individual'[4] to his own prudence, and this is logical: 'Every man is certainly, in every respect, fitter and abler to take care of himself than of any other person. Every man feels his own pleasures and his own pains more sensibly than those of other people.'[5] A man should eat when he is hungry, drink when he is thirsty, and avoid extremes of heat and cold. In doing so, he is sure of attracting the full sympathy of the impartial spectator:

Regard to our own private happiness and interest . . . appear upon many occasions very laudable principles of action. The habits of economy, industry, discretion, attention and application of thought, are generally supposed to be cultivated from self-interested motives, and at the same time are apprehended to be very praiseworthy qualities, which deserve the esteem and approbation of every body.[6]

A man must, of course, show self-command, as excessive self-love can easily become anti-social: an obsession with wealth could lead to over-work,[7] destroy mental tranquillity,[8] and cause the neglect of justice and fair-play in the race for riches.[9] The impartial spectator cannot be expected to sympathise with such perversions of self-love. On the other hand, proper and moderate self-seeking attracts approbation, and this is particularly the case in the economic sphere. In *The Moral Sentiments* he points out that a tradesman 'is thought a poor-spirited fellow among his neighbours, who does not bestir himself to get what they call an extraordinary job, or some uncommon advantage'.[10] In other words, propriety of sentiments wins the tradesman both sympathy and pecuniary benefit. In *The Wealth of Nations* he telescopes this argument by focusing directly on results: 'The uniform, constant, and uninterrupted effort of every man to better his condition (is) the principle from which public and national, as well as private opulence is originally derived.'[11] In both books, however, the idea is the same, that there are clearly desirable actions 'to which self-love alone ought to be sufficient to prompt us'.[12] Benevolence is simply not necessary in the economic sector: 'It is not from the benevolence of the butcher, the brewer, or the baker, that we expect our dinner, but from their regard to their own interest.'[13]

The individual is, however, simultaneously involved in other sectors of society which evoke from him a greater degree of personal engagement. In his relationship with family and friends, the 'economic man' may display a degree of benevolence that his customers would never have expected. This is not the Christian idea of benevolence as a desirable goal, but a simple positive statement that close contact breeds 'that cordial satisfaction, that delicious sympathy, that confidential openness and ease, which naturally take place in the conversation of those who have lived long and familiarly with one another'.[14] Close contact means that the parties are well acquainted and in the habit of sharing one another's feelings with the greatest delicacy. A man's sympathy with close associates 'is more precise and determinate than it can be with the greater part of other people. It approaches nearer, in short, to what he feels for himself.'[15] Moreover, because contact means understanding and because man desires sympathy, we tend to moderate our various personal characteristics so as to make ourselves more acceptable to those with whom we most often come in contact: we have 'a natural disposition to accommodate and to assimilate, as much as we can, our own sentiments, principles, and feelings, to those which we see fixed and rooted in the persons whom we are obliged to live and converse a great deal with'.[16] Benevolence, in short, becomes a special topic in the theory of sympathy.

Benevolence towards the members of one's family results from contiguity, not from consanguinity: while on the one hand 'affection is in reality nothing but habitual sympathy',[17] on the other 'the force of blood . . . exists nowhere but in tragedies and romances'.[18] Children educated away from home may cease to experience particular feelings of benevolence towards their parents;[19] and a father reserves his 'warmest affections'[20] for his family, provided however that they 'usually live in the same house with him'.[21] Benevolence is the product of intense relationships and close contacts in a stable, intimate social group. This explains why there is greater sympathy between the children of brothers and sisters than between those of cousins; and also why colleagues at work who know one another well feel benevolent to one another and call one another brother.[22]

Benevolence arises spontaneously from sympathy, but may not in practice be totally without advantage in return. As Smith points out, 'no benevolent man ever lost altogether the fruits of his benevolence'.[23] Because of the existence of sympathy, one man's gain is not necessarily another man's loss: your gain is my gain since I have the pleasure of sympathising with (and sharing) your happiness (so long as it is proper). It is enjoyable to tell a joke to a friend, since in that way we obtain pleasure from the joke plus pleasure from sympathy with our friend's pleasure. Sympathy thus 'enlivens joy by presenting another source of satisfaction'.[24] Moreover, a man who has behaved with proper benevolence will be rewarded with the full approbation of the impartial spectator. However, although 'kindness is the parent of kindness',[25] an act motivated solely by a desire for kindness in return or for 'the most extravagant praises',[26] cannot be defined as benevolent: an act performed for applause or reward, however great the self-sacrifice involved, is no more than a prudent action. Propriety of sentiments and not utility of outcome is in this, as in all things, the criterion: thus parents feel benevolent towards their children and care for them because of habitual sympathy, not because of their social duty to take responsibility for those over whom they have the greatest influence and power. Nonetheless, utility is the unintended outcome.

An individual feels most benevolent towards himself and, 'after himself'[27] to those relatives and friends with whom he is in constant and close association. He also feels benevolent, albeit still less so, to his fellow citizens, with whom he shares a common language and culture. Contiguity, sympathy, assimilation, a sense of group identity, coupled with the fact that the individual, his family, friends and members of his class are encompassed in the nation, stimulate the sense of patriotism:

> We do not love our country merely as a part of the great society of mankind — we love it for its own sake, and independently of any such consideration. That wisdom which contrived the system of human affections, as well as that of every other part of nature, seems to have judged that the interest of the great society of mankind would be best promoted by directing the principal attention of each

individual to that particular portion of it which was most within the sphere both of his abilities and of his understanding.[28]

Patriotism nonetheless has unintended utilitarian side-effects. The fact that people predictably identify with their group helps to maintain the domestic and international balance of power. Also, by identifying himself with his country, the individual can vicariously bask in its superiority and enjoy reflected admiration: 'Its prosperity and glory seem to reflect some sort of honour upon ourselves.'[29] And in any case, the prosperity and security of the individual depends in large measure on the prosperity and security of the country. Patriotism, however, arises from the passions and not from rational calculation of advantage: we feel properly benevolent towards our country simply because we are able to sympathise with our fellow citizens.

Benevolence stops with patriotism. There is a fourth concentric circle surrounding the individual, namely mankind as a whole; but here, since there is no contiguity, there is little or no sympathy. Two nations 'are placed at so great a distance that they are almost quite out of sight',[30] and a man's sense of involvement with complete strangers is small indeed: he would be more upset by the loss of a finger than if 'the great empire of China, with all its myriads of inhabitants, was suddenly swallowed up by an earthquake'.[31] Clearly Smith did not share Voltaire's anguished reproach that 'Lisbonne est abimée et l'on danse à Paris': on the contrary, he found it natural that 'we should be but little interested . . . in the fortune of those whom we can neither serve nor hurt, and who are in every respect so very remote from us'.[32] We cannot help the miserable in China, and will only make ourselves miserable in the process: 'To what purpose should we trouble ourselves about the world in the moon?'[33] Armchair philanthropy is no substitute for proper, if more mundane kinds of benevolence: 'To man is allotted a much humbler department, but one much more suitable to the weakness of his powers, and to the narrowness of his comprehension — the care of his own happiness, of that of his family, his friends, his country.'[34]

Benevolence is 'the perfection of human nature'[35] but it is neither as necessary as justice nor as dependable as self-love. It is 'the ornament which embellishes, not the foundation which supports the building', and the want of benevolent sentiments 'tends to do no real positive evil'.[36] Thus, even though benevolence cannot be made compulsory by law, social solidarity would not be threatened by its absence. After all, socially-desirable but highly unintended outcomes might result from the most surprising sources: national 'wealth and prosperity' from 'the

natural effort of every individual to better his own condition',[37] an
increasing population from 'the passion which unites the two sexes',[38]
social cohesion from the 'agreeable bands of love and affection'[39] which
propriety of moral sentiments generates. Whatever the manifest
function, the latent function appears everywhere to be such as to promote human welfare; and the philosopher, contemplating the beauty
and utility of the social machine, the perfect adjustment of means to
ends may be forgiven his temptation to convert empiricism into
teleology by searching for 'final causes' concealed behind observable
'efficient causes'. He may be unable not to suspect the existence of an
'Author of Nature', a 'great superintendent of the Universe', a 'great
Architect', a highly skilled machine-maker who alone knows the secrets
of the social machine and who alone can be trusted to be equally
benevolent in all four concentric circles of human undertaking. In
short, he may be unable not to 'admire the wisdom of God, even in the
weakness and folly of men'.[40]

God's intentions are known: 'The happiness of mankind, as well as
of all other rational creatures, seems to have been the original purpose
intended by the Author of Nature when he brought them into
existence.'[41] A sceptic can convince himself, not by reading the Bible,[42]
but 'by the examination of the works of Nature, which seem all
intended to promote happiness, and to guard against misery'.[43] Thus, in
the last analysis, utility is the supreme unintended outcome of a social
machine in which each individual orientates himself simply to
considerations of propriety. As Dr Campbell concludes,

> Utility is, therefore, very much *the* meta-principle for Smith, It is to
> be found at the basis of his whole moral outlook, but it operates
> most typically at the level of contemplation, when men adopt a
> God's-eye-view of society, enter into His universal benevolence and
> feel admiration and approval for what they observe . . . Smith
> considers God to be a utilitarian.[44]

Our argument, in summary, is this: Smith believed that knowledge of
God can be obtained by a study of nature's laws, that nature is
demonstrably moral since it clearly promotes men's happiness, and that
there is hence no necessary contradiction between an inductivist,
empiricist theory of morality, utilitarianism, and Deism. In other words,
Smith may have felt a sense of proper filial piety towards his creator in
the same way that a child honours his father,[45] but he also had a
particular reason for his sympathy with God: both belonged to the same
school of philosophy. It seems at times, however, that Smith is only

indulging in wishful thinking, as for example when he says of God that no other end but 'the happiness of mankind . . . seems worthy of that supreme wisdom and divine benignity which we necessarily ascribe to him'.[46] Calvin and Knox would not have accepted as self-evident the optimistic view that God desires the greatest happiness of the greatest number on this earth; while latter-day pessimists (to say nothing of Smith himself in his more pessimistic moods) would argue that the natural order itself can be productive of considerable misery.

As an empiricist, Smith knew that no one had seen God; but he also recognised the psychological void that would result if man had no certainty about his origins and his future. The fear of death and sense of our own inadequacy causes us to seek consolation in the opium of the masses: 'Our happiness in this life is thus, upon many occasions, dependent upon the humble hope and expectation of a life to come . . . The virtuous man who has the misfortune to doubt of it, cannot possibly avoid wishing more earnestly and anxiously to believe it.'[47] Smith himself, having more or less repudiated Christ, may have had such melancholic doubts: it is interesting that he qualifies his view on the life to come with phrases such as 'we suppose' and 'we think'.[48] Although he may have been an agnostic, however, it is doubtful if he was an atheist: his need for the psychological tranquillity that only a belief in God can bring was too great.

In any case, God is assigned an active role to play in the Smithian scheme of things by providing a supernatural sanction for natural norms: 'Religion, even in its rudest form, gave a sanction to the rules of morality, long before the age of artificial reasoning and philosophy.'[49] Although the moral code is not based on absolute, universal, eternal, inflexible rules (as would be the case with revelation and casuistry) but simply on observed standards of propriety in a given place at a given time, such standards are nonetheless 'to be regarded as the commands and laws of the Deity, promulgated by those vice-regents which he has thus set up within us'.[50] Any set of moral sentiments, so long as it genuinely and spontaneously arises from sympathy, thus receives the seal of sanctification. It is *as if* some great designer had consciously prescribed those sentiments in order to ensure the smooth functioning of the social machine; but this need not mean he actually did so. The moral code might have arisen automatically in a concrete material situation, and the members of a society, perceiving the supra-individual constraint of such collective representations, might then have deified this sensation of moral support from an external, anonymous, all-seeing, seemingly impersonal source.

Durkheim argues that a society itself has all that is necessary to arouse the sentiment of 'the sacred', of 'mana' or 'wakan', in its members, since it imposes certain modes of acting and certain universally held beliefs on its members in the interests of some higher ends for which the individual is prepared to make sacrifices. Religion, he argues, is founded neither on revealed Truth nor on systematised hallucination, but on social reality. God is simply the symbolic or figurative expression of society: 'The god of the clan ... can ... be nothing else than the clan itself.'[51] Smith would not have denied that social reality, group exaltation, and the love of sympathy, create supra-individual sentiments which can neither be obtained by physical force nor even explained rationally by the actor in terms of his individual utility; and it is therefore possible that Smith would have found much in Durkheim's secular, functionalist theory of religion that he could have accepted. Certainly, whether or not Smith actually believed in God, he would have argued that men in society have considerable freedom to create God in their own image. For example: 'Men are naturally led to ascribe to those mysterious beings, whatever they are, which happen in any country to be the objects of religious fear, all their own sentiments and passions. They have no other, they can conceive no other, to ascribe to them.'[52]

If God did design the social machine, he appears to have done so in a fit of absence of mind, since the end product shows signs of unskilled workmanship. It is well known that the natural order not uncommonly favours the 'knave' to the detriment of the 'man of virtue',[53] and that 'a campaign at Versailles or St. James's is often worth two either in Germany or Flanders'.[54] Man may, of course, quite naturally endeavour to 'turn away the arrow that is aimed at the head of the righteous', and to 'accelerate the sword of destruction that is lifted up against the wicked', but the task of rectifying nature's mistakes is not an easy one: more often than not in the natural course of things, 'the current is too rapid and too strong for him to stop it'.[55] In such a situation, Panglossian optimism can be defended only by bringing in the *deus ex machina* of Heaven and Hell, of 'a place provided for the punishment of the wicked, as well as one for the reward of the just'.[55] This confidence in the omnipresence of an 'all-seeing Judge of the world'[57] goes some way towards explaining Smith's residual Stoicism.[58] Yet the introduction of a supreme Big Brother and the fear of Hell Fire does also suggest Smith is admitting the failure of sympathy and fellow-feeling (at least in some instances), and is attempting to buttress them with a new concept, the prudence of propriety. In this he anticipated Paley and the Christian Utilitarians. Unfortunately, he also admits that the shadow can well prove as unreliable as the substance: the punishment of injustice in the after-life 'cannot serve to deter the rest of mankind, who see it not, who know it not'.[59]

III. Character

Character is not accidental or arbitrary. It is a stock of reflexes conditioned by habitual association in a given social context: 'The degree of politeness which would be highly esteemed, perhaps would be thought effeminate adulation, in Russia, would be regarded as rudeness and barbarism at the court of France. That degree of order and frugality which, in a Polish nobleman, would be considered as excessive parsimony, would be regarded as extravagance in a citizen of Amsterdam.'[1] No-one wants to be as ridiculous and out of place as a sow in a drawing-room: 'We are embarassed, and put to a stand, and know not how to address ourselves to a character which plainly affects to be of a different species from those with which we should have been disposed to class it.'[2]

What is customary and habitual in one country is not necessarily customary and habitual in another. These differences are not random and arise because of differences in the situation. Thus: 'In general the style of manners which takes place in any nation may commonly, upon the whole, be said to be that which is most suitable to its situation.'[3] And elsewhere: 'The different situations of different ages and countries are apt . . . to give different characters to the generality of those who live in them.'[4]

Moreover, by 'situation', Smith means 'economic situation': 'The objects with which men in the different professions and states of life are conversant being very different, and habituating them to very different passions, naturally form in them very different characters and manners.'[5] Such character-patterns, therefore, are not only customary but uniquely appropriate. Men learn when they must and what they must: 'The peculiar character and manners which we are led by custom to appropriate to each rank and profession, have sometimes, perhaps, a propriety independent of custom, and are what we should approve of for their own sakes, if we took into consideration all the different circumstances which naturally affect those in each different state of life.'[6] It is a weak proposition to say that we approve of what we are used to seeing: 'In each species of men, we are particularly pleased, if they have neither too much nor too little of the character which usually accompanies their particular condition and situation.'[7] For example: 'We expect in each rank and profession a degree of those manners which, experience has taught us, belonged to it . . . A man, we say, should look like his trade and profession.'[8] It is a much stronger proposition to impute causation to that trade and profession, and to argue that his character was moulded by it: 'The understandings of the greater part of men are necessarily formed by their ordinary employments.'[9]

Smith gives many examples of how character is formed directly by the imperatives of the work-function. Consider the case of the sailor: 'Every man naturally, or rather necessarily, familiarizes his imagination with the distresses to which he foresees that his situation may frequently expose him. It is impossible that a sailor should not frequently think of storms and shipwrecks.'[10] Customs-inspectors, on the other hand, develop a 'hardness of character': their 'duty obliges them to be frequently very troublesome to some of their neighbours',[11] and 'mercy and generosity' would simply not be appropriate in their particular material situation.

To take another example, Smith says, 'We cannot expect the same sensibility to the gay pleasures and amusements of life in a clergyman which we lay our account with in an officer.'[12] The clergyman is grave and severe because of his professional preoccupation with the 'awful futurity' awaiting mankind, and because he feels himself obliged by his office to set a good example to his flock by avoiding triviality, frivolity and dissipation. Such conduct may be customary and to be expected from a clergyman, but it is also uniquely well suited to his profession. The soldier too is conditioned by his work. He is dissolute, not by nature, but because of the need to put out of his mind the hazards to which he is continually being exposed, and because a professional killer is bound to experience some lessening of his more humane sentiments. (Thus a city-guardsman, unlike other soldiers, is sober and careful, and not dissolute: his life, after all, is never at risk. Yet he is an exception, and men are so little used to associating serious-mindedness with the military that they 'laugh at the grave and careful faces of a city-guard, which so little resemble those of their profession'.[13] On the surface his character is unexpected, out of place and ridiculous; but in fact he is acting with perfect propriety, since his situation differs from that of most other soldiers.) A second reason why the soldier is dissolute is that his income is assured: he is paid by the week and not by the job. An industrial labourer could not afford such dissipation: 'The manufacturer has always been accustomed to look for his subsistence from his labour only: the soldier to expect it from his pay. Application and industry have been familiar to the one; idleness and dissipation to the other.'[14]

Like the soldier, the bureaucrat has a guaranteed income. The result is that the typical bureaucrat is inefficient, not because the promise of a specified salary regardless of work performed tends to attract inefficient and lazy men, but rather because the lack of incentive tends to make otherwise hard-working clerks lazy. Such character-defects are the fault of the situation, not of the clerks: 'It is the system of government, the situation in which they are placed, that I mean to censure; not the character of those who have acted in it. They acted as their situation naturally directed.'[15] On the other hand, men working in large organisations do at least learn patience and self-command in a way that the outside observer cannot comprehend if he has 'never experienced the insolence of his superiors, the jealous and malignant envy of his equals, or the pilfering injustice of his inferiors'.[16]

As another example of the relationship between character and work, take the case of the criminal. Smith does not see him as the victim of Original Sin, debased and depraved from birth, but as more probably a virtuous man placed in a debasing and depraving economic situation. In feudal Europe, for example, noblemen kept large numbers of retainers, and such dependence is not likely to bolster a man's self-respect: 'Nothing tends so much to corrupt mankind as dependency, while independency still increases the honesty of the people.'[17] These retainers were corrupted still further when the lords began to spend their wealth on consumption rather than on private armies: when turned out, they 'had no other way of getting their subsistence but by committing robberies, and living on plunder'.[18] In general, the solution to the problem of crime is not to devise laws which prevent criminals from acting, but to generate an economic situation which does not produce criminals:

> The establishment of commerce and manufactures, which bring about . . . independency, is the best policy for preventing crimes. The common people have better wages in this way than in any other, and in consequence of this a general probity of manners takes place through the whole country. Nobody will be so mad as to expose himself upon the highway, when he can make better bread in an honest and industrious manner. [19]

Unfortunately, commerce and manufacturers may also have deleterious effects on men's character. The repetitive work-function of the factory operative under a system of extensive division of labour makes him 'exceedingly stupid'.[20] This stupidity is induced and not intrinsic: men do not become workers because they are stupid, they are stupid because they are workers. The difference between the character of the porter and that of the philosopher 'seems to arise not so much from nature, as from habit, custom, and education', and is not 'so much the cause, as the effect of the division of labour'.[21] An agricultural labourer, whose 'view of things beyond his own trade'[22] is more extensive than that of an industrial worker, escapes this 'mental mutilation':[23] 'When the mind is employed about a variety of objects, it is somehow expanded and enlarged, and on this account a country artist is generally acknowledged to have a range of thoughts much above a city one.'[24]

Similarly, in a wealthy commercial society, martial virtues may become vestigial organs and wither away. Division of labour, preoccupation with a full-time job, lack of experience in following leaders, lack of practice in the arts of war, physical deterioration due to lack of exercise in the open air, mental deterioration due to diminished opportunities for inventiveness at work, an obsession with affluence and 'the arts of luxury',[25] all mean that 'the natural habits of the people render them altogether incapable of defending themselves'.[26]

On the other hand, however, the martial character flourishes in primitive societies, particularly among shepherds (who have considerable property to defend), and least among hunters (who do not).[27] The conditions of the situation 'breed and form'[28] men: in savage societies, the very preservation of life depends on characteristics such as 'contempt of danger' and 'patience in enduring labour, hunger and pain', that is, on 'self-denial'.[29] To a savage, living a hand-to-mouth existence in a world characterised by the survival of the fittest, self-sufficiency and abstinence from pleasure are more proper to the material conditions of his existence than 'civility and politeness'. It is no accident that he is insensitive to the feelings of others: 'Before we can feel much for others, we must in some measure be at ease ourselves. If our misery pinches us very severely, we have no leisure to attend to that of our neighbour: and all savages are too much occupied with their own wants and necessities to give much attention to those of another person.'[30] The savage is so lacking in humanity that he even practices infanticide; but neither the missionary (even if he is not of the 'stupid and lying'[31] variety) nor the philosopher (even if he correctly sees infanticide as a 'barbarous prerogative', 'horrible abuse', and 'violation of humanity') can deny its propriety in given material conditions. The savage quickly perceives that 'it is frequently impossible for him to support both himself and his child':[33] 'the weakness of love ... is regarded among savages as the most unpardonable effeminacy',[34] and this is perfectly proper where society is a perpetual game of musical chairs for the right to stay alive. It would be highly improper for the savage to act in a way that contradicts the demands of his material environment; but his character can be reformed, not by law or education, but by changing the economic situation in which he lives. In a civilised society, justice and security of contract and property[35] mean that one no longer needs to be continually on one's guard against aggression; while opulence and assured subsistence mean a man can afford the luxury of treating defenceless children with humanity. Meanwhile, leisure and tranquillity[36] provide encouragement for sympathy, the precondition for cohesion based on norms and not on force. As society progressed, 'love, which was formerly a ridiculous passion, became more grave and respectable'.[37] Indeed, one of the greatest advantages of economic progress is precisely the effect that it has on the character of the Ignoble Savage: 'A polished people . . . become frank, open, and sincere. Barbarians, on the contrary, being obliged to smother and conceal the appearance of every passion, necessarily acquire the habits of falsehood and dissimulation.'[38]

Consider now the character of the landowning aristocrat, the product of quite a different economic situation from the savage. As a landowner, his revenue accrues to him automatically year after year from the rent of land farmed by others, and is thus independent of his own effort or outlay. As an aristocrat, power and prestige are his birth-right, and he does not need to win status (say, by maximising returns on his investment or treating landowning as a business). Thus, a 'man born to a great fortune' can afford to indulge his love of 'extravagant vanity'.[39] He has, after all, no reason to be frugal: 'The situation of such a person naturally disposes him to attend rather to ornament which pleases his fancy, than to profit for which he has so little occasion. The elegance of his dress, of his equipage, of his house, and household furniture, are objects which from his infancy he has been accustomed to have some anxiety about.'[40] In any case, in some societies 'to trade was disgraceful to a gentleman'.[41]

It is to be expected that such a man becomes 'indolent' and 'incapable of that application of mind which is necessary in order to foresee and understand the consequences of any public regulation'.[42] After all, the greatest challenge his situation has ever called upon him to meet has been 'to figure at a ball' or 'to succeed in an intrigue of gallantry'.[43] Surrounded by sycophants who need him more than he needs them, he can afford to be 'proud and unfeeling'.[44] Never having felt the need to develop either his intrinsic intelligence or his sensitivity, however, he is forced to rely on men with developed faculties of reasoning and the habit of industry:

He shudders with horror at the thought of any situation which demands the continual and long exertion of patience, industry, fortitude, and application. These virtues are hardly ever to be met with in men who are born to those high stations. In all governments accordingly, even in monarchies, the highest offices are generally possessed, and the whole detail of the administration conducted, by men who were educated in the middle and inferior ranks of life, who have been carried forward by their own industry and abilities. [45]

Smith's interest in men 'carried forward by their own industry and abilities', coupled with his desire for more rapid economic growth, caused him to devote particular attention to the character of the rising commercial and industrial middle classes. Business, he argued, creates habits of thrift and industry: 'A merchant is commonly a bold; a country gentleman, a timid undertaker . . . The habits . . . of order, oeconomy and attention, to which mercantile business naturally forms a merchant, render him much fitter to execute, with profit and success, any project of improvement.'[46]

The virtues of the businessman ('industry, frugality, and attention'[47]) and even his vices ('mean rapacity'[48] and 'avarice and ambition'[49]) are precisely those one would have expected from a man not born into the aristocracy, a man whose revenue and social position depend on nothing but 'the labour of his body and the activity of his mind'.[50] He has no other way of distinguishing himself than by over-coming some obstacle, responding to some challenge:

He must acquire superior knowledge in his profession, and superior industry in the exercise of it. He must be patient in labour, resolute in danger, and firm in distress. These talents he must bring into public view, by the difficulty, importance, and, at the same time, good judgement of his undertakings, and by the severe and unrelenting application with which he pursues them. Probity and prudence, generosity and frankness, must characterize his behaviour upon all ordinary occasions. [51]

Consider Smith's description of the 'prudent man', a sort of ideal type of the businessman. First of all, he is practical, down-to-earth, and single-minded in his pursuit of prosperity. Thus he avoids gay and riotous gatherings which 'might too often interfere with the regularity of his temperance, might interrupt the steadiness of his industry, or break in upon the strictness of his frugality'.[52] Similarly, a divorce between civil society and the state occurs, since he prefers not to get caught up in politics: he would 'be much better pleased that the public business were well managed by some other person, than that he himself should have the trouble, and incur the responsibility, of managing it'.[53] His desire to avoid responsibilities outside business extends to personal relationships as well. Although scrupulous in his observance of social conventions and usages, and polite and correct to others, such a man nonetheless is 'not generally the most sensible and compassionate'.[54] It is easy to see why prudence 'commands a certain cold esteem, but seems not entitled to any very ardent love or admiration'.[55]   .

Secondly, he is able to evaluate new investments carefully: 'If he enters into any new projects or enterprises, they are likely to be well concerted and well prepared.'[56] He is able to discount future satisfactions and to compare them with the utility of current consumption; and, having self-command, to 'postpone the present enjoyment for the sake of a greater to come'.[57] He knows that accumulation makes a man rich,[58] and thus suffers from a Faustian conflict: because he is a businessman and wishes to retain his status as such, he must abstain from 'the passion for present enjoyment'[59] and plough back his profits in an effort to defend and improve his fortune and position. He is aware that the very definition of a capitalist is a man with capital, and that if he fritters away this capital on unproductive labourers and luxury goods he will sink back into the lower classes; while if he yields to what we all know to be a stronger desire than that of mere 'present enjoyment', namely 'the desire of bettering our condition' ('a desire which . . . comes with us from the womb, and never leaves us till we go into the grave'[60]), then he will advance along the social scale. The capitalist suffers from a fundamental insecurity: lacking a recurring revenue or hereditary title, he must win by his function what he failed to acquire through his birth, and thus to him investment is more than merely deferred consumption opportunities. His fundamental insecurity causes him to accumulate capital and makes him the engine of economic and social development.

Thirdly, the prudent man attempts at all times to avoid excessive risks capable of destroying what he has already built up. His aim is thus insurance as well as prosperity, defensive as well as offensive. After all, 'we suffer more . . . when we fall from a better to a worse situation, than we ever enjoy when we rise from a worse to a better'.[61]

Fourthly, the prudent man is honest at all times. This he must be, since a businessman with a reputation for crooked dealings would be ostracised from the business community. An ambassador can afford to be unscrupulous, since nations 'treat with one another not above twice or thrice in a century';[62] but merchants make 'perhaps twenty contracts in a day'[63] and cannot afford to lose the trust of their associates. At all times, therefore, 'a dealer is afraid of losing his character'.[64] Smith's contemporary, Adam Ferguson, with whom he had so much in common, took a similar view of the effects of commercial activity:

> Even in China, we are informed, where pilfering, fraud, and corruption, are the reigning practice with all the other orders of men, the great merchant is ready to give, and to procure confidence: while his countrymen act on the plans and under the restrictions of a police adjusted to knaves, he acts on the reasons of trade, and the maxims of mankind.[65]

Thus, like Weber, Smith identified the capitalist entrepreneur as being hard-working, rational, honest, ascetic in his preference of abstinence to ostentation, possessing business acumen and an ability to weight future against present utilities.[66] Whereas, however, to Weber the constraint was ideal (notably Calvinist attitudes to work and consumption), to Smith it was material: years of activity as a businessman cannot but breed habits of frugality, industry and self-command, as without these no individual can survive and prosper in business, and in this sense capitalism generates its own *Geist*. Smith would not have disagreed with Alfred Marshall's view that 'man's character has been moulded by his every-day work, and the material resources which he thereby procures, more than by any other influence unless it be that of his religious ideals'.[67]

Moreover, again like Weber, Smith explained the businessman's pursuit of prosperity not simply in terms of utilitarian egocentrism, but with respect to some supra-individual end. To Weber, this end (at least in the early stages of capitalism) was sacred (the doctrine of predestination, with its implication that material success in this life could be taken as an indication of one's fate in the next), while to Smith it was profane (the love of sympathy from the impartial spectator). The capitalist conforms to those behaviour-patterns habitually associated with a capitalist in order to win approval for playing his chosen role with propriety. These behaviour-patterns are uniquely proper as they will also make him a successful capitalist; but, as is so often the case in Smith's work, utility appears to be an unintended outcome. In other words, both wealth (the end) and frugality, industry and self-command (the means) attract 'the entire approbation of the impartial spectator',[68] and this approval is 'as much under the aspect of propriety as under that of utility'.[69] There are prizes for trying as well as succeeding: what matters is propriety in playing the game.

Clearly, abstinence from consumption need not be painful. A capitalist might legitimately divert expenditure from conspicuous consumption to conspicuous investment and actually improve his social standing as a result. Prudence is, after all, so much more proper to one in his station:

> His parsimony to-day must not arise from a desire of the particular threepence which he will save by it, nor his attendance in his shop from a passion for the particular tenpence which he will acquire by it: both the one and the other ought to proceed solely from a regard to the general rule, which prescribes, with the most unrelenting severity, this plan of conduct to all persons in his way of life. In this consists the difference between the character of a miser and that of a person of exact economy and assiduity. The one is anxious about small matters for their own sake; the other attends to them only in consequence of the scheme of life which he has laid down to himself.[70]

The economist often tends to theorise in terms of an upward-sloping supply-curve of savings and a downward-sloping demand-curve for investment with respect to the rate of return. Smith accepted the existence of these schedules but, like Marx and Keynes, must have questioned their sensitivity. Capital formation was likely to be affected to some extent by a change in the rate of interest or profit, but it was also likely to be far more dependent on sociological factors which might cause the capitalist to accumulate for non-pecuniary reasons: the desire for status, the love of sympathy, a hunger for power ('the pride of man makes him love to domineer'[70] and he needs an opportunity to indulge 'that tyrannic disposition which may almost be said to be natural to mankind'[72]), combined with his ingrained capitalistic habits and customs which cannot be altered at a stroke. In any case, Smith believed that commodity-consumption yielded little satisfaction save in so far as it was ostentatious; and proper frugality and conspicuous investment are bound to yield the capitalist at least as much approbation, besides increasing his capital as well. The implication seems to be that, because the proportion of sociological causation in the capital market is so great relative to purely economic causation, there is no reason to think that the savings and investment schedules will necessarily intersect at a reasonable rate of interest. In other words, although Smith the economist championed Say's Law, Smith the sociologist appears to have pioneered the theory of underemployment equilibrium.

Smith was aware that in certain situations even businessmen might prefer extravagant consumption, luxury and leisure, to prudence, parsimony, application and accumulation. For example, at very high rates of profit the supply curve of savings bends backward: 'The high rate of profit seems every where to destroy that parsimony which in other circumstances is natural to the character of the merchant. When profits are high, that sober virtue seems to be superfluous, and expensive luxury to suit better the affluence of his situation.'[73] The character of the prudent man is poised on a razor's edge: if he were richer he would substitute luxury for thrift, while if he were poorer his 'parsimonious frugality'[74] would be aimed at physical, not social survival. It appears only possible to experience the virtue of prudence in a narrow and clearly defined income band, and for maximum economic growth the accumulating classes should be confined to it. Fortunately the rate of profit will be kept low by continued economic growth (since competition for factor-services in a growing economy causes the break-down of cartels established by capitalists to impose maximum wage-incomes[75]) and by the operation of the free market mechanism in the goods market (where competition, replacing monopoly and collusive oligopoly, means more modest prices[76]). Whereas to Marx and Keynes, the threat to capitalism was expected to come from a low rate of profit, to Smith excessively high as well as excessively low returns could cause the capitalist to lose his peculiarly capitalist *Geist*.

His prognosis for the future of capitalism becomes particularly grim if we examine the mass, rather than the rate, of profit: even at a modest rate of profit, great mercantile and industrial fortunes can nonetheless over time be built up. This wealth might then be withdrawn from industry and trade and invested in stately homes and country estates, once these can be afforded and consumed with propriety: 'Merchants are commonly ambitious of becoming country gentlemen, and when they do, they are generally the best of all improvers.'[77] This marriage of landed property and capitalistic virtues need not be so happy, however. A merchant who became a landowner might think he 'ought to live like other men of large revenues; and to spend a great part of his time in festivity, in vanity, and in dissipation'.[78] In such a case, not only is capital accumulation sacrificed, but the capitalistic ethos is abandoned as unsuitable. Extravagance replaces prudence, often causing fortunes to be exhausted.[79] The time is then ripe for prudence to replace extravagance and, presumably, for the whole cycle to begin anew.

There is another situation in which the middle classes might be led by existential conditions to eschew parsimony in favour of luxury. This is the case of the wealthy tax-farmers, bankers and financiers, who have already climbed as far as institutions will permit up the social ladder:

> Such people are commonly men of mean birth, but of great wealth, and frequently of great pride. They are too proud to marry their equals, and women of quality disdain to marry them. They frequently resolve, therefore, to live bachelors, and having neither any families of their own, nor much regard for those of their relations, whom they are not always very fond of acknowledging, they desire only to live in splendour during their own time, and are not unwilling that their fortune should end with themselves.[80]

Just as the character of the individual is largely the product of his work-activity, so the national character is largely the product of the nation's economy. For example: 'When the greater part of people are merchants, they always bring probity and punctuality into fashion, and these, therefore, are the principal virtues of a commercial nation.'[81] It is no surprise that the Dutch are particularly thrifty and industrious: in a rich country like Holland, where the rate of interest had fallen so low that only the very wealthiest could afford to live as rentiers, almost everyone had some sort of trade or business ('As it is ridiculous not to dress, so is it, in some measure, not to be employed, like other people'[82]). Smith believed that mercantile virtues arise from mercantile activity, and that other nations, if placed in a similar economic situation, would acquire similar habits:

> Whenever commerce is introduced into any country probity and punctuality always accompany it. These virtues in a rude and barbarous country are almost unknown. Of all the nations in Europe, the Dutch, the most commercial, are the most faithful to their word. The English are more so than the Scotch, but much inferior to the Dutch . . . This is not at all to be imputed to national character, as some pretend; there is no natural reason why an Englishman or a Scotchman should not be as punctual in performing agreements as a Dutchman.[83]

Clearly, economic change has far-reaching sociological consequences in so far as it brings about a revolution in national character. One and only one mentality is proper to a given economic basis, and the only way the philosopher can destroy a mentality of which he disapproves is by dissolving the infrastructure and selecting another. Whereas some economists have advocated changes in national character as the price of economic growth, it appears at times as if Smith believed economic growth to be the price of changes in the national character.

In altering the material infrastructure of society, economic growth very often acts through the redistribution of income, and thus of effective demand for labour. The distribution of the national income as between classes which demand productive labourers (such as factory operatives) and those which demand unproductive labourers (such as private armies and domestic servants) necessarily 'determines in every country the general character of the inhabitants as to industry or idleness. We are more industrious than our forefathers; because in the present times the funds destined for the maintenance of industry, are much greater in proportion to those which are likely to be employed in the maintenance of idleness, than they were two or three centuries ago.'[84] The proof is that in England and Holland, the labouring classes are 'industrious, sober and thriving', while in towns such as Rome or Versailles (where they are unproductive rather than productive), the masses remain 'idle, dissolute, and poor'.[85] Workers tend to be more industrious when employed by 'prudent' businessmen than when employed by 'indolent' aristocrats: 'If the employer is attentive and parsimonious, the workman is very likely to be so too; but if the master is dissolute and disorderly, the servant who shapes his work according to the pattern which his master prescribes to him, will shape his life too according to the example which he sets him.'[86] The source of the capital used to maintain labour is as important for national character as its absolute size and rate of growth are for the level of employment.

Civilisation results from opulence, and opulence results from commerce. Economic progress is to be welcomed because it leads to cultural progress, as moderation, sincerity and industry replace the inhumanity of the savage and the indolence of the landowner. Yet whereas a civilised society is characterised by 'love . . . gratitude . . . friendship, and esteem',[87] a commercial society is characterised by the shopkeeper's utilitarian watchword, a 'mercenary exchange of good offices according to an agreed valuation'.[88] Opulence may breed 'the agreeable bands of love and affection',[89] but the means of attaining opulence is 'a base and selfish disposition'.[90] In short, Smith appears to have been involved in a fundamental dilemma: the only way to construct a society in which 'mutual love or affection'[91] were possible was by means of its negation, the merchant/customer relationship and the worship of the *quid pro quo*. The virtues associated with the level of the national income are contradictory to those associated with its rate of change.

One way of escaping this contradiction might have been to advocate economic growth based on the agricultural rather than the industrial and commercial sectors:

> Nations . . . which, like France or England, consist in a great measure of proprietors and cultivators, can be enriched by industry and enjoyment. Nations, on the contrary, which, like Holland and Hamburgh, are composed chiefly of merchants, artificers and manufacturers, can grow rich only through parsimony and privation. As the interest of nations so differently circumstanced, is very different, so is likewise the common character of the people. In those of the former kind, liberality, frankness, and good fellowship, naturally make a part of that common character. In the latter, narrowness, meanness, and a selfish disposition, averse to all social pleasure and enjoyment.[92]

Economic growth based on agriculture is not without its advantages. Agriculture enjoys lower risk than other branches of the economy (such as industry, trade or transport) and also provides a greater number of jobs: 'No equal capital puts into motion a greater quantity of productive labour than that of the farmer.'[93] Yet this statement loses much of its force when one remembers, both that Smith tends to lump 'labouring cattle'[94] together with human labourers as productive of accumulation, and that he in any case believed endemic unemployment not to be a problem in contemporary Britain: in an economy characterised by wages substantially above subsistence, the need is not to divert capital towards labour-intensive employment, but to improve the mobility of the existing labour force.[95]

Moreover, economic growth based on agriculture had substantial disadvantages. First of all, in Britain the classes that benefited most from agriculture were the great landowners (the Crown, aristocracy and clergy) with whom Smith had the least sympathy: rather than strengthening their influence, he hoped to weaken it through greater countervailing power from the new middle classes. And secondly, because he wanted to raise the living standards of the lower classes, Smith saw a case for maximum capital accumulation. In agriculture, however, there was less opportunity for raising factor-productivity than in industry, as (partly for seasonal reasons) there was less scope for the division of labour.[96]

In any case, progress from agriculture to industry is 'in the nature of things': when factor-endowments are right, manufactures will *naturally* be introduced in an agricultural country. The cause of this

change is the profit motive, which alone can optimally allocate capital
in such a way as to ensure not just the natural balance of employments
but also the maximum rate of growth of national income *per capita*.
Hence Smith would have opposed any kind of government intervention
aimed at redirecting capital towards one employment (say, agriculture)
and away from another (say, industry). In general, 'every derangement
of the natural distribution of stock is necessarily hurtful'.[97]

In the early stages of a country's development, its economy is
naturally agricultural. In the North American colonies, for example,
land was abundant and cheap, while labour and capital were scarce and
expensive.[98] In other words, rents were low while wages and profits
remained high. Clearly, British restrictions on industrialisation in the
North American colonies were ridiculous and irrelevant, since American
factor-endowments naturally induced the colonies to be agricultural
anyway: the welfare of a new colony is unquestionably maximised by
exchanging its primary produce for manufactures from abroad. Indeed,
government measures to encourage premature industrialisation would
be just as misguided: 'artificers and manufacturers' in the towns are
'the most important of all markets for the rude produce of the land',[99]
but before agriculture can release labourers to the towns it must be
capable of producing an adequate surplus with a reduced labour force.

In the later stages of its development, a country naturally becomes
industrial. Hence in Europe pressure on land caused rents to rise while
a growing population and an increasing capital stock moderated the rise
in wages and actually caused average profit rates to fall. In Europe, high
rents made manufacturing more attractive relative to agriculture; which
meant in turn that if the living standards of the masses were to improve
at a reasonable pace, if the national character was to be humanised
through emancipation from material cares, the impetus would have to
come from the capital accumulation of merchants and industrialists.

As the economy becomes ever more commercial, of course, the
danger becomes ever more real that the traits associated with commerce
might outweigh those associated with civilisation. Society might come
to depend for its continuance on the exchange of 'trinkets and baubles',
on utility and justice, on cohesion by contract, rather than on the warmth
of human sympathy. The price of cultural progress might be a sort of
relapse into cultural barbarism. 'In a commercial state', as Adam Ferguson
warned, 'man is sometimes found a detached and a solitary being.'[100]

4 CONSUMER BEHAVIOUR

Introduction

Adam Smith attacked mercantilism for trying to maximise the stock of bullion rather than the flow of commodities, and championed the interest of the consumer as against that of the producer: 'The interest of the producer ought to be attended to, only so far as it may be necessary for promoting that of the consumer. The maxim is so perfectly self-evident, that it would be absurd to attempt to prove it.'[1] Yet at the same time he dismissed many consumer goods as 'trifling' and 'frivolous'[2] and described much commodity consumption as 'the gratification of the most childish, the meanest and the most sordid of all vanities'.[3] Thus, on the one hand, he appears to have been a commodity-utilitarian concerned with free trade, economic growth, the ending of restrictive practices, and other ways of providing 'a plentiful revenue or subsistence for the people';[4] while on the other hand he seems to have been determined to prove that higher material standards of living do not, except for the poor, represent a significant change in human happiness. The purpose of this chapter is to discuss this apparent contradiction in Adam Smith's theory of consumer behaviour.

In Section I we will argue that Adam Smith saw commodity consumption as a social action, an attempt by each man to acquire the symbols he needs to identify his status in a given society. By relating consumer preferences to role-playing and human interaction rather than to scarcity of resources and individual utility, Smith was underlining his belief that the struggle for physical survival was (except for the poor) a thing of the past. In an affluent society, the most urgent need is for social survival, and this necessitates propriety of behaviour patterns, observance of the established rules of decency, acceptance of the normal conventions of *bienséance:* a scholar dressed as a fop, for example, would undoubtedly offend the sensibilities of his friends at a salon, and make himself as ridiculous as a sow in a drawing-room. The point is, as Polanyi reminds us, that man in society must adapt to the social as well as to the physical environment:

> The outstanding discovery of recent historical and anthropological research is that man's economy, as a rule, is submerged in his social relationships. He does not act so as to safeguard his individual interest in the possession of material goods; he acts so as to safeguard his social standing, his social claims, his social assets. He values material goods only in so far as they serve this end.[5]

Man in society seeks happiness and shuns misery; but in truth 'happiness and misery . . . reside altogether in the mind'.[6] Pleasure is derived not so much from the consumption of 'trinkets of frivolous utility'[7] as from the acceptance, approbation and standing which those trinkets procure for their faithful consumer. The impartial spectator is known to sympathise with the habitual (and proper) association of symbol and subject, an expected conjunction which also restores tranquillity to the mind and presents an aesthetically satisfying spectacle to the eye; and the actor, as usual possessed of an enviable certainty as to the nature of these symbols in a given society at a given time, coupled with admirable sensitivity and a praiseworthy desire to satisfy the impartial spectator, glories in his conformity to social norms of consumption-patterns.

Moreover, in a stratified society, by increasing his wealth and thereby his proper conspicuous consumption of symbols, a man can increase his power and prestige. It cannot be denied that wealth and greatness are the 'natural objects' of respect, since empirical proof is at hand (they 'almost constantly obtain it'[8]), and 'it is chiefly from this regard to the sentiments of mankind, that we pursue riches and avoid poverty'.[9] A Trobriand Islander or a disciple of Gandhi might find other ways of achieving respect than through 'vanity and ostentation'[10] and the consumption of expensive trinkets.

Wealth fosters respect; respect leads to political power. The 'undistinguishing eyes of the great mob of mankind'[11] can easily perceive riches and greatness, whereas they can hardly be expected to identify wisdom and virtue. Indeed, the implication is that there might be anarchy if political power ever came to depend on respect for men of learning rather than on respect for men of property.

Men desire to better their condition primarily to acquire greater sympathy and standing in their society: 'It is not ease or pleasure, but always honour, of one kind or another, though frequently an honour very ill understood, that the ambitious man really pursues.'[12] In this process of social advancement, however, there is an argument for making haste slowly. Gradual promotion along the social scale ensures the actor continued sympathy from his fellows, whereas a rapid leap forward would arouse their jealousy. As Montesquieu says, 'nobody likes to be poorer than somebody whom he recently saw just below him'.[13] Fortunately, gradual progression seems to be the typical case: a peasant does not in practice usually become king, whereas many a frugal small shopkeeper is promoted by the market-mechanism to frugal medium-sized shopkeeper.

In Section II we will consider why Smith, despite his love of permanency, propriety and tranquillity, sought to use ambition and economic growth as the instruments to produce social change and thereby to create a new set of habitual associations of subject and symbol in the market-place.

It is easy to accuse Smith of arrogance in wilfully rejecting the empirically observed taste patterns of sovereign consumers. It must, however, also be remembered that functionalism is a harder taskmaster than methodological individualism. If individual desires are reduced to symbols in a social matrix, then we can only compare two positions of want-satisfaction by comparing two whole social organisms. Moreover, if wants are contingent, relative to a particular social context, then, by altering the context, we alter the wants. The situation becomes absurd and meaningless, since to an economic determinist such as Smith the ends are in good measure the product of the means: the desire to have cheaper, more efficiently produced maypoles two centuries ago triggered off an industrial revolution and continuous economic growth, with the result that today different people consume different commodities produced in different ways and live in a different institutional environment with different norms and values. In short, everything is different, and there is no positivist method of comparing the second historical state with the first. Yet the second resulted from the economist's desire, in the first state, to use scarce means to attain a particular end: by trying to satisfy the demand for maypoles in a highly stratified society with limited suffrage, economic change eventually created a demand for colour televisions and trips to the Moon in a relatively open society with political democracy. Different societies generate different wants; to satisfy those wants is both to alter that society and to create new wants. By demanding a good, the consumer helps to transcend it; and a consumer who loves both the good and the social matrix within which it is with propriety consumed would be well advised not to demand it too intensively, lest both good and social matrix vanish as result.

Adam Smith recognised the fundamental absurdity that, as Berger says, ' "Truth" . . . is not only a matter of geography but of the time of day'.[14] Hence, consumer-preferences need not be treated as sacred, since they are only cultural values, changing when society changes; and even market prices are not so much a measure of the 'true' demand for a good as of the transitory distribution of income.[15] Market reality is a thing of the moment; and possibly this is why Smith chose a non-empirical, absolute standard of value in the form of labour-embodied. His love of permanence is also reflected in his praise of tranquillity and political continuity, in his admiration for durable goods and for productive labour.

Yet Smith also believed in economic growth, and this is surprising both since he was convinced that tastes and preferences in considerable measure arise from the process of economic and social change itself, and since he did not accept that increased material satisfactions necessarily increase men's enjoyment of life. He would have shared Durkheim's view that 'our capacity for happiness is very limited',[16] that 'the normal savage can be quite as happy as the normal civilized man'.[17] In his own private life he was, as Millar describes him, 'a man of no personal expense',[18] generous in sharing with others but with strictly limited individual wants (albeit he was a 'beau in his books', treasuring good books and the best hand-made writing paper). Clearly, to Smith the teleology of economics must be sought elsewhere than in the satisfaction of consumer desires. Smith sought to use a rising GNP to combat moral pollution (not least as represented by the aristocracy and clergy), and would not have hesitated to use a declining GNP for the same purpose, had it been expedient for his purpose of actualising philosophy on earth to do so.[19] The teleology of economics to Smith seems to have been the fashioning of a new world which a philosopher can behold with pleasure.

I. Consumption And Social Status

Adam Smith felt that, by and large, work is not enjoyable, and that 'it is the interest of every man to live as much at his ease as he can'.[1] Yet men do work, and Smith was in no doubt about the reason for this: 'The consumptibility . . . of goods, is the great cause of human industry.'[2] It can be taken as axiomatic that 'consumption is the sole end and purpose of all production'.[3] Actual job-satisfaction is rare, and most people work for money:

> In the inferior employments, the sweets of labour consist *altogether* in the recompence of labour. Those who are soonest in a condition to enjoy the sweets of it, are likely soonest to conceive a relish for it, and to acquire the early habit of industry. A young man naturally conceives an aversion to labour, when for a long time he receives no benefit from it.[4]

Moreover, man's desire for consumer goods can never be fully satisfied The pleasures of the affluent society 'seem to be altogether endless'[5] and have 'no limit or certain boundary'.[6] There is no end to the continuing process of demand-led growth and thus no end to the progress of national felicity, provided that growth in happiness is proportional to growth in commodity-consumption. Smith, however, took the view that this was not really the case. He clearly and consistently refers to consumer goods as 'trinkets and baubles',[7] 'trinkets of frivolous utility',[8] 'a few trifling conveniencies',[9] as goods 'fitter to be the playthings of children than the serious pursuits of men'.[10] The luxuries of the rich are 'contemptible and trifling',[11] while the 'baubles' that most men carry about with them are so trivial that 'the whole utility is certainly not worth the fatigue of bearing the burden'.[12] Indeed, the very belief that there is a causal connection between commodity-consumption and happiness is a 'deception':[13]

> To what purpose is all the toil and bustle of the world? . . . Is it to supply the necessities of nature? The wages of the meanest labourer can supply them . . . Do (the upper classes) imagine that their stomach is better, or their sleep sounder, in a palace than in a cottage? The contrary has been so often observed, and, indeed, is so very obvious . . . that there is nobody ignorant of it.[14]

Naturally, some consumption is necessary to sustain life and to satisfy the 'great wants of mankind' (for food, clothing and lodging[15]). Fortunately, in all but the most primitive societies, it is not difficult to provide for these 'necessities and conveniences of the body':[16] so modest are these needs that they can be gratified 'by the unassisted labour of the individual'[17] long before the division of labour. In the Smithian world, basic wants have long since been satisfied and 'the whole industry of human life is employed not in procuring the supply of our three humble necessities, food, clothes and lodging, but in procuring the conveniences of it according to the nicety and delicacy of our taste'.[18] In short, mankind has moved from 'the gratification of the bodily appetites'[19] to the satisfaction derived from the gratification of cultural needs, from the realm of physical survival to that of social survival.[20]

This is not the poverty-stricken society which Professor Galbraith argues that Smith, in common with other classical economists, had in mind, but an opulent world where energy is diverted to satisfying 'many insignificant demands, which we by no means stand in need of'.[21] Smith, like Galbraith himself, was concerned to explain why the individual chose one trinket and rejected another which was certainly no more useless. The Galbraithian answer is want-creation, that the individual's desires only become evident to him once they have been 'synthesized, elaborated, and nurtured by advertising and salesmanship'.[22] Smith, however, was not troubled by the dangers of taste manipulation: the possibility that the seller 'may sometimes decoy a weak customer to buy what he has no occasion for' is 'of too little importance to deserve the publick attention'.[23] The agony of choice only exists where the individual is confused about his desires and where ends are random; but in the Smithian world the choice of trinkets is prescribed by habitual association, and ends are not random but part of a social system. Once an individual knows his station, he knows the symbols normally connected with it: it is proper for a stockbroker to have a bowler hat, for the king to have a crown, for a cowboy to have a horse. Even an advertising industry of Madison Avenue proportions could not convince a stockbroker that it would be proper to ride through the City on a horse, and wearing a crown. He would be as ridiculous as a sow in a drawing-room.

Only a consumer like Robinson Crusoe or Wild Peter of Hanover could be in any doubt as to what society expects of him. Otherwise, in the process of socialisation man builds up a stock of images of what is usual in different situations, and the love of sympathy from the spectator of his actions causes him to respect the social norms of propriety:

> To one who was to live alone in a desolate island, it might be a matter of doubt perhaps, whether a palace, or a collection of such small conveniencies as are commonly contained in a tweezer-case, would contribute most to his happiness and enjoyment. If he is to live in society, indeed, there can be no comparison, because in this, as in all other cases, we constantly pay more regard to the sentiments of the spectator than to those of the person principally concerned, and consider rather how his situation will appear to other people than how it will appear to himself.[24]

Consumption-patterns are social facts, exogenous to the individual's psychology or to his biological make-up, and exercising constraint over him through sanctions such as ridicule. Standards of taste are truly collective phenomena, common to all members of the group. As Durkheim says,

> If I do not submit to the conventions of society, if in my dress I do not conform to the customs observed in my country and in my class, the ridicule I provoke, the social isolation in which I am kept, produce, although in an attenuated form, the same effects as a punishment in the strict sense of the word . . . We can no more choose the style of our houses than of our clothing — at least, both

are equally obligatory.[25]

Consider the case of diet. In Great Britain, beer and ale are luxuries. Partly this is because they are not necessary for physical survival, but partly too because they are not necessary for social survival. In Britain, 'custom nowhere renders it indecent to live without them'.[26] If, however the 'established rules of decency' made it necessary for, say, a rugby player to be seen from time to time with a pint in his hand, then beer and ale would cease to be luxuries and become necessities: 'By necessaries I understand, not only the commodities which are indispensably necessary for the support of life, but whatever the custom of the country renders it indecent for creditable people, even of the lowest order, to be without.'[27] Similarly, 'it may indeed be doubted whether butchers meat is any where a necessary of life'.[28] It is not necessary for physical survival (the masses thrive on vegetables and dairy products, and in any case the intake of food is limited 'by the narrow capacity of the human stomach'[29]), and, equally important, it is not necessary for social survival either: 'Decency no where requires that any man should eat butchers meat.'[30]

Again, in the case of clothing, standards of dress must be proper to the identity of the actor in a given situation: 'A man would be ridiculous who should appear in public with a suit of clothes quite different from those which are commonly worn, though the new dress should in itself be ever so graceful or convenient.'[31] Thus custom has rendered leather shoes a necessity in England for both sexes and all classes, while in Scotland lower-class women 'may, without any discredit, walk about bare-footed', and in France 'the lowest rank of both sexes' can appear publicly and with perfect propriety 'sometimes in wooden shoes, and sometimes bare-footed'.[32] As well as leather shoes, an Englishman who wishes to avoid the contempt and ridicule of his fellow Englishmen should wear a linen shirt.[33] The warmth of fellow-feeling from his peers as they 'enter into' and 'sympathise with' the propriety of his sentiments, the awareness that the appropriateness of his dress makes him a thing of beauty, will more than compensate him, should he have an individual dislike for linen shirts. As Adam Ferguson pointed out, a costume is chosen not because of its intrinsic utility but because it is capable of winning respect and admiration for the wearer:

Vanity is not distinguished by any peculiar species of dress. It is betrayed by the Indian in his phantastic assortments of his plumes, his shells, his party-coloured furs, and in the time he bestows at the glass and the toilet. Its projects in the woods and in the town are the same: in the one, it seeks, with the visage bedaubed, and with teeth artificially stained, for that admiration, which it courts in the other with a gilded equipage, and liveries of state.[34]

Finally, let us examine the case of lodging. Smith points out that it is improper in England for a respectable family to live in a flat. The 'peculiar manners and customs of the people . . . oblige every master of a family to hire a whole house from top to bottom'.[35] On the other hand, in France or Scotland it is the done thing for such a family to occupy 'no more than a single story'[36] without anyone questioning their respectability or wondering if their choice did not denote 'that disgraceful degree of poverty, which, it is presumed, no body can well fall into without extreme bad conduct'.[37] As a family was expected to demand more living space in England than in Scotland or France, it is no surprise rents were higher there, and the practice of taking lodgers more common. Whereas, however, a modern utilitarian positivist economist would content himself with identifying the equilibrium price at which the market allocates scarce housing (and possibly with relating it to alternative claims on the same resources), Smith went behind the demand curve and examined the social conventions which gave rise to the subjective sensation of scarcity.[38] A respectable family in England is expected to live in a house, and respectable families would be ashamed not to play their proper roles. For the same reason, they do not have a free hand in decorating: 'There seems to be an absurdity . . . in ornamenting a house after a quite different manner from that which custom and fashion have prescribed.'[39] Once again, propriety takes precedence over utility, and sociology takes precedence over economics.

Man is a social animal, and his consumption patterns, rather than being individual or random, are laid down by society: 'When we say that a man is worth fifty or a hundred pounds a-year . . . we mean commonly to ascertain what is or *ought to be* his way of living, or the quantity and quality of the necessaries and conveniencies of life in which he can with propriety indulge himself.'[40] Just as in a planned economy the consumer is at the mercy of the Commissars, or in a Galbraithian affluent society a sitting target for the ad-man, in the Smithian world society is a prison imposing its own strict standards of propriety on the consumer. In this sense, economics to Smith was not so much about choice as about the denial of choice. In place of individual free will and consumer sovereignty, he recommends Sartrian 'bad faith' and conformity to norms. These norms are not moral absolutes. Their propriety 'can be founded upon nothing but habit and custom';[41] but that is enough to ensure the smooth functioning of the social machine.

So far our analysis has been static. We have argued that individuals work to earn money and spend that money on commodity-consumption for two reasons, for physical survival (a threshhold reached very early in human history) and for social survival (the consumption of those goods proper to their particular station in life). Neither reason, however, tells us why people should want to work *harder* in order to consume *more* trinkets. Smith's theory of consumer behaviour can only be made dynamic by recognising that, not only does conspicuous wealth attract sympathy, but that increased wealth attracts increased sympathy. Thus, to improve our standing, to obtain 'rank and credit among our equals',[42] to win greater approbation from our fellow men, we must improve our fortune:

> It is chiefly from this regard to the sentiments of mankind, that we pursue riches and avoid poverty . . . What is the end of avarice and ambition, of the pursuit of wealth, of power, and pre-eminence?. . . To be observed, to be attended to, to be taken notice of with sympathy, complacency, and approbation . . . The rich man *glories* in his riches, because he feels they naturally draw upon him the attention of the world . . . At the thought of this his heart seems to swell and dilate itself within him, and he is fonder of his wealth, upon this account, than for all the other advantages it procures him. The poor man, on the contrary, is ashamed of his poverty. He feels that it either places him out of the sight of mankind, or, that if they take any notice of him, they have, however, scarce any fellow-feeling with the misery and distress which he suffers.[43]

In other words, individuals strive to better their condition[44] not because of the voluptuous utilitarian pleasures that arise from the consumption of more trinkets and baubles, but principally because the spectator is more likely to 'sympathise' with success and comfort than with wretchedness and misery. At all times, 'humanity does not desire to be great, but to be beloved';[45] but we must face the fact, deplorable as it may be, that being great is sometimes the precondition for being beloved. It is easier to sympathise with the inhabitants of a palace than of a prison, although a prison is more useful to society than a palace.[46] The rule seems to be that 'Our respect for the great . . . is most apt to offend by its excess — our fellow-feeling for the miserable, by its defect'.[47] Consider two examples: on the one hand, 'all the innocent blood that was shed in the civil wars, provoked less indignation than the death of Charles I'.[48] On the other hand, a virtuous poor man, no matter how proper his behaviour, is overlooked and ignored: 'When in the midst of a crowd (he) is in the same obscurity as if shut up in his own hovel.'[49] For such a man, however, Smith, like Guizot, had a message of hope: 'Enrichissez-vous!'

Wealth attracts respect, but only when it has become conspicuous wealth. For this reason, 'with the greater part of rich people, the chief enjoyment of riches consists in the parade of riches'.[50] In the consumption of goods, 'it is the vanity, not the ease, or the pleasure, which interests us ':[51] 'The rich not being able to distinguish themselves by the expence of any one dress, will naturally endeavour to do so by the multitude and variety of their dresses.'[52] It is a Veblenesque world of conspicuous consumption as an index of 'relative ability to pay',[53] a world characterised by a 'pecuniary canon of reputability'[54] and dominated by emulation and ostentation in an attempt to demonstrate status. The following passage from Veblen might well have come from Smith: 'In order to gain and to hold the esteem of men it is not sufficient merely to possess wealth or power. The wealth or power must be put in evidence, for esteem is awarded only on evidence.'[55]

Thus, as Smith points out, the rich might purchase an object precisely *because* it is expensive (and therefore an object for which 'nobody can afford to pay but themselves'[56]), and scorn an object 'which the meanest of the people can have as well as they'.[57] For this reason the sculpture of trees, being inexpensive and therefore widespread, was never accepted by the British upper classes: such ornamentation, although intrinsically harmonious, was disgraced by its 'vulgarity'.[58] Cheap goods are common in every sense of the word: 'In the cabbage-garden of a tallow-chandler we may sometimes perhaps have seen as many columns and vases, and other ornaments in yew, as there are in marble and porphyry at Versailles . . . The rich and the great, the proud and the vain, will not admit into the gardens an ornament which the meanest of the people can have as well as they.'[59] In France, on the other hand, the sculpture of trees was more widely practised in the gardens of the rich; it was, after all, relatively more expensive. Here we have a clear example of what Veblen called the pecuniary canons of taste' according to which commodities such as expensive flowers, fashionable dresses, books in limited editions, Angora cats, fast horses, are judged beautiful when in fact they only gratify 'our senses of costliness masquerading under the name of beauty'.[60] Aesthetic beauty, Veblen says, is so tied to our concepts of the pecuniarily honorific that often 'a beautiful article which is not expensive is accounted not beautiful'.[61] So it was in England, according to Smith, with the sculpture of trees.

Smith demystifies and personifies the downward-sloping demand-curve for goods by identifying it as a continuous chain of social groups with different amounts of money to spend. High prices are paid by 'the rich and great' with substantial fortunes, while low prices are paid by 'the inferior ranks of people' without great fortunes.[62] Consider, for example, the following picture of how the rich prove they are rich in the market-place:

> If two persons have an equal fondness for a book, he whose fortune is largest will carry it . . . Upon this principle, everything is dearer or cheaper according as it is the purchase of a higher or lower set of people. Utensils of golds are comeatable only by persons in certain circumstances. Those of silver fall to another set of people, and their prices are regulated by what the majority can give.[63]

Smith's marginalism is evidently not so much a theory of marginal individual desires as of marginal social classes.

The rich lead in fashion ('that is not the fashion which every body wears, but which those wear who are of a high rank or character'[64]), and, by association with themselves, make even aesthetically indifferent dress seem 'genteel and magnificent'. If the very same costume were commonly worn by 'the inferior ranks of people', however, it would seem by association 'to have something of their meanness and awkward-ness'.[65] The point is that not only do clothes make the man, but the man makes the clothes. The symbol must be appropriate to the subject, so that the ideas habitually associated with each be mutually reinforcing: 'The graceful, the easy, and commanding manners of the great, joined to the usual richness and magnificence of their dress, give a grace to the very form which they happen to bestow upon it.'[66] Elegant clothes are the badges of office of an elegant man; they are a source of ridicule rather than admiration if worn by a pastry-cook.

Consumption-patterns should be appropriate to the station of the consumer, as determined empirically by observing approved habitual associations in a given culture. Smith would certainly have agreed with Veblen's description of this mechanism:

> The accepted standard of expenditure in the community or in the class to which a person belongs largely determines what his standard of living will be. It does this directly by commending itself to his common sense as right and good, through his habitually contemplating it and assimilating the scheme of life in which it belongs; but it does

so also indirectly through popular insistence on conformity to the accepted scale of expenditure as a matter of propriety, under pain of disesteem and ostracism.[67]

Excessive modesty will lead to loss of status. Smith warns that a person who consumes less than is proper for a man of his station will be taken for an imposter: 'Men of no more than ordinary discernment never rate any person higher than he appears to rate himself.'[68] The king eating fish and chips in the East End would be as out of place as a sow in a drawing-room: 'As in point of dignity, a monarch is more raised above his subjects than the chief magistrate of any republic is ever supposed to be above his fellow-citizens; so a greater expence is necessary for supporting that higher dignity. We naturally expect more splendor in the court of a king, than in the mansion-house of a doge or burgo-master.'[69] A king who lives like a commoner will be thought to be in doubt about his own merit.

On the other hand, however, inadequate modesty will not lead to acquisition of superior status. A person whose 'dress', 'equipage', and 'way of living'[70] are too splendid for his station will be dismissed as an 'ostentatious and empty pretender',[71] a 'hypocrite of wealth and greatness'.[72] Moreover, a fraud with any sensitivity at all would, even if he succeeded in impressing his peers with his excessively conspicuous consumption, suffer from a perpetually guilty conscience. A successful masquerade in the uniforms of prestige and power yields little satis-faction for the simple reason that 'man naturally desires, not only to be loved, but to be lovely; or to be that thing which is the natural and proper object of love'.[73] Again, a coxcomb, an economic Tartuffe, cannot afford continually to purchase the status symbols of a superior order: diamonds are expensive, and he is certain eventually to make himself bankrupt. There is no point in trying to look like a Lord if one cannot in all ways act the part of a Lord. The only solution is to accumulate wealth so as to *deserve* approbation.

For the well-to-do, the unintended outcome of propriety in consumption is political power. The rich are admired not so much because of their happiness as because of the suitability of the means they possess for attaining the end of happiness. There is beauty in the fact that they have expensive country-houses, servants, and all the other fittings of a perfectly-arranged machine: 'It is the ingenious and artful adjustment of those means to the end for which they were intended, that is the principal source of . . . admiration.'[74] The poor obey the rich, not out of fear or hope of advancement, but out of a desire to 'assist them in completing a system of happiness that approaches so near to perfection'.[75] A natural affection develops in the masses for those very social groups 'upon whose safety often depends that of the whole society',[76] and for this reason the 'great mob of mankind'[77] entrust political power to those very classes which have both the means and the incentive to defend the property rights of the haves from the jealousy and aggression of the have-nots, the *raison-d'être* of the state in the first place.[78]

Rather than being a source of discord, inequality of wealth becomes a source of social peace and continuity, a psychological barrier to revolution purchased at the cost of some corruption of our moral sentiments (as when we ignore the crimes of the great, so powerful is our sympathy with them[79]). But this respect is dependent on the wealth being transformed into ostentation. A nobleman must not only be a nobleman but must be seen to be nobleman: 'His air, his manner, his deportment, all mark that elegant and graceful sense of his own superiority, which those who are born to inferior stations can hardly ever arrive at. These are the arts by which he proposes to make mankind more easily submit to his authority.'[80] It is not enough for his pedigree to be immaculate; he must also *appear* noble. Thus the Athenians reproached Alcibiades 'for wearing a dress somewhat more splendid than was ordinarily worn by the citizens':[81] he had made himself a threat to their egalitarian and democratic form of government by purchasing goods superior to those consumed by the common rank of men. The Romans, on the other hand, were not offended by the luxury of Lucullus or the splendour of Pompey: ostentatious consumption is not only proper in a stratified society but indeed is functionally necessary to ensure the power of the oligarchy.

Perhaps Smith regretted that the rich and great were so much more respected than the wise and virtuous, that in the real world 'the external graces, the frivolous accomplishments, of that impertinent and foolish thing called a man of fashion, are commonly more admired than the solid and masculine virtues of a warrior, a statesman, a philosopher, or a legislator'.[82] Yet he recognised the fact that there was a direct link going from wealth to consumption, consumption to sympathy, sympathy to prestige, prestige to authority. In the Middle Ages, wealth was directly a source of power as, in the absence of a market, the upper classes used their riches to maintain standing armies of retainers.[83] In commercial society the principle is the same,[84] except that wealth must first be converted into consumables. In this way the rich can both have their cake and eat it too.

The struggle for wealth and consumer goods thus turns out to be a struggle for prestige, position and power: 'Place, that great object which divides the wives of aldermen, is the end of half the labours of human life; and is the cause of all the tumult and bustle, all the rapine and injustice, which avarice and ambition have introduced into this world.'[85] For this reason, a person who is able from the outset to choose a high-prestige, high-power occupation might be willing to dispense with high remuneration and conspicuous consumption. For example: 'The office of judge is in itself so very honourable, that men are willing to accept of it, though accompanied with very small emoluments.'[86] And, speaking of lawyers in general: 'It is the eminence of the profession, and not the money made by it, that is the temptation for applying to it, and the dignity of that rank is to be considered as a part of what is made by it.'[87] Similarly, a person will scorn higher income if it deprives him of social standing. In the Middle Ages, no amount of money could have induced an aristocrat to become a merchant, since 'to trade was disgraceful to a gentleman';[88] and in Smith's own time, since yeomen farmers were regarded as social inferiors not only to merchants and manufacturing capitalists but even to craftsmen and skilled artificers, 'it can seldom happen, therefore, that a man of any considerable stock should quit the superior, in order to place himself in an inferior station'.[89] As with prestige, so with power: since 'the desire of being believed, the desire of persuading, of leading, and directing other people, seems to be one of the strongest of all our natural desires',[90] ambitious men are attracted to professions like politics, despite the improbability of financial success.[91]

In this section we have attempted to show how, according to Adam Smith, society is integrated by roles, not rules; and that, therefore, to know what part an actor is playing it helps to know what he consumes (where he lives, how he dresses, what he eats, the school he went to, the books he reads, the car he drives). Such a theory of consumption patterns as predetermined by standards of propriety arising out of habitual association in a given context suggests two implications:

First, since ends are not random and individual but prescribed group ends, a unique set of subject-symbol relationships, an economic planner could feed a profile of predicted changes in the social structure into a computer and get back a prediction of what consumer goods will be demanded (weighted, of course, by the proportion of the population known to be sensitive to what society regards as proper). In the absence of a computer or reliable economic planners, the same information can be obtained *ex post* through laissez-faire and the market mechanism. But this is a far cry from the econo-mystification of utilitarian consumer sovereignty: the consumer votes in the market-place, but there is only one name on the ballot.

Secondly, in a rapidly-changing society (the product of a rapidly-changing economy), norms of propriety are in a state of flux and may become blurred, thereby generating status insecurity and uncertainty about one's proper style of life. There is no reason to think that the subject/symbol relationship is as clear today as it was in the eighteenth century, or that people are as willing to do society's thing rather than their own, to play their assigned roles with propriety. In a permissive society, even Hamlet might 'begin to do somersaults and sing dirty ditties'.[92] Perhaps Galbraith is right to say that people are so overwhelmed by the abundance of unnecessary gadgets in a modern society that they actually need the hidden persuasion and sales strategies of the ad-man to tell them what they want (even if it is only a toaster that prints an inspirational message on each piece of toast[93]). Perhaps it is too late to argue, as Smith did, in terms of prescription. In economics as in philosophy, perhaps modern man is condemned to be free. Smith would have been the first to admit that his theory of consumption might have been overtaken by events.

II. Tranquillity, Ambition and Progress

Production takes place at a psychological cost. To acquire money, consumer goods, position and power, a man is obliged to sacrifice leisure and 'the composure of the mind'.[1] The philosopher, reflecting on the nature of true satisfaction, is in no doubt that the cost outweighs the benefit:

> In ease of body and peace of mind, all the different ranks of life are nearly upon a level, and the beggar, who suns himself by the side of the highway, possesses that security which kings are fighting for . . . Happiness consists in tranquillity and enjoyment. Without tranquillity there can be no enjoyment; and where there is perfect tranquillity there is scarce anything which is not capable of amusing. . . Examine the records of history, recollect what has happened within the circle of your own experience, consider with attention what has been the conduct of almost all the greatly unfortunate, either in private or public life, whom you may have either read of, or heard of, or remember, and you will find that the misfortunes of by far the greater part of them have arisen from their not knowing when they were well, when it was proper for them to sit still and to be contented.[2]

The paradox of the human condition is that each person is capable of attaining happiness, not by increasing his efforts, but simply by restricting his demands. Smith accepts the Stoic view that, in terms of happiness, there is little difference between one permanent situation and another, and that the security of having a permanent situation is in itself a source of satisfaction. Tranquillity of mind is 'so necessary to happiness'[3] that even a prisoner would be well advised not to plot to escape lest he upset his psychological equilibrium. Smith praised 'the man who struggles the least, who most easily and readily acquiesces in the fortune which has fallen to him':[4] such a man wisely recognises that acceptance of one's lot is the precondition for peace of mind.

An ambitious man, however, despises what he has and 'sacrifices a real tranquillity that is at all times in his power'[5] in the hope of regaining tranquillity at a higher level of wealth, desiring thereby to combine tranquillity with a better standard of living and greater sympathy from his fellow men. Yet the oasis of 'artificial and elegant repose'[6] may turn out to be a mirage. Consumer goods themselves, in terms of direct utility yielded, are a 'deception', and may indeed cause an ambitious man to enjoy less sympathy rather than more from his peers: men tend to resent 'upstart greatness'[7] and his former friends may reject him unless he foregoes the conspicuous consumption proper to his new station and 'affects the same plainness of dress, and the same modesty of behaviour, which became him in his former station'.[8] The fact is that men tend to be envious of the rapid rise of their former neighbours; while the wealthy tend to be too proud to accept a *parvenu* as their equal, even if he goes into debt to impress them with his ostentation. The *nouveaux riches,* like *nouveaux pauvres,* may well end up social outcasts.

An ambitious man might be unsuccessful in his bid to attain a higher level of wealth; and, even if he is successful, tranquillity of mind might not be restored, if he ascends one peak only to discover a higher one behind it. Thus a poor man's son 'whom heaven in its anger has visited with ambition'[9] would be well advised not to try to better his condition by an 'augmentation of fortune':[10] the peaks he is able to ascend by even the greatest of exertions are insignificant, and he will never rise high enough to command real respect. Anyway, the best things in life are free: health, freedom from debt, a clear conscience, the 'ease and indolence of youth',[11] the aesthetic pleasure of contemplating the tranquillity of 'order' and the beauty of 'arrangement'.[12] Peace of mind can so easily be 'the natural and ordinary state of mankind';[13] it would be foolish to sacrifice it for power and riches which, even if a man could attain them, would 'afford him no real satisfaction'.[14] In truth, 'wealth and greatness are more trinkets of frivolous utility, no more adapted for procuring ease of body or tranquillity of mind, than the tweezer-cases of the lover of toys'.[15]

Ambition is a threat to the moral sentiments which are the cement of society. The insatiable drive for wealth might mean prudence swells until it leaves no room for the other virtues of justice and benevolence; and acceleration of expectations may cause men to live in an unhealthy fantasy world of their own, making them insensitive to the feelings of others. In the violence of passion, the impartial spectator is ignored and moral judgements are deformed: in this respect frenzied ambition is only the economic counterpart of (political) faction and (religious) fanaticism, which Smith felt were the greatest 'corrupters of moral sentiments'.[16] Ambition is the enemy of the 'soft virtue of humanity' which flourishes best 'in the mild sunshine of undisturbed tranquillity'.[17] Moreover, it leads to profound economic and social changes which might upset the delicate balance of power necessary for political stability: after all, the 'stability and permanency' of the political order depends on the 'stability and permanency' of the social order.[18]

Given that each permanent situation is a source of satisfaction in itself, and that any change threatens social continuity and mental tranquillity, it seems surprising that Smith also sought functionally to harness the 'deception' that 'trinkets and baubles' yield utility to produce the unintended outcome of economic growth.[19] In fact, however, the contradiction is more apparent than real:

To begin with, it is important to remember that tranquillity to Smith implies moderation and balance, but not a complete state of rest. Some self-love, as we have already seen, is actually virtuous if combined in the proper proportions with some justice and some benevolence; and thus some economic growth is possible without loss of psychological equilibrium. So important to Smith is 'the balance of the affections'[20] that he feels the want of proper self-love to be no less surely a 'failing'[21] than the presence of excessive benevolence. Tranquillity thus comes to mean smooth change, change taking place in a gradual and tranquil manner without any sudden disruption of the time-honoured patterns of activity. As for the individual, 'he is happiest who advances more gradually to greatness':[22] he alone is able to combine increasing wealth with peace of mind and the sympathy of his fellow men. Nonetheless, advance he does: by tranquillity Smith does not mean 'ease and idleness' and would have agreed with Hume that 'human happiness . . . seems to consist in three ingredients; action, pleasure, and indolence'.[23] In other words, alongside his needs for consumption and rest, man thrives on activity. At the same time, the idea of the importance of challenge in overcoming obstacles (whether challenge to the merchant,[24] the scholar,[25] the gamester[26] or the hunter[27]) that is so central to the theories of progress of both Hume and Ferguson is absent in Smith. Ferguson eulogised warfare and sport as giving stimulating and beneficial outlet to man's animal passions, and believed that men seek out difficulties in order to exert and stretch themselves. To him, happiness was not the tedium of freedom from care, but arose 'more from the pursuit, than from the attainment of any end whatever'.[28] Stress is placed on striving, not arriving, and means become ends in themselves. To Smith, on the other hand, activity is explained more modestly in terms of social standards of propriety. Man does not seek out challenge, but on those occasions when it habitually arises he deals with it in the habitual manner, and in that way wins the entire approbation of the impartial spectator.[29] Certainly this is a more sociological approach than Ferguson's theory, which is founded on the psychological premise that man is forever in search of antagonists since 'he loves to bring his reason, his eloquence, his courage, even his bodily strength, to the proof'.[30]

Again, there is little danger, in the Smithian world, of consumer-preferences in the course of economic growth becoming infinite, and thereby replacing mental tranquillity with feelings of frustration, discouragement and pessimism. Durkheim states the problem as follows: 'An insatiable thirst cannot be slaked. If certain actions are to give us pleasure, we must feel that they serve some purpose, that is to say, bring us progressively closer to the goal we seek. One cannot bring some objective nearer that, by definition, is infinitely far away. The remaining distance is always the same, whatever route we take.'[31] But Durkheim also provides a solution to the problem (in terms of self-command, social discipline and moral sentiments), as well as a description of consumption-patterns based on prescription which illustrates clearly why in Adam Smith's view men have determinate goals rather than unlimited objectives:

> According to accepted ideas . . . a certain way of living is considered the upper limit to which a workman may aspire in his efforts to improve his existence, and there is another limit below which he is not willingly permitted to fall unless he has seriously bemeaned himself. Both differ for city and country workers, for the domestic servant and the day-laborer, for the business clerk and the official, etc. Likewise the man of wealth is reproved if he lives the life of a poor man, but also if he seeks the refinements of luxury overmuch. Economists may protest in vain; public feeling will always be scandalized if an individual spends too much wealth for wholly

superfluous use, and it even seems that this severity relaxes only in times of moral disturbance. A genuine regimen exists, therefore, although not always legally formulated, which fixes with relative precision the maximum degree of ease of living to which each social class may legitimately aspire.[32]

Finally, although Smith is inclined to recommend Stoic apathy to the masses, he does reserve to the philosopher the right to rank permanent situations and to reject the less harmonious in favour of the more harmonious. Social change may then be necessary so as to render the world a more beautiful object of contemplation for the philosopher, so as to restore the mental tranquillity not of the actor but of the student of action.

Smith rejected the liberal view that all goods are equal in the sight of the market and that a commodity is worth producing if there is an effective demand for it. He did not hesitate to evaluate consumer preferences, and made no secret of his scorn for many of the commodities that people chose to buy. Thus 'a pair of diamond buckles' is found 'frivolous and useless',[33] while silver is dismissed as 'one of the most proper subjects of taxation, a mere luxury and superfluity'.[34] Clearly all goods are not of equal importance to the philosopher: 'Corn is a necessary, silver is only a superfluity.'[35] Similarly, in the market for housing, Smith not only disaggregated the demand for rented property in London into three categories ('trade and business', 'pleasure and society', and '*mere* vanity and fashion'[36]), but also used this disaggregation to justify a tax on house-rents. It would, after all, be *de facto* progressive, since the poor reserve their meagre incomes mainly for subsistence, and the justification for the tax lies precisely in this wilful reshaping of the free market:

> The luxuries and vanities of life occasion the principal expence of the rich; and a magnificent house embellishes and sets off to the best advantage all the other luxuries and vanities which they possess. A tax upon house-rents, therefore, would in general fall heaviest upon the rich; and in this sort of inequality there would not, perhaps, be any thing very unreasonable. It is not very unreasonable that the rich should contribute to the public expence, not only in proportion to their revenue, but something more than in that proportion.[37]

Elsewhere, he laughs at the 'folly' of a 'capricious man of fashion' who preferred foreign goods to cheaper and better domestic ones 'merely because they were foreign'.[38] And, although a free trader (one, however, who ended his life, similarly to his father and other relatives before him, as a Commissioner of Customs), he does not hesitate to disaggregate imports from America into three clearly-defined categories: those for 'conveniency and use', those 'for pleasure', and those 'for ornament'.[39]

Again, he evaluates the 'gaudy finery' of the court and finds it to be 'splendid, but insignificant pageantry', involving as it does 'costly trinkets' which only satisfy 'frivolous passions'.[40] The court employs unproductive labourers (ranging from physicians to actors) whose work 'perishes in the very instant of its production',[41] and this is unfortunate as no capital is generated 'which could afterwards purchase or procure an equal quantity of labour'.[42] Of course, the court probably had goals other than economic growth or full employment, and the money to back up those ends in the market-place. Nonetheless the philosopher feels free to disagree with the verdict of the market, and offers his own opinion, that he prefers productive to unproductive labour, and goods to services. Perhaps because of his residual Puritanism, even among tangible goods Smith tended to prefer the more durable to the less durable. A 'great wardrobe of fine clothes' is the 'most trifling of all'[43] since it wears out in a short time and must be replaced; a 'stock of houses', on the other hand, 'well built and properly taken care of, may last many centuries',[44] and is hence an admirable investment in the nation's future.

Finally, consider the state of the market in China. There the price of gold and silver was abnormally high for institutional reasons: wealth was concentrated in the hands of traditional aristocrats or 'grandees' with no desire to invest and a vested interest in preventing others from doing so. These 'grandees' sought to distinguish themselves by the elegance of their consumption-patterns, and hence the precious metals, being 'singular and rare', became 'the great objects of the competition of the rich'.[45] Meanwhile, because the economy was stationary, the incomes of the masses tended to the subsistence level. The common people practiced infanticide and dined off the carcasses of dogs at the very time that the upper classes squandered money on 'conveniency and luxury'.[46] This Smith found unacceptable. Although both rich and poor were consuming the trinkets proper to their status in a given situation, Smith saw no reason to accept that situation. The philosopher can reject the appropriateness of the existing natural equilibrium in the market on the grounds that his tranquillity is disturbed by it; and replace what society wants by what society needs and ought to want, considered, of course, in an 'abstract and philosophical light'.[47] One way of imposing such a salubrious structure of effective demand would be by a political revolution and the 'dictatorship of the philosophers'; but a more gradual and practical way of altering the convection of market preferences is by enlisting economic change in the service of philosophy to bring about a structural transformation of society. It is sometimes said that the market is like an election in which the consumer 'votes' for a commodity. If so, then Smith is like the absolute monarch described by Brecht who, displeased by the way his people voted, dissolved the people and elected another.

Sustained economic growth means competition for labour, rising wages, redistribution of the national income in favour of the lower classes, and a new set of market preferences. In comparing positions of general market equilibrium (positions of 'Paretian' optimality), Smith, like Pareto, was not afraid to identify some positions as more optimal than others.

Sustained economic growth also means institutional change. The temporal power of the feudal aristocracy and clergy, for example, was eroded by the development of markets, as they began to trade their agricultural surplus for consumables rather than using it to maintain armies of retainers. Smith is scornful of their priorities, of course: 'For the gratification of the most childish, the meanest and most sordid of all vanities, they gradually bartered their whole power and authority.'[48] He nonetheless welcomes the decline in their influence resultant from their reallocation of expenditure with such enthusiasm that it is impossible not to conclude that, if economics is the science of choice between alternatives, then Smith follows this to its logical conclusion by proposing to analyse not only choice between goods in a given situation, but between different situations, different moments in history. Whereas most modern economists tend to take a rising standard of living as the goal and institutional change as the means, Smith seems to reverse the process by treating the 'deception' of a rising standard of living as the means and institutional change as the end.

If the unintended outcome of commodity-consumption is economic growth, and the unintended outcome of economic growth is historical progress, then the revolutionary upheaval of *The Wealth of Nations* must be interpreted as a two-stage functionalist exercise in social engineering aimed at creating a world in which it is possible for a philosopher to be tranquil. Unfortunately, however, the revolution by spontaneous combustion may go too far: work may become 'mental mutilation', mere 'trinkets and baubles' may begin to be worshipped for their own sake, men may become obsessed with a desire to get on at any price, and tranquillity may become an inferior good. Economic growth, by breeding the very acquisitiveness which heightens the sense of scarcity and deprivation, may ensure that the series never converges on a subjective feeling of affluence, and even diverges increasingly from it. Smith realised that progress might have its limits; but, like many another academic Sorcerer's Apprentice, chose to ignore the danger that he would be unable to stop the machinery he had set in motion once its work was done.

5 THE UPPER CLASSES

This chapter, like all others in this book, is a study in the relationship between economic basis and social superstructure. In Section I we shall state Adam Smith's case against the feudal aristocracy and clergy: society in the Middle Ages was characterised by insecurity, aggression, waste, superstition, and faction. In Section II we shall discuss how, by moving along Smith's four-stage growth-path from an agricultural to a commercial economy, the power of the landed classes was reduced: the growth of the market created a new material situation in which it was possible to spend wealth on consumption rather than simply on private armies of retainers. This social revolution was unplanned and unintended, the landed classes wanting only 'to gratify the most childish vanity', the merchants acting 'merely from a view to their own interest, and in pursuit of their own pedlar principle of turning a penny wherever a penny was to be got'.[1] In Section III we shall argue that, since to Smith free trade in religion was analogous to free trade in corn, competition among many small sects would establish natural religion, just as competition among many small corn-merchants would establish a natural price of corn; while clergymen should be remunerated on the same principle as capitalists, that is, neither too poorly nor too well.

To Adam Smith, a vote for economic growth was not simply a vote for a higher material standard of living. Economic change also brought with it a change in the institutions of society itself, since to each economic basis, be it hunting, pasturage, farming or commerce, there corresponds a unique political and social superstructure. A philosopher could reject the 'deception' of commodity consumption or the formation of equivocal new patterns of conduct and character arising from new forms of economic activity, and yet still welcome economic change as the peaceful means of bringing about desired social changes. Here, however, the science of economics collapses into the philosophy of history.

Smith knew that history could not be expected to *écraser l'infame*; nor would it mean the strangulation of the last nobleman with the guts of the last priest. Historical change would bring about a sort of millenium, but that millenium would be based, as Smith believed most good things in life to be, on moderation and compromise.

I. Aristocracy, Clergy and Feudalism

In the chaos following the fall of Rome, great proprietors engrossed land and formed huge feudal estates. Great estates were necessary since, in a state of near anarchy, land was the 'means, not of subsistence merely, but of power and protection'.[1] Estates were 'a sort of principalities'[2] and every great landowner was 'a sort of petty prince'.[3] In a pre-market economy, it was impossible for the landowner to exchange the surplus product of his lands for other commodities, and hence he used it to maintain private armies of retainers and dependants.[4] The opportunity cost of such 'rustic hospitality' was zero since the surplus would otherwise have been 'thrown away as things of no value'.[5] Feudal authority seems thus to have depended on a residual; in the absence of commerce, and despite the 'natural selfishness and rapacity'[6] of the rich, there was simply no alternative use for the landlord's agricultural surplus but to maintain followers and hangers-on, who in return made the landlord's power absolute on his estates. The landlord did not choose consciously between consumption and autocracy. Rather, feudalism was thrust upon him.

The feudal system appears to have been self-reinforcing, acquiring a momentum of its own. For one thing, in the 'barbarous times of feudal anarchy',[7] there was no separation of powers, no impartial administration of justice. Contracts were unenforceable, and subsistence itself depended upon the 'good pleasure'[8] of the local lord. Outside the towns, 'order and good government'[9] were not to be found, and the business climate was far too uncertain for serious commercial and industrial undertakings:

> That irregular and partial administration of justice . . . often protects the rich and powerful debtor from the pursuit of his injured creditor, and . . . makes the industrious part of the nation afraid to prepare goods for the consumption of those haughty and great men, to whom they dare not refuse to sell upon credit, and from whom they are altogether uncertain of repayment.[10]

Moreover, in the Middle Ages, continual conflict between the private armies of rival lords, or between lords and king, could mean loss or destruction of a businessman's product. Such insecurity led to waste: because the open country 'continued to be a scene of violence, rapine, and disorder',[11] because in time of peace the retainers of the lords often turned to crime,[12] many men frequently preferred to bury their wealth to prevent it from being seized, rather than employing it productively.[13] In short, the 'violence of the feudal government'[14] stifled any move towards economic growth and a consumer-orientated society.

Again, feudalism was self-perpetuating because of its waste of capital. An industrial capitalist would employ his capital in setting to work productive labourers who reproduce and increase the capital. The landlord wastes his revenues on unproductive labourers such as servants, entertainers and retainers, which means the capital is used up and will not in future maintain labour. Frugality is analogous to the foundation 'of a public workhouse',[15] while prodigality exhausts the stock that might have reduced unemployment or raised the wages of the poor. It is no surprise that Smith concludes that 'every prodigal appears to be a public enemy':[16]

> Like him who perverts the revenues of some pious foundation to profane purposes, he pays the wages of idleness with those funds which the frugality of his forefathers had, as it were, consecrated to the maintenance of industry. By diminishing the funds destined for the employment of productive labour, he necessarily diminishes, so far as it depends upon him, the quantity of that labour which adds a value to the subject upon which it is bestowed, and, consequently, the value of the annual produce of the land and labour of the whole country, the real wealth and revenue of its inhabitants. [17]

Moreover, Smith believed, as we have already seen, that national character is intimately related to the imperatives of the national economy, that 'the understandings of the greater part of men are necessarily formed by their ordinary employments'.[18] This means that, in feudal conditions, the nation tends to be extravagant and wasteful rather than industrious and parsimonious. The upper classes can afford to squander their wealth since, being agricultural in origin, it replenishes itself annually. They have no incentive to save their revenues, and to trade or accumulate would be a disgrace for a nobleman.[19] Their social position is hereditary and independent of their own efforts, being based on an irrevocable title to land; and thus their indolence is 'the natural effect of the ease and security of their situation'.[20] The breaking-up of large estates was prevented by primogeniture and the practice of entailing;[21] and in this way the law itself, arising directly from 'the state of property and manners',[22] provided further reinforcement for feudal institutions.

The lower classes too are moulded by their economic situation; and have, moreover, a tendency to emulate their superiors. They turn out to be 'idle, dissolute, and poor'[23] if unproductively employed (say, as servants to a great lord). They would have been 'industrious, sober, and thriving'[24] if productively employed (say, as factory operatives); but, in feudal conditions, the suppression of the industrious and parsimonious capitalist class substantially reduced the opportunities for such employ-

ment, and thus prevented the formation of character-patterns favourable
to industry and trade. In general, 'the proportion between capital and
revenue . . . seems every where to regulate the proportion between
industry and idleness'.[25] The absence of a commercial mentality thus
joins the lack of justice, security and capital accumulation in explaining
why feudalism was self-perpetuating.

Smith was no less disapproving of clerical landowners in their
capacity as clerics than in their capacity as landlords. Like the temporal
lords, the church had used its agricultural surplus to maintain retainers,
ostensibly out of 'hospitality and charity', but in reality to have on
hand private armies which might be 'called out at pleasure, in order to
fight in any quarrel in which the clergy might think proper to engage
them'.[26] Unlike other private armies, however, the church's armies in
the Middle Ages had 'one head' and 'one uniform plan',[27] and operated
on a multinational scale, directed by 'one man'.[28] The monolithic,
concentrated power of the Roman Catholic Church had made it 'the
most formidable combination that ever was formed against the
authority and security of civil government, as well as against the liberty,
reason, and happiness of mankind'.[29] Moreover, it was able to reinforce
its temporal power with spiritual sanctions. Religions do not hesitate
to play on fears of 'eternal misery'[30] and 'the grossest delusions of
superstition'[31] to win influence. A church can be a permanent fifth
column and threat to political stability within the state since, in a
dispute with the secular monarch, it can at any time 'employ all the
terrors of religion in order to oblige the people to transfer their
allegiance to some more orthodox and obedient prince'.[32]

In any case, quite apart from the threat to pluralism and political
stability that an appeal to the supernatural could represent, Smith felt
that magic and superstition, as they are 'out of all danger from any
assault of human reason',[33] are the enemies of empiricism. In his
'History of Astronomy' he described how the savage, victim as he is of
'impotence of mind', seeks to explain the complex (the Heavenly
bodies) in terms of the known (men similar to himself, called 'gods,
daemons, witches, genii, fairies'[34]). In his *Lectures on Justice* he
showed that superstition is the result of fear and ignorance: 'Every
person is superstititous in proportion to the precariousness of his life,
liberty, or property, and to their ignorance. Gamesters and savages are
remarkably so.'[35] And in *The Wealth of Nations* he returned to the
curiosity aroused by the Heavenly bodies and argued that superstition
and scientific method cannot be reconciled: 'Superstition first
attempted to satisfy this curiosity, by referring all those wonderful
appearances to the immediate agency of the gods. Philosophy afterwards

endeavoured to account for them, from more familiar causes, or from
such as mankind were better acquainted with, than the agency of the
gods.'[36]

Religions have tended to opt for the 'cobweb science' of metaphysics,
and to neglect the scientific approach of 'experiment and observation'.[37] Yet even knowledge of right and wrong can be obtained,
not from 'the abstruse syllogisms of a quibbling dialectic',[38] but only
through observation of the reactions of the impartial spectator in a
given society at a given stage in its development: 'The general maxims
of morality are formed, like all other general maxims, from experience
and induction.'[39] Moral philosophy is unable to flourish if moral
judgements are laid down by revelation and casuistry, if immutable
rules of universal applicability are taught without regard to differences
in the concrete (material) situation.[40] Moreover, because religions often
tend to be ascetic and anti-sensual,[41] they frequently condemn both
the search for happiness in this world and the epistemological validity
of obtaining moral knowledge through individual sense-perception. Yet
both of these points are central to Smith's own theory of the moral
sentiments, as indeed to his theory of capitalism and economic
growth.[42]

Because religions refuse to learn from nature, religious norms can
have a corrupting influence. Historically, 'false notions of religion' have
often caused a 'very gross perversion of our natural sentiments'.[43] One
example is in Voltaire's play *Mohomet*, where a 'horrid murder' is
committed because of 'the strongest motives of a false religion'.[44]
Smith is no more charitable to religions which put belief before deeds
or offer absolution of sins. Possibly he was thinking of the church with
'one head' and 'one uniform plan' when he described how, according to
one religion, people can 'by sacrifices, and ceremonies, and vain
supplications . . . bargain with the Deity for fraud, and perfidy, and
violence'.[45]

Finally, Smith distrusted organised religion because churches are
subject to in-fighting among rival factions. This means popular judgements on ethical questions become confused: 'Of all the corrupters of
moral sentiments . . . faction and fanaticism have always been by far
the greatest.'[46] It would be particularly destabilising to the established
government if religious factions made common cause with dissatisfied
political factions, hoping in the event of victory to 'have some share
in the spoil'.[47] An established church, especially where it is not
dependent on 'humouring the people . . . for a subsistence',[48] can
become cut off from the masses. It then becomes the target for an
attack by new religious leaders of simple customs and charismatic

personality, and this can be the cause of civil war. The Protestant Reformation was only possible because of the unpopularity of the Roman Catholic Church.[49]

Conflict between factions of fanatics ('stupid and ignorant enthusiasts'[50] as Smith calls them) are particularly ugly when they pit one great confession against another. In France, disagreements between Protestant and Catholic culminated in the massacre of St Bartholomew's Day,[51] while in Ireland the social structure is founded not on the normal sources of stratification ('birth and fortune') but on 'the most odious of all distinctions, those of religious and political prejudices'.[52] This fanaticism and intolerance carried with it the threat of civil war if not counterbalanced by direct rule from Westminster: 'Without a union with Great Britain, the inhabitants of Ireland are not likely for many ages to consider themselves as one people.'[53]

Hence, Smith felt the church, as well as being a great landowner and thus a pillar of feudalism, was also a source of false doctrines based on superstition, revelation and casuistry; and a threat to political stability because of its tendency to faction and fanaticism, backed up by an appeal to the supernatural. Smith was however, optimistic about the future.

II. Historical Evolution

Aristocracy and clergy had not always been the dominant classes in the past; nor would they be the dominant classes in the future. Adam Smith identified four stages in historical evolution (hunting, pasturage, farming and commerce),[1] each with a unique political, social and intellectual superstructure arising from its economic infrastructure. Feudalism appeared in the third (farming) stage. It would decline in the fourth (commerce). The most the philosopher can do is suggest ways of accelerating the transition. Every dog has his day. By choosing the day, one chooses the dog.

There are two pre-feudal forms of social organisation. The first arose when the economy was based on hunting. The imperatives of the chase limit the size of the band (to, say, two or three hundred men[2]), and hence such societies do not need formal government: they are small enough to debate collectively in a general assembly. Where subordination exists, it is based on superior qualities of body and mind, and especially on age,[3] often reinforced by ties of family. Moreover, in such societies property is insignificant, 'universal poverty establishes there universal equality',[4] and there is thus no need to protect one member of society from the jealousy and aggression of the others: 'Where there is no property, or at least none that exceeds the value of two or three days labour, civil government is not so necessary.'[5] Hence, tribal society was acephalous among hunters for three reasons: because their common cause was so well discerned', because the society was small enough for all to debate together, and because all were 'upon the same level'.[6]

The second pre-feudal form of social organisation is based on pasturage. The rise of private property in the form of herds meant inequality of fortunes, privilege, social tension, and the need for government: 'Wherever there is great property, there is great inequality. For one very rich man, there must be at least five hundred poor, and the affluence of the few supposes the indigence of the many. The affluence of the rich excites the indignation of the poor, who are often both driven by want, and prompted by envy, to invade his possessions. It is only under the shelter of the civil magistrate that the owner of that valuable property, which is acquired by the labour of many years, or perhaps of many successive generations, can sleep a single night in security . . . The acquisition of valuable and extensive property, therefore, necessarily requires the establishment of civil government.'[7]

The hierarchy of wealth among shepherds *is* a hierarchy of power. In the absence of a market economy among the Tartars or the Arabs, wealth is used to maintain retainers:

> The authority of riches . . . though great in every age of society, is perhaps greatest in the rudest age of society which admits of any considerable inequality of fortune. A Tartar chief, the increase of whose herds and flocks is sufficient to maintain a thousand men, cannot well employ that increase in any other way than in maintaining a thousand men. The rude state of his society does not afford him any manufactured produce, any trinkets or baubles of any kind, for which he can exchange that part of his rude produce which is over and above his own consumption. The thousand men whom he thus maintains, depending entirely upon him for their subsistence, must both obey his orders in war, and submit to his jurisdiction in peace. He is necessarily both their general and their judge, and his chieftainship is the necessary effect of the superiority of his fortune. In an opulent and civilized society, a man may possess a much greater fortune, and yet not be able to command a dozen of people . . . The authority of an Arabian scherif is very great; that of a Tartar khan altogether despotical.[8]

Power appears to be the unintended outcome of the reluctant repression of the urge to consume: once again, there was no alternative use of wealth. Meanwhile, presents to the chief increase his wealth,[9] and owners of small flocks (not unlike Marx's petty bourgeoisie) rally to defend men of great property so that the rich will help to defend them against the aggression of men with no flocks at all.[10] Chieftainship becomes hereditary, and nobility of birth joins greatness of wealth as a basis for authority.

Smith is convinced that this form of economic and social organisation is dangerous to its neighbours. Shepherds are barbarous in combat because they are not only fighting for their lives but for their property.[11] Moreover, inequalities of fortune mean a pool of property-less retainers who have no choice but to follow the commands of the rich or go without their supper. Again, shepherds are a threat because social units are large: whereas hunters travel in small bands so as not to exhaust the game, shepherds can travel as a nation (two or three hundred thousand strong, or more[12]), herding their flocks before them. Shepherds are nomads without any attachment to the soil, and thus there is a constant threat that they will take the offensive; while, as nomads, they have acquired the habit of following a leader even in peacetime, and are ready to follow the same leader when he becomes their commander in war.[13] This habit the Highlanders never acquired since they were stationary rather than nomadic shepherds.[14] Shepherds are in the prime of physical condition since they spend much time in the open air, and they have considerable leisure to devote to military training. They are obsessed with combat: even their games are 'the images of war'.[15]

The second stage in historical evolution, therefore, was characterised by a hierarchy of wealth, creating a hierarchy of power; and a nomadic economy based on pasturage, making shepherds dangerously aggressive. Yet man's 'insatiable desires'[16] cause him to want more and more:

> If a number of persons were shipwrecked on a desert island their first sustenance would be from the fruits which the soil naturally produced, and the wild beasts which they could kill. As these could not at all times be sufficient, they come at last to tame some of the wild beasts that they might always have them at hand. In process of time even these would not be sufficient; and as they saw the earth naturally produce considerable quantities of vegetables of its own accord, they would think of cultivating it so that it might produce more of them.[17]

Thus pasturage gives way to sedentary agriculture, which in Europe took the form of the feudal system. This was the third stage in historical evolution, and the stage in which the dominance of aristocracy and clergy was absolute. Moreover, since feudalism offered no security for accumulation or contract, it appeared to be self-perpetuating and an effective bar to further historical progress. Only by altering the economic basis from farming to commerce could one hope to alter the social superstructure and weaken the power of the upper classes; but it was impossible to ignite even the sparks of commerce in feudal conditions.

Meanwhile, however, 'tradesmen and mechanics' had concentrated in towns. Here they were subject to the direct authority of the king. Initially they were nothing more than 'a very poor, mean set of people'[18] who hawked their wares from fair to fair; but the king saw in them potential allies in the struggle against the common enemy, the barons. 'Mutual interest, therefore, disposed them to support the king, and the king to support them against the lords. They were the enemies of his enemies.'[19] To win their support, the king made considerable concessions to them: the towns were given their fiscal independence in exchange for 'a rent certain never afterwards to be augmented'[20] and allowed to be self-governing, through a town-council, as if they were 'independent republics'.[21] They were allowed to raise a militia for their defence and to construct fortifications. The townspeople, freed from the arbitrary power both of the barons and of the king, instituted the rule of law. Security led to prosperity and small traders became substantial burghers, trading at first with burghers in other lands, but eventually hitting upon the idea of trading with their own hinterland by offering imported manufactured luxuries in exchange for the landlords' agricultural surplus: 'The inhabitants of trading cities, by importing the improved manufactures and expensive luxuries of richer countries, afforded some food to the vanity of the great proprietors, who eagerly purchased them with great quantities of the rude produce of their own lands.'[22] Encouraged by the growth of a domestic market, some merchants even became manufacturers and produced in the towns the sort of goods they had used to import.

The vicious circle of feudalism had been broken. The towns had proven its weakest link. The exchange of agricultural produce for manufactured goods unleashed a flood of pent-up consumer demand. Barons and clergy no longer needed to waste their agricultural surplus on retainers and supernumeraries as they could now exchange it for commodities, mainly new luxuries, destined for their own personal consumption. They were driven by greed to dismiss their private armies and dependents, and lost thereby their political dominion:

What all the violence of the feudal institutions could never have effected, the silent and insensible operation of foreign commerce and manufactures gradually brought about. These gradually furnished the great proprietors with something for which they could exchange the whole surplus produce of their lands, and which they could consume themselves without sharing it either with tenants or retainers. All for ourselves, and nothing for other people, seems, in every age of the world, to have been the vile maxim of the masters of mankind. As soon, therefore, as they could find a method of consuming the whole value of their rents themselves, they had no disposition to share them with any other persons. For a pair of diamond buckles perhaps, or for something as frivolous and useless, they exchanged the maintenance, or what is the same thing, the price of the maintenance of a thousand men for a year, and with it the whole weight and authority which it could give them. The buckles, however, were to be all their own, and no other human creature was to have any share of them. . . For the gratification of the most childish, the meanest and the most sordid of all vanities, they gradually bartered their whole power and authority.[23]

So as to spend their entire revenues on themselves, the landlords dismissed their retainers; so as to augment their revenues, they made their tenants-at-will into independent farmers. Such farmers would only be willing to pay higher rents if leases were long and tenure secure, as only then would they be able to improve the land and raise its productivity. This meant the end of personal obligations between farmer and landlord: pecuniary advantages having become 'mutual and equal',[24] the tie between them was simply a cash nexus, a business contract, and no other services were called for. In short, serfdom declined for the same reason as slavery: as soon as output becomes exchangeable, a premium is placed on efficiency, and serfdom and slavery are simply less productive than the employment of labour on contract.[25]

Once armies of retainers were disbanded and ties of personal service broken, the central government was able to extend its influence to all parts of the nation: 'A regular government was established in the country as well as in the city, nobody having sufficient power to disturb its operations in the one, any more than in the other.'[26] Moreover, the growth of multiple fortunes led to the dispersion of power within the state. A mixed constitution, with powers divided between Monarch, Lords and Commons resulted from the king's need for finance from, among others, the new and opulent non-aristocratic, non-clerical classes:

> The king, on account of his urgent necessities, was forced to grant whatever they asked, and thus the authority of the parliament established itself . . . The parliament consists of about 200 peers and 500 commoners. The Commons in a great measure manage all public affairs, as no money bill can take its rise except in that House. Here is a happy mixture of all the different forms of government properly restrained, and a perfect security to liberty and property.[27]

Nor was it only political power that was shared more widely because of the dispersion of wealth. Economic power too was dispersed, the tradesman in a market economy being dependent on a large number of customers: 'Each tradesman or artificer derives his subsistence from the employment, not of one, but of a hundred or a thousand different customers. Though in some measure obliged to them all, therefore, he is not absolutely dependent upon any one of them.'[28] Economic dependence is thus dispersed, power becomes indirect (via the market), and obligations come to be defined by the contractual exchange of equivalents rather than by traditional relationships of status and personal service. Both political and economic power come to be related increasingly to considerations of utility rather than authority.

At the same time, the existence of impartial judges independent of both legislative and executive branches, and unable to be swayed by magnates (old or new) guaranteed that even the poorest could 'get redress of injuries from the wealthiest and most powerful'.[29] The rule of law meant that the indolent could no longer oppress the industrious,[30] and even in the countryside capital accumulation became possible:[31] once men 'are secure of enjoying the fruits of their industry, they naturally exert it to better their condition and to acquire not only the necessaries, but the conveniencies and elegancies of life'.[32]

Meanwhile, the gap between middle and upper classes was narrowing. The landlords were coming to have a business mentality, and to think in terms of maximisation of returns, efficiency, the market, the law of contract, while simultaneously their ranks were being diluted by the presence of successful merchants (who bought land as an investment or for prestige, but no longer for power). In terms of power, the market economy had made the aristocrat 'as insignificant as any substantial burgher or tradesman in a city',[33] while in terms of wealth the merchants were rapidly gaining ground. The increasing similarities (in mentality, power and wealth) between the middle and upper classes meant businessmen ceased to be looked down upon and acquired greater status in the community. It was no longer a disgrace to be in trade. Previously, the 'mean and despicable' idea which people had of merchants had 'greatly obstructed the progress of commerce'.[34]

Thus, economic change had brought about a social revolution. The upper classes rushed to sell their birthright 'for trinkets and baubles, fitter to be the playthings of children than the serious pursuits of men',[35] and committed class suicide. As result, security, pluralism and the balance of powers became possible: 'Commerce and manufactures gradually introduced order and good government, and with them, the liberty and security of individuals, among the inhabitants of the country, who had before lived almost in a continual state of war with their neighbours, and of servile dependency upon their superiors.'[36] Moreover, the dispersion of political and economic power, the impartial administration of justice, the increasing prestige of businessmen, all helped to make the new capitalist system self-perpetuating.

Only after the transformation of the economic basis has almost completely succeeded in transforming the social superstructure does it make sense to suggest ways in which governmental policy can accelerate the process. Smith calls for further checks and balances to the abuse of power, coupled with an absolute reduction in the power of the state, to prevent the transition from feudalism to utilitarian capitalism from stopping at mercantilism or enlightened despotism. He also advocates the use of discriminatory taxation to disadvantage further the upper classes — for example, a highway toll levied most heavily on luxury carriages to penalise 'the indolence and vanity of the rich',[37] or *ad valorem* taxation rather than taxes on bulk (precious commodities are often light[38]). Moreover, the abolition of entailing and primogeniture would, by creating a free market in land, allow existing holders to sell land to finance their love of 'expensive vanity'.[39] This would break the link with the land. As for the clergy, state education could be used as a means of combatting superstition and weakening the hold of established religion: 'Science is the great antidote to the poison of enthusiasm and superstition; and where all the superior ranks of people were secured from it, the inferior ranks could not be much exposed to it.'[40] Laissez-faire, taxation, law reform or education can, however, only provide the *coup de grâce* to an outdated social form. The decline in the feudal power of aristocracy and clergy must result in the main from a change in the material basis upon which all power depends.

Like so much of eighteenth-century historicism, however, Smith's four-stage growth-path seems to be more an expression of belief than an impartial inquiry into the nature of historical evolution. The progression he describes is neither inevitable nor complete.

First, it is not inevitable. Demonstrably, not all societies have followed the same path. Some (such as the inland parts of Africa or Siberia) 'seem in all ages of the world to have been in the same barbarous and uncivilized state in which we find them at present'[41] because of poor water communications. Others (such as China) have become stationary at a pre-commercial stage because of their 'laws and institutions':[42] 'the real progress is not always the most natural',[43] as Dugald Stewart reminds us, and in the case of China human action had clearly diverted historical progress from its natural course. Still others (such as Bengal[44]) were in a state of decay. Clearly, stagnation can set in before an economy has escaped from the farming stage and become commercial.

There may even be a social cycle, albeit probably around a rising trend in national income and refinement of institutions. In one place Smith describes how military monarchy 'came to share that fated dissolution *that awaits every state and constitution whatever*'.[45] And elsewhere, referring specifically to Great Britain, he comments that 'it is now more than two hundred years since the beginning of the reign of Elizabeth, a period *as long as the course of human prosperity usually endures*'.[46] Such passages are strikingly reminiscent of Adam Ferguson, who observed that 'The pavement and the ruins of Rome are buried in dust . . . The tents of the wild Arab are even now pitched among the ruins of magnificent cities . . . The most remarkable races of mankind, it is true, have been rude before they were polished. They have in some cases returned to rudeness again.'[47] It is not inconceivable that Smith shared with Ferguson (and indeed with Machiavelli, Vico, Montesquieu and Pareto) a belief in a rise and fall in the life of a society.

Second, the path is incomplete. For Smith history seems to stand still at the instant in which the fruits of the industrial revolution are being harvested, just as for Hegel time stops immediately the world spirit has become fully self-conscious. Yet since Smith saw the past as a process of becoming, not being, it is strange that he saw commercial society as the end of the progression rather than as a half-way house to something different.

The failure to treat the present as part of a dynamic and on-going historical process is particularly serious since Smith leaves a number of questions unanswered. Economically, his growth-path stops with the restoration of small-scale commerce and manufacturing and the breaking up of imperfections artificially maintained by the mercantile system. Yet he also recognises the existence of large-scale capital-intensive plant necessitating huge outlays,[48] and thus leaves the reader wondering whether, at some future date, oligopoly and monopoly could not represent some sort of threat to the economic balance of power. Politically, his growth-path stops with rule by 'aristocracy' (which comes to include the mercantile plutocracy). Yet class-consciousness among the workers[49] and bitterness about the division of the product,[50] coupled with the replacement of a respected traditional aristocracy by the 'upstart greatness'[51] that results from greater social mobility, could mean that the lower classes might cease to consent to their own exclusion from the political process. Democracy might result, creating a new political balance of power Smith would hardly have welcomed.

Moreover, Smith's approach is teleological and partial, and seems at times to be more a philosophy of human development then a scientific investigation into the laws of history. He seems to prefer impressions of the past to empirical evidence on what actually happened (as in his discussion of the Middle Ages, where his analysis is vague and fails to distinguish between periods and countries). *Histoire raisonnée* need not apparently imply reasoned judgement, and the reader is left with a general feeling of curiosity as to what variables have been suppressed, as to how their inclusion might modify Smith's idealised historical schema.

Even if his growth-path is neither inevitable nor complete, however, Smith's work still represents a valuable methodological contribution to the study of social dynamics. The approach is comparative (treating history as a museum and human nature as a constant, so that institutions can be situated in the context of their appropriate stage) and grand in conception (in the case of each stage, the entire social matrix changes: like Parsons,[52] Smith demonstrates that historical change means changes in economy, society, polity and morality, and shows how these changes are interrelated). Smith shows an awareness of the need for theory as well as simple collection of facts, and attempts at all times to stress interdependence, connection, and particularly causality. In this context he brings in economic determinism and argues that each convection of social, political and moral phenomena results directly from a particular economic basis: stages are hence characterised by the division of labour, ownership of property and nature of economic dependence rather than by social, political or moral factors, which are mere dependent variables.

Finally, Smith's approach was evolutionary. He applied both the Lamarckian concept of adaptation (for example, the adaptation of the businessman to the changed environment caused by the decline of feudalism) and the Darwinian notion of natural selection (for example, the selection represented by perfect competition in the market-place), and was thus a pioneer in the use of the evolutionary method in sociology (even if he believed, as he probably did, that the natural, physical and organic environment remains static and does not evolve in the same way that societies do).

The direction of evolution to Smith was unmistakably upward: change was not a shapeless kaleidoscopic flux, determined at random (as Holbach argued), but could be expected to pass successively and successfully through four stages in social morphology, and to end up by promoting maximum social welfare. Of course, the argument is not necessarily true: the progression might be neither inevitable nor complete, it might bring with it unpleasant side-effects such as 'mental mutilation',[53] and it might lead, at the end of the road, to stagnation and a stationary state.[54] The most that can be said is that Smith's optimistic historicism should be viewed as an expression of hope, the dream of an ideal society. Perhaps Bagehot was not far from the target when he described Smith's theory of history as an attempt to show 'how, from being a savage, man rose to be a Scotchman'.[55]

III. Clergy and Commerce

The impact of market society was particularly hard on the clergy. Not only were they no longer able to support private armies of retainers, not only were they no longer willing to waste their precious exchangeable surplus on charity and the relief of the poor, but their greed and their opulent standard of living alienated the sympathies of the masses:

> The inferior ranks of people no longer looked upon that order, as they had done before, as the comforters of their distress, and the relievers of their indigence. On the contrary, they were provoked and disgusted by the vanity, luxury, and expence of the richer clergy, who appeared to spend upon their own pleasures what had always before been regarded as the patrimony of the poor.[1]

Thus, whereas to Max Weber, commerce was the result of religious reformation, to Smith it was the cause. The selfish and frivolous love of luxury, the market mechanism, the 'gradual improvements of arts, manufactures, and commerce'[2] destroyed the temporal power of the clergy as surely as it had destroyed that of the barons. The church still retained considerable power over the minds of men, however, and was still able to challenge the government by appealing to the 'superstition' and 'enthusiasm' of its followers. Smith considered four solutions to the problem of the state within the state; he rejected all but those which were based on the analogy with commerce.

One way of neutralising the church would have been through the union of church and state. It would have been possible to make the church dependent on the state for its offices and benefices, as Martin Luther had done,[3] and as was the practice of the Church of England in Smith's own time. This has the advantage of making the clergy obedient to the ruler so as to obtain preferment, and is thus 'favourable to peace and good order, and to submission to the civil sovereign'.[4] If, however, the church were made subservient to the state, the masses might regard the clergy as mere mercenary dependents of the court rather than as sincere men of God. Moreover, an institutionalised clergy, like all civil servants whose income is independent of effort, becomes indolent and complacent. In either case, the church ceases to have influence with the masses and becomes unable to defend itself 'against the most ignorant enthusiast who chuses to attack them'.[5] Thus, ultimately the challenge from dissenters must destroy the union of church and state.

Alternatively, the problem of established religion could be solved by making the church into a propaganda instrument of the state. Religion has, after all, often been used as the justification for actions that were politically expeditious, such as colonialism: 'In consequence of the representations of Columbus, the council of Castile determined to take possession of countries of which the inhabitants were plainly incapable of defending themselves. The pious purpose of converting them to Christianity sanctified the injustice of the project.'[6] Smith did not have a very flattering view of clergymen. He described with considerable irony how the Jesuit Gumila, convinced of the reality of Eldorado, 'expressed with great warmth, and I dare to say, with great sincerity, how happy he should be to carry the light of the gospel to a people who could so well reward the pious labours of their missionary.'[7] Very often missionaries have a deplorable tendency to be 'stupid and lying';[8] and the state could naturally make it attractive for a clergyman without doctrinal scruples to preach unqualified obedience, holy war, the divine right of kings, or anything else it felt to be in the public interest.

Smith preferred, however, not to recommend such a supernatural sanction to temporal power. Possibly this was because he was aware of the conflict between science and superstition, and was unwilling to buttress the era of empiricism with magic; possibly, too, because he felt an alliance between two monoliths would make the government too strong relative to other interests in the country; or possibly it was because he knew the church was not always a friend to commerce, as the examples of Spain and Portugal show.[9] Again, he was aware that the power of doctrine should not be overestimated: in practice religions tend either to teach what the flock wants to hear or to be ignored. Thus the fact that the Quakers in Pennsylvania released their slaves indicated to Smith 'that their number cannot be very great',[10] particularly since in other colonies Christianity had not led to the abolition of slavery, although 'our planters are all Christians';[11] and the mercy a Christian conqueror shows to a Christian country he has occupied is only the mercy he would have shown anyway, so as better to govern his new subjects[12] (the proof is the considerable lack of Christian charity in a sea-war). Ideas have consequences; but the consequences of ideas not arising directly out of the concrete situation in which men live and work are minimal, unless supported by the threat of supernatural terror, a *deus ex machina* Smith would have regarded as spurious, fictitious, and in any case despicably Catholic.

Whatever his reasons, Smith nowhere suggests that religion should be harnessed to provide a particular set of social norms in the service of the government. In his discussion of the ideal curriculum for charity schools, he does not even mention religious knowledge;[13] and where he does relate education to the 'benefit of religion', he seems to take the view that the advantage to the 'low people' of reading the Bible should be estimated not only 'in a pious sense', but also in light of the fact that it 'affords them subject for thought and speculation'.[14] In other words, study of, and reflection upon, problems of God and ethics, are desirable actions for their own sake, and independent of the specifically Christian norms contained in the New Testament. It was, after all, a century of religious tolerance, the century of Voltaire's *Zadig* and Lessing's *Nathan The Wise*, the century of Montesquieu's *The Spirit of the Laws*.[15]

Smith sought to deal with organised religion directly, through the reformation of its material bases. Specifically, he suggests two reforms. First of all, instead of one church (official or not), there should be 'two or three hundred, or perhaps . . . as many thousand small sects',[16] competing with one another for customers. Each clergyman would have to exert himself to attract business. Of course, a 'ghostly practitioner'[17] can always play on the baser passions of fear and superstition to steer the congregation out of his neighbour's shop and into his own; but Smith seems to regard excessive fanaticism as a problem of oligopoly, not perfect competition. In an oligopolistic situation, the 'interested and active zeal'[18] of, say, two or three large sects can be a threat to social stability, but in perfect competition, no sect would be large enough to disturb public tranquillity. Just as competition among purveyors of fish leads to convergence on a 'natural price', just as competition among purveyors of education leads to convergence on true knowledge,[19] so competition among suppliers of religion leads to convergence on a common body of doctrine, 'that pure and rational religion, free from every mixture of absurdity, imposture, or fanaticism, such as wise men have in all ages of the world wished to see established'.[20]

Competition among many sects (not necessarily Christian) means that religion ceases to be 'popular superstition and enthusiasm' and becomes the product of 'philosophical good temper and moderation'.[21] Rather than being imposed by revelation (and, equally deplorable, upheld by a confessional church of the Roman Catholic type, to which Enlightenment writers seldom were keen to extend their much-valued tolerance), religious norms grow naturally out of the conditions of the situation. This is a very conservative approach to theology since 'pure and rational' doctrine is the result of events and institutions, not their cause. At the same time, it gives an extra dimension to the empirical investigation of nature in the form of a final cause. Whatever naturally is, is not only good, but God.

Each religious sect should aim to socialise the individual; and, by rescuing him from anonymity[22] and the 'temptations of bad company'[23] (say, in the new industrial towns), by subjecting him to scrutiny and thus to group discipline, strive to improve his moral behaviour. In this way Smith's sects (like Durkheim's 'corporations') were to be an antidote to incipient normlessness. Each sect should reinforce its teachings by reminding the individual of the existence of a Tartarus and an Elysium, and that abuses left uncorrected in this life will be dealt with in the next. Although religious norms may reflect no more than 'philosophical good temper and moderation', the fear of some supernatural super-Lord may be necessary to compel the lower classes to respect them. Historically, in little religious sects 'the morals of the common people have been almost always remarkably regular and orderly; generally much more so than in the established church'.[24]

A second reform Smith proposes is in the system of remunerating clergymen. If they are poorly paid, they will tend to resort to extreme devices to attract donations. Mendicant preachers, for example, are 'obliged . . . to use every art which can animate the devotion of the common people'.[25] Poverty inspires fanaticism: 'No plunder, no pay.'[26] If, on the other hand, they are very well paid, and especially if their income comes to them regardless of their work, they will tend to be luxury-loving and indolent, to say nothing of 'contemptuous and arrogant'.[27] Here as in most things the solution lies in moderation. The ideal situation seems to be the presbyterian church in Scotland, where rewards to clergymen, while not inadequate, are moderate. Such men cannot with propriety indulge in luxury and ostentation, which would be unsuitable not only to their status as clergymen, but also to their economic status:

> Nothing but the most exemplary morals can give dignity to a man
> of small fortune. The vices of levity and vanity necessarily render
> him ridiculous, and are, besides, almost as ruinous to him as they
> are to the common people. In his own conduct, therefore, he is
> obliged to follow that system of morals which the common people
> respect the most. He gains their esteem and affection by that plan
> of life which his own interest and situation would lead him to
> follow.[28]

The clergyman is similar to the capitalist. Perfect competition and
moderate rewards stimulate hard work and good morals, while imperfect
competition and excessively high or excessively low rewards lead to
idleness and corruption.[29] After all, men respond to the demands of
their material situation. The philosopher who wants to form and reform
character must also be an economist.

6 THE LOWER CLASSES

All classes in society benefit from increasing prosperity. In an affluent and growing economy such as Britain a day-labourer 'has more luxury in his way of living than an Indian sovereign',[1] and 'the accommodation of a European prince does not always so much exceed that of an industrious and frugal peasant, as the accommodation of the latter exceeds that of many an African king, the absolute master of the lives and liberties of ten thousand naked savages'.[2]

Such prosperity is not obtained without a cost. To the lower classes, the costs of economic growth are intellectual deprivation (resulting from the division of labour) and class antagonisms (resulting from conflict between worker and capitalist over relative shares). In this chapter we shall investigate how far mental challenge and harmony of interests must be sacrificed to gain a higher material standard of living.

In Section I we shall consider the division of labour and conclude that it improves the worker's mental powers only in those trades where excessive specialisation does not deprive him of the opportunity to invent and innovate. In those industries where technology is complex, however, invention will become the province of specialists. They will enjoy the thrill of discovery (and there is more challenge in a growing economy than in a stagnant one) while the 'low people' become 'exceedingly stupid': 'The Dutch vulgar are eminently so, and the English are more so than the Scotch. The rule is general; in towns they are not so intelligent as in the country, nor in a rich country as in a poor one.'[3] The progression is a historical one, from the Scotch to the English to the Dutch mentality; and education, although it can raise the workers' dexterity and teach respect for the existing social structure, cannot reverse the material results of the work function on character. Since 'the understandings of the greater part of men are necessarily formed by their ordinary employments',[4] the division of labour is as much about the production of character and the allocation of social roles as about the production and allocation of material commodities.

In Section II we shall examine the possibility that exploitation of the labourer is implicit in Smith's theory of value. This theory is, of course, not without ambiguity: Smith offers both a labour-commanded ('measure of value') and a labour-embodied ('source of value') theory, and exploitation can only arise as an objective fact in the latter case. Here capitalist and landlord are not productive of value added, and yet have a share in the national product (the sum of all the value added by productive labour). Naturally, such transfers may be necessary deductions from labour's class income, essential to reward capitalist and landowner for the performance of vital but non-productive functions such as entrepreneurship, risk-taking, or participation in the allocative process. Moreover, such deductions are the price of maintaining the desirable and diversified three-class system (which was already coming into being and had in any case to be accepted as the new *status quo*). Nonetheless, if Smith did tend towards the labour-embodied theory of value, he must have been aware that the labourer was yielding up a surplus product to two non-productive and sterile classes.

Smith's theory of value and distribution was forward-looking. He was conscious of the incipient industrial and social upheaval that was happening under his very eyes, and recognised that wages, profits and rents were not theoretical abstractions but rewards to groups or classes in society that were becoming ever more distinct.[5] Matter is in motion, and a world where the small independent craftsman is also the proprietor of his own means of production was increasingly being replaced by the separation of labour and capital. In the modern world, 'the labourer is one person, and the owner of the stock which employs him another'.[6] Classes as well as functions become differentiated and separate, and this development is closely correlated with the development of productive forces. In this sense the anatomy of civil society is truly to be sought in political economy.

Through his use of the labour theory of value, Smith was able to 'demystify' the monetary forms of these new social relationships, and to emphasise that exchange means not just the exchange of anonymous money for inanimate goods, but of personal labour for the products of personal labour. Goods cost labour, and a labour theory of value enables the economist to make interpersonal comparisons of sacrifice. It also allows him, having classified men in groups according to which sort of factor-income they receive, to show that some class-incomes are deductions from others.

The presence of the objective fact of economic exploitation in a society may be a barrier to cordiality and social solidarity: exchange can only be a bond of union and friendship where both parties to a contract believe that fairness and justice are not being neglected. Smith does not explain how his general optimism about interdependence and the mutual gratification of desires is to be reconciled with the problem of shares implicit in his labour theory of value. Nor does he consider what would happen to the distribution of the product in the absence of landowners and capitalists; but this is part of his general refusal to consider non-capitalist forms of industrialisation or single-class economic and political systems.

In Section III we will turn from the objective evidence for exploitation (if in fact Smith believed it existed) to the subjective perception of exploitation; and here Smith made clear that the lower classes, rightly or wrongly, did not have the sensation of living in a blissful state of natural harmony with other orders and classes. The worker appears to be aware that relative shares depend not on some unique functional relationship between the productivity of factors but on bargaining strength alone, and that there are a vast number of possible market equilibria depending on different distributions of economic power. This sort of survival of the fittest in the market is not likely to promote social cohesion; and in any case a truce has no moral power to reconcile subjective feelings of antagonism.

The problem is that even if the worker were to accept the verdict of the labour-market as 'fair' and the result of 'natural justice', there might still be discontent about the very fact of sharing, quite apart from the equity of shares. It is not just 'want' but 'envy' that causes the rich to fear the aggression of the poor. In a stratified industrial society the lower classes may suffer from (relative) deprivation by comparison, particularly where the rich are the new rich (a case of mere 'upstart greatness'[7]); and may resent the dependency implicit in a system whereby the employer advances wages and raw materials to the worker at the start of the period, and claims in return the whole product of the labourer's work at the end.

Such resentment might, objectively speaking, be difficult to justify. A contemporary marginalist economist is able to demonstrate mathematically to the worker (with the aid of first and second derivatives, Lagrangean multipliers and Euler's Theorem) that there will be no actual exploitation, provided that factor rewards are equal to the marginal revenue product that results from the employment of one more unit of the factor.[8] Such a proof can be translated into social philosophy by bringing in the utilitarian doctrine of the natural identity of interests: given individual freedom, all classes can be expected to work together in concert and thus to secure maximum output from scarce inputs. Some writers have attempted to identify Adam Smith with this tradition.[9] There is, however, an alternative tradition, which was reluctant to identify natural identity of interests with natural harmony of social classes. Durkheim, of course, writing in this tradition, believed that a subjective sense of social solidarity would automatically result from the objective condition of interdependence and the division of labour. Max Weber, on the other hand, offered what is possibly a more realistic view of the perversion of rational perceptions that can result in the real world. Consider the following discussion of class antagonisms:

> It is not the rentier, the share-holder, and the banker who suffer the ill will of the worker, but almost exclusively the manufacturer and the business executives who are the direct opponents of workers in price wars. This is so in spite of the fact that it is precisely the cash boxes of the rentier, the share-holder, and the banker into which the more or less 'unearned' gains flow, rather than into the pockets of the manufacturers or of the business executives.[10]

Smith's views on the natural identity of interests may have been ambiguous, but it is difficult not to detect a similar awareness of social malintegration based on just such a subjective sense of disharmony between groups in society.

Finally, in Section IV, we will argue that Smith desired the accumulation of capital not simply because it increased the supply of 'trinkets and baubles' available to all consumers in the society, but specifically because it provided jobs for the lower classes (so long as a 'reserve army' of the unemployed continues to exist) and also improved their absolute and relative living standards (since the bargaining power of labourers *vis-à-vis* capitalists improves as the point of full employment is approached). Better living standards, in turn, both encourage an increase in the population (the potential labour force) and stimulate the worker to exert himself (thereby raising his productivity). Presumably, too, higher wages would attract the underemployed and the incorrectly employed (such as domestic servants and other unproductive labourers) into the industrial sector of the economy.

Unlike later Malthusians, Smith tended to the view that a growing population was both possible and desirable (even if he was less extreme in his enthusiasm than Montesquieu[11] and Kames,[12] who actually feared depopulation). Unlike contemporary mercantilists, who preached the 'utility of poverty', Smith believed high wages would stimulate industry, not idleness, in the lower classes. In this, his view resembles that of Hume, who had argued that an increase in the supply of money within a state (at least in the transitional period before inflation resulted) would encourage both employment and diligence: 'If workmen become scarce, the manufacturer gives higher wages, but at first requires an Encrease of labour; and this is willingly submitted to by the artisan, who can now eat and drink better, to compensate his additional toil and fatigue.'[13]

To Adam Smith, the solution to the problem of unemployment and low (in the limiting case, subsistence) wages that resulted inevitably

from the excess of labour relative to capital was to increase the supply
of capital relative to labour. This could be done by removing artificial
restraints and constraints on the optimal allocation of resources (such
as the Navigation Laws,[14] which kept profits unnaturally high in trades
that were unusually roundabout, and thereby wasted capital that could
have been used more intensively and productively elsewhere). The
problem is not a technological one (as would have been the case with
non-transferable resources), but is institutional in nature, namely the
inefficiency that results from a limitation of the market, restrictions
on factor-mobility and competition, and a slow rate of economic growth.

Smith's views on the socially beneficial effects of capital accumulation
are ambiguous in so far as he related falling unemployment and rising
standards of living to an increasing supply of capital *in toto*. Capital is,
after all, of two types, circulating and fixed, and an increase taking
place in machinery rather than in payment to the workers could
actually worsen the lot of the labouring classes. Moreover, even
circulating capital can be disaggregated into wage-goods and raw
materials. In both cases Smith is vague as to the allocation of total
capital between its various uses. He nonetheless was optimistic in his
belief that a rising capital-stock could not but better the lot of the
lower classes. Indeed, his whole theory of capital accumulation and
economic growth appears to be an attempt to skew the distribution of
the national income (without state intervention in the labour market).
Increasing wealth is not an alternative to redistribution; it *is*
redistribution, and towards the have-nots. Such redistribution promotes
greater equality, and this is basically a good thing. Smith would have
agreed with Hume's view that 'a too great disproportion among the
citizens weakens any state'.[15]

The emphasis in this chapter on employment and living standards on
the one hand, and social conflict on the other, suggests at least a
superficial similarity between Smith and Hobbes. In both cases, the
aim (for the individual and the society alike) is to stay alive. As Smith
puts it, 'self-preservation, and the propagation of the species, are the
great ends which nature seems to have proposed in the formation of all
animals'.[16] In both cases, wealth is seen as a means to power. To Hobbes
this meant the ability to accumulate a stock of friends and servants for
defence in case of aggression in a world where the weakest man can kill
the strongest. To Smith it meant command over labourers and the
produce of labour:

> Wealth, as Mr. Hobbes says, is power. But the person who either
> acquires, or succeeds to a great fortune, does not necessarily acquire

or succeed to any political power, either civil or military . . . The power which that possession immediately and directly conveys to him is the power of purchasing; a certain command over all the labour, or over all the produce of labour which is then in the market.[17]

In both cases men are naturally equal, and it is the accumulation of wealth which conveys unequal power.

Moreover, both Hobbes and Smith took a supply-and-demand approach to the value of a human being, and the following passage from the *Leviathan* is reminiscent of Smith's whole theory of collective bargaining: 'The *Value*, or WORTH of a man, is as of all other things, his Price; that is to say, so much as would be given for the use of his Power: and therefore is not absolute; but a thing dependant on the need and judgement of another.'[18] It might be objected that Hobbes means political power while Smith is thinking of economic power. Professor Macpherson, however, has reinterpreted Hobbes as the creature of nascent capitalism, not the Civil War. While Macpherson's approach has been much criticised for relating ideas mainly to the economic basis of a society, it must be remembered that this would probably have been Adam Smith's own method, had he chosen to write a study of Hobbes. According to Macpherson, Hobbes argued backwards from the possessive individualism of his own market society to the state of nature. Man's love of power is not natural, nor is the state of war a constant threat, except in a market society with inequalities of wealth, power and property. Human nature is not independent of time and place.[19]

If one accepts Macpherson's view that Hobbes modelled his state of nature on modern market society, then it is possible to argue that the Smithian theory of conflict is similar to the Hobbesian *bellum omnium contra omnes:* in the Smithian world weak and strong struggle in the market place for relative shares in the national product, and know that they are struggling. Indeed, since Hobbes neglected social stratification and an explicit class-struggle, Smith, by emphasising class-conflicts over relative shares, appears to have been a bridge between Hobbes and Marx. In his discussion of the position of the lower classes, Smith thus appears paradoxically to have been opening a debate which was, in the nineteenth and twentieth centuries, to bring into question the very social stability he valued so highly.

I. The Division of Labour

In the opening sentence of Book One of *The Wealth of Nations*, Smith makes clear the central role he assigns to the division of labour in the process of economic growth: 'The greatest improvement in the productive powers of labour, and the greater part of the skill, dexterity, and judgement with which it is any where directed, or applied, seem to have been the effects of the division of labour.'[1] As Schumpeter observed: 'Nobody, either before or after A. Smith, ever thought of putting such a burden upon division of labor. With A. Smith it is practically the only factor in economic progress.'[2]

The division of labour is the road to prosperity. Specialisation on one operation improves the worker's dexterity and also means a saving of time previously wasted moving from one task to another. Moreover, it stimulates the worker and others to raise productivity by developing new techniques and machinery to 'facilitate and abridge labour'. There is no limit to the division of labour save the size of the market, which in turn could be both widened (by an extension of transport facilities and the freedom of trade) and deepened (by economic growth itself, a synonym for rising incomes and expenditure of all classes).

The worker has a share in increasing prosperity: there will only be full employment and rising standards of living if the stock of capital is growing more rapidly than the working population,[3] but in an affluent and growing economy such as Britain a day-labourer 'has more luxury in his way of living than an Indian sovereign'.[4] The reason for that luxury is specialisation: 'It is the division of labour which increases the opulence of a country'[5] and ensures that 'a general plenty diffuses itself through all the different ranks of the society'.[6]

Yet the division of labour can also mean something else to the worker: psychological deprivation and narrowed horizons. In more primitive societies of hunters, shepherds and peasant farmers, consumer satisfactions were rare, but at least variety of occupations and scope for problem-solving innovation prevented intellectual decay: 'Invention is kept alive, and the mind is not suffered to fall into that drowsy stupidity, which, in a civilized society, seems to benumb the understanding of almost all the inferior ranks of people.'[7] In modern society, the cost of affluence seems to be the 'mental mutilation' of the lower classes.

This conclusion is not immediately obvious for two reasons:

Firstly, increasing dexterity could have a favourable rather than an unfavourable effect on the worker's intelligence. Pre-industrial society was far from idyllic:

The habit of sauntering and of indolent careless application, which is naturally, or rather necessarily acquired by every country workman

who is obliged to change his work and his tools every half hour, and
to apply his hand in twenty different ways almost every day of his
life; renders him almost always slothful and lazy, and incapable of
any vigorous application even on the most pressing occasions. [8]

Before the division of labour, therefore, the worker was seldom very
dexterous because the way in which work was organised made him
inefficient. He was 'slothful and lazy' because of frequent interruptions
in his work, because of the psychological adjustment and readjustment
needed as he moved from one set of tools and techniques to a
completely different set.

This is not, however, intellectual sloth or mental laziness. Smith is
simply stating the well-known fact of life that most men need to have
a break between one sort of job and another. This is true for the
scholar as for the labourer: 'When a person has been reading he must
rest a little before he begins to write.'[9] As far as the mind is concerned,
a man who is daily confronted by a variety of tasks (such as the
country weaver with a small farm,[10] acquainted as he is with sowing,
reaping and threshing as well as weaving) enjoys a considerable degree
of intellectual challenge. He may be 'slothful and lazy' because of the
need to react to one stimulus after another, but at least his multiplicity
of jobs prevents him from becoming 'stupid and ignorant', as he would
if he had to concentrate on reacting to a single stimulus.

Specialisation on one simple operation means that 'a frequency of
action insensibly fits men to a dexterity in accomplishing it';[11] but,
since this improvement in dexterity results from the elimination of
the unknown and the obsolescence of challenge, since the conversion
of the production process into a set of simple habitual associations
reduces the probability that Suprise and Wonder will arise, specialisation also makes intelligence into a vestigial organ which starts to
wither away.

Secondly, greater opportunities to invent and innovate following
the division of labour might stimulate the worker's mental activity:
'A great part of the machines made use of in those manufactures in
which labour is most sub-divided, were originally the inventions of
common workmen, who, being each of them employed in some very
simple operation, naturally turned their thoughts towards finding
out easier and readier methods of performing it.'[12] The worker is
more likely to be capable of inventing and innovating if his mind is
focused on a single operation than if his attention is divided among a
variety of things.[13]

Man has a natural fascination with machines and an instinctive desire to improve them: 'Such is the delicacy of man alone, that no object is produced to his liking. He finds that in everything there is need of improvement.'[14] The worker has a further incentive to improve on the technology he uses in so far as it abridges his own labour. Thus 'some miserable slave who had perhaps been employed for a long time in grinding corn between two stones, probably first found out the method of supporting the upper stone by a spindle',[15] while a boy 'who loved to play with his companions' discovered that manual operation of a valve could be superseded by tying a string from the valve to another part of the machine.[16] A farmer probably made the 'original plough'.[17] In all these cases, self-interest had unintended consequences: the aim of each technological advance (however modest) was simply to 'facilitate and abridge' the inventor's labour, but it nonetheless had a favourable effect on his intelligence by presenting him with a challenge and thus providing intellectual relief from mere repetition.

Apart from the workers, however, there are other groups in society who invent and innovate. There are the capitalist entrepreneurs (whose propensity to make discoveries we will investigate elsewhere in this chapter). There are the specialist producers of capital goods: 'Many improvements have been made by the ingenuity of the makers of the machines, when to make them became the business of a particular trade.'[19] In his example of the grinding mill, Smith shows there was a division of labour in invention between the miller (who made simple discoveries such as the feeder and shoe) and the millwright (who made more complex discoveries such as the cog wheel and trundle). Here the more advanced technology clearly bears 'the most evident marks of the ingenuity of a very intelligent artist'.[20] Finally, there are the full-time experts, 'philosophers or men of speculation, whose trade it is not to do any thing, but to observe every thing; and who, upon that account, are often capable of combining together the powers of the most distant and dissimilar objects'.[21] In the course of the division of labour, even the craft of inventing itself becomes a full-time occupation, improving the dexterity of the inventor, saving his time, and rendering his understanding 'both acute and comprehensive'.[22]

Thus, although the worker may be encouraged by the division of labour to invent and innovate in the early stages of the industrial revolution, it appears that sooner or later that same division of labour brings with it a separation of mental and physical labour: 'In opulent and commercial societies . . . to think or to reason comes to be, like every other employment, a particular business, which is carried on by a very few people.'[23] The worker does not have advanced education, and concentration on a single job-function (say, the production of one-eightieth of a pin) gives him neither 'leisure' nor 'inclination'[24] to 'observe every thing'. Yet 'they must have extensive views of things, who . . . bring in the assistance of new powers not formerly applied'.[25] In an advanced and technologically sophisticated economy, the lower classes are increasingly excluded from the creative and mind-stretching processes of invention and innovation, which become the province of philosopher-specialists. As a result, the intelligence of the philosopher becomes more acute and that of the operative more blurred: 'Notwithstanding the great abilities of those few, all the nobler parts of the human character may be, in a great measure, obliterated and extinguished in the great body of the people.'[26]

Fortunately, the picture may not be quite so bleak as it seems. For instance, although increasingly only the mind of the philosopher might be able to 'think of the application of new powers, which are altogether unknown, and which have never before been applied to any similar purpose',[27] the 'meer artist' might still be able to innovate even after he has given up inventing. Consider the case of steam-power: 'It was a real philosopher only who could invent the first engine, and first form the idea of producing so great an effect, by a power in nature which had never before been thought of',[28] and yet, as we have already seen, a common workman using the machine was quick to improve it by attaching a string from valve to piston, so that the valve would open and shut automatically.[29] Similarly, 'it must have been a philosopher who, in the same manner first invented, those now common and therefore disregarded, machines, wind and water mills. Many inferior artists may have afterwards improved them.'[30] In other words, in a sophisticated economy the division of the labour of discovery between philosopher and artisan may come to be a straightforward division between invention and innovation. It is not however clear how much even such opportunities to innovate will continue to arise once the worker comes to specialise on one or two simple operations. There is limited scope for tying strings to valves when one is working with computers or supersonic aircraft, and Smith never denied that the labourer is able to simplify his work only where 'the nature of it admits of such improvement'.[31]

In short, therefore, it appears that neither increasing dexterity nor greater opportunities to invent and innovate following the introduction of the division of labour can prevent the eventual 'mental mutilation' of the lower classes. Perhaps industrialisation does cause an initial improvement in the intellectual powers of the worker (since in large-scale production alone can the labourer concentrate adequately on one operation as to be able to improve it); but it later causes those mental powers to deteriorate (since as technology becomes more complex, the worker increasingly loses the opportunity to exercise his mind as well as his hands). Basically Smith's view is pessimistic:

> In the progress of the division of labour, the employment of the far greater part of those who live by labour, that is, of the great body of the people, comes to be confined to a few very simple operations; frequently to one or two. But the understandings of the greater part of men are necessarily formed by their ordinary employments. The man whose whole life is spent in performing a few simple operations, of which the effects too are, perhaps, always the same, or very nearly the same, has no occasion to exert his understanding, or to exercise his invention in finding out expedients for removing difficulties which never occur. He naturally loses, therefore, the habit of such exertion, and generally becomes as stupid and ignorant as it is possible for a human creature to become.[32]

Such pessimism was part of the intellectual capital of the Scottish Enlightenment. Lord Kames believed that excessive division of labour and concentration on a single monotonous operation 'confines the mind to a single object and excludes all thought and invention: in such a train of life the operator becomes dull and stupid like a beast of burden'.[33] Intellectual inaction, said Kames, makes men 'degenerate into oysters'.[34] Adam Ferguson warned that, since a man's character is so much the product of his work-function, repetitive work is likely 'to contract and to limit the views of the mind',[35] and pointed out that such intellectual decay is paradoxically a considerable aid to industrial efficiency:

> Many mechanical arts, indeed, require no capacity; they succeed best under a total suppression of sentiment and reason; and ignorance is the mother of industry as well as of superstition. Reflection and fancy are apt to err; but a habit of moving the hand, or the foot, is independent of either. Manufactures, accordingly, prosper most, where the mind is least consulted, and where the workshop may, without any great effort of imagination, be considered as an engine, the parts of which are men.[36]

And John Millar deplored the fact that in modern society workmen become 'like machines' in the absence of any need for reflection and intellect: 'As their employment requires constant attention to an object which can afford no variety of occupation to their minds, they are apt to acquire an habitual vacancy of thought, unenlivened by any prospects, but such as are derived from the future wages of their labour, or from the grateful returns of bodily repose and sleep.'[37]

Clearly, Smith was not alone in expecting dehumanising and brutalising consequences for the lower classes to result from the division of labour, at least once the stage of early industrialisation had been passed. Here as elsewhere he is thinking of an optimum position which is fortunately reached and then regrettably abandoned; similar argumentation applies to the process by which inadequate commodity-consumption becomes adequate and then degenerates into the worship of 'trinkets and baubles', or to the possibility that in certain situations prudence could become so great as to blot out the other virtues of justice and benevolence. The dilemma with the division of labour, however, is that an argument for moderation is no argument at all, since the worker has a triple identity (as a producer, as a consumer, and as an actor in a given institutional framework). The division of labour means less job-satisfaction (at least, beyond the optimum point), but also more consumer-gratifications, and a transformed social superstructure resulting from economic change. It appears to be the case that the optimum point for the worker as producer is reached before the optimum institutional structure for society as a whole (the reformed institutional environment discussed in Chapter 5) is in place, and this implies that some mental deterioration of the labouring classes is inevitable: it is the vale of tears through which some must pass in order that all may reach Paradise.

Some groups are able to escape this mental deterioration, however. Thus, in agriculture, where there is less scope than in industry for the division of labour and improvement in productivity, the labourer's intellect is more alert. He has a 'great variety of knowledge and experience'[38] since, rather than concentrating on one 'simple operation' (such as making 'the seventeenth part of a pin or the eightieth part of a button'), he performs a number of different tasks: 'When the mind is employed about a variety of objects, it is somehow expanded and enlarged, and on this account a country artist is generally acknowledged to have a range of thoughts much above a city one.'[39] Moreover, in agriculture, 'custom' is not allowed to deaden 'the vivacity of both pain and pleasure'.[40] Habitual associations do not simply repeat themselves, each situation is different, and the worker is forced to make decisions:

The man who works upon brass and iron, works with instruments and upon materials of which the temper is always the same, or very nearly

the same. But the man who ploughs the ground with a team of
horses or oxen, works with instruments of which the health,
strength, and temper, are very different upon different occasions.
The condition of the materials which he works upon too is as
variable as that of the instruments which he works with, and both
require to be managed with much judgement and discretion.[41]

There is an aesthetic satisfaction in such variety: 'A smooth surface is
more agreeable than a rough one. Variety is more pleasing than a
tedious undiversified uniformity.'[42] Of course, just as 'uniformity tires
the mind' ('a long uniform wall is a disagreeable object'), so 'too much
variety, too far increased, occasions an over-dissipation of it'.[43] Some
division of labour is clearly necessary to prevent excessive variety from
leading to mental and physical exhaustion. Moderation, however, has
obtained in agriculture, and the resulting effects on the lower classes
are to be welcomed: 'How much the lower ranks of people in the
country are really superior to those of the town, is well known to every
man whom either business or curiosity has led to converse much with
both.'[44]

Another group which has escaped the brutalising effects of the
division of labour is that of men 'of some rank or fortune'. Their work
tends to 'exercise the head more than the hands', and obviously 'the
understandings of those who are engaged in such employments can
seldom grow torpid for want of exercise'.[45] Moreover, they 'generally
have a good deal of leisure' in which to develop creative hobbies and
other outside interests, many of them acquired in the long years spent
at school ('people of rank or fortune' normally continue to receive
education until they are at least eighteen or nineteen years of age[46]).
This contrasts with the situation of lower-class children who leave
school at an early age and are forced into a repetitive and exhausting
job: 'That trade is generally so simple and uniform as to give little
exercise to the understanding; while, at the same time, their labour is
both so constant and so severe, that it leaves them little leisure and less
inclination to apply to, or even to think of anything else.'[47]

Men's character is mainly formed by the imperatives of their
economic situation. It is therefore understandable, even predictable,
that boring and routine work produces boring and routine men, 'as
stupid and ignorant as it is possible for a human creature to become'.[48]
Smith believed, however, that 'a man without the proper use of the
intellectual faculties of a man . . . seems to be mutilated and
deformed'[49] in an essential part of his nature, and called for state
encouragement to schooling for the worker, whose 'dexterity at his

own particular trade seems . . . to be acquired at the expence of his intellectual, social, and martial virtues. But in every improved and civilized society this is the state into which the labouring poor, that is, the great body of the people, must necessarily fall, unless government takes some pains to prevent it.'[50] This suggests that Smith saw education as an antidote to the ill-effects of the division of labour, a means of retarding or even reversing the effect of employment on the formation of character. This was, for example, James Mill's optimistic interpretation of Smith's views on education. He wrote that, according to Smith, 'the minds . . . of the great body of the people are in danger of really degenerating, while the other elements of civilization are advancing, unless care is taken, by means of the other instruments of education, to counteract those effects which the simplification of the manual processes has a tendency to produce'.[51]

It is clear that Smith both deplored the 'gross ignorance and stupidity'[52] of the lower classes which resulted from the division of labour and advocated state aid to education. What is less clear, however, is the exact mechanism through which education was to work its miracles. After all, Smith was not thinking of a general liberal education to raise the worker's cultural level and give him leisure-time interests. Smith does complain that, as for the masses, 'their work through half the week is sufficient to maintain them, and through want of education they have no amusement for the other, but riot and debauchery'.[53] The education he proposed, however, was strictly practical:

If, instead of a little smattering of Latin, which the children of the common people are sometimes taught (in the charity schools), and which can scarce ever be of any use to them; they were instructed in the elementary parts of geometry and mechanics, the literary education of this rank of people would perhaps be as complete as it can be. There is scarce a common trade which does not afford some opportunities of applying to it the principles of geometry and mechanics.[54]

In short, education to Smith meant an investment in human capital that would raise the worker's productivity and accelerate economic growth. Acquired talents, 'as they make a part of his fortune, so do they likewise of that of the society to which he belongs. The improved dexterity of a workman may be considered in the same light as a machine or instrument of trade which facilitates and abridges labour, and which, though it costs a certain expence, repays that expence with a profit.'[55]

Perhaps Smith felt that, since the division of labour is inescapable, at

least a semi-educated, semi-skilled worker would have more opportunity to exercise his intelligence than if he were uneducated and
unskilled. What he says, however, is quite different. A man destined to
be a porter will be a better porter if he has had some education:

> Though the common people cannot, in any civilized society, be so
> well instructed as people of some rank and fortune, the most
> essential parts of education, however, to read, write, and account,
> can be acquired at so early a period of life, that the greater part even
> of those who are to be bred to the lowest occupations, have time to
> acquire them before they can be employed in those occupations.[56]

Education should thus be both useful and appropriate to the future
needs of the pupil. Like many other eighteenth-century writers on
education, Smith believed that a different sort of education should be
provided to 'people of some rank or fortune' from that offered to the
masses, as their future employments and stations in life will make
different demands on them. In all cases, his basic principle appears to
be that education is first and foremost preparation for 'the real business
of the world, the business which is to employ (the pupils) during the
remainder of their days'.[57] Hence the excellence of education for
women (which was privately and competitively provided) lies precisely
in the fact that 'every part of their education tends evidently to some
useful purpose . . . In every part of her life a woman feels some conveniency or advantage from every part of her education. It seldom
happends that a man, in any part of his life, derives any conveniency or
advantage from some of the most laborious and troublesome parts of his
education.'[58] Education should be appropriate to the role the pupil will
later play in society. A woman will become the 'mistress of a family',
and hence women should be educated in such a way as 'either to
improve the natural attractions of their person, or to form their mind
to reserve, to modesty, to chastity, and to oeconomy'.[59]

This is perhaps surprisingly limited in view of Smith's experience in
France where women held salons and were significant contributors to
intellectual life; but Smith had a keen sense of what was proper in a
given situation, at a given time. In Britain it was proper for the masses
to be taught simple skills, for upper-class men to be prepared for a
profession, and for women to be groomed for the vocation of wife and
mother. Education was thus to be both practical and conservative:
rather than raising the cultural level of the nation or accelerating social
mobility, it was to reinforce the existing social structure by helping each
group to play its assigned role with even greater dexterity.

Moreover, education could be a means of shaping public opinion. Locke had put forward the psychological premise that children are 'white Paper, or Wax, to be moulded and fashioned as one pleases',[60] and argued that 'of all the Men we meet with, Nine Parts of Ten are what they are, Good or Evil, useful or not, by their Education'.[61] Helvétius, a Lockean sensationalist of the most extreme type, advocated the use of this power to improve public morals along whatever lines the philosopher-legislator (the origin of goodness) should prescribe. Smith, heir to this tradition and personally acquainted with Helvétius and other *philosophes*, was certainly not unaware of the propaganda function of education, particularly with regard to the lower classes:

> The state . . . derives no inconsiderable advantage from their instruction. The more they are instructed, the less liable they are to the delusions of enthusiasm and superstition, which, among ignorant nations, frequently occasion the most dreadful disorders. An instructed and intelligent people besides, are always more decent and orderly than an ignorant and stupid one. They feel themselves, each individually, more respectable, and more likely to obtain the respect of their lawful superiors, and they are therefore more disposed to respect those superiors. They are more disposed to examine, and more capable of seeing through, the interested complaints of faction and sedition, and they are, upon that account, less apt to be misled into any wanton or unnecessary opposition to the measures of government.[62]

Education for citizenship has thus both a religious and a civil function. The religious function is mainly negative, to combat the 'superstition and dogma' to which an ignorant people is more likely to fall victim, but it can also be positive in so far as the 'benefit of religion' (not of the Church, however) makes men more aware of the community and the need for ethics.[63] The civil function is positive, to teach men the benefits they receive from the existing social structure, and to recognise the shallowness of factions and revolutionaries. Moreover, educated men feel that they themselves have become more deserving of 'respect', and are more likely to identify with the Establishment.

The power of education to civilise a nation by instructing it is not, however, unlimited. Although at birth the mind might have been a *tabula rasa*, reflexes are rapidly conditioned, as we saw in Chapter 3, by the imperatives of man's material situation as perceived through the impartial spectator mechanism. Man is not infinitely malleable, not because he has in him some unique and uncorrupted individual essence, but because each economic basis generates a particular intellectual superstructure. The educator should never forget the limits to manipulation imposed by ingrained 'habits' and 'dispositions'[64] resulting from the process of social conditioning.

Education can reinforce existing norms and values, but it cannot simply inculcate new ones unless the pupil is kept isolated from society (the case in Rousseau's *Emile*). Thus a social religion would be no more successful than a revealed religion in a world of empiricism if the doctrines it taught did not first arise from the conditions of a given situation. A society generates the ideology necessary to hold itself together, and no use of the pleasure/pain principle in the classroom can seriously affect the quasi-Mannheimean struggle for the minds of men that is the inevitable concommitant of economic change. In that sense the propaganda function of education is largely superfluous: it can, for example, teach respect for the rich and powerful, but will only really be successful if such respect already exists.[65]

In places, however, Smith writes as if he believed 'the bulk of mankind' to be substantially less sensitive to the approbation or disapprobation of the impartial spectator, substantially more indifferent to social norms supposedly internalised by sympathy, than are 'men of refinement'. Clearly, if the masses are unable to see themselves reflected in the social mirror, then education becomes a particularly powerful instrument. Men 'of the happiest mould' (like Plato's philospher-kings) become able to impose their perceptions on the masses:

> None but those of the happiest mould are capable of suiting, with exact justness, their sentiments and behaviour to the smallest difference of situation, and of acting upon all occasions with the most delicate and accurate propriety. The coarse clay of which the bulk of mankind are formed, cannot be wrought up to such perfection. There is scarce any man, however, who by discipline, education, and example, may not be so impressed with a regard to general rules, as to act upon almost every occasion with tolerable decency, and through the whole of his life to avoid any considerable degree of blame.[66]

Education does not circumvent the passions but acts through them. Smith says that 'the great secret of education is to direct vanity to proper objects',[67] and clearly prefers this emotional appeal to the rationalist approach of 'precept and exhortation'. But if vanity has to be *directed* to proper objects, this means that propriety of sentiments does not invariably result from an automatic reflex-mechanism: socially conditioned reflexes, as we have seen before, do not have to be taught. The educator thus acquires considerable power to impose his own notions of propriety on his pupils, and this indicates that the propaganda function of education may in fact be more extended than we have suggested. Fortunately, Smith's more usual view appears to be that all members of society, whatever their class, are able through their passions to perceive that society's standards of right and wrong.

This being the case, the social function of education becomes a more modest one: it is not a remedy for the mental mutilation that results from overspecialised and unrewarding work (since it is impossible to escape from the effects of employment on character) and it is unable to impose spurious idealistic norms (since most people are already aware of society's true standards of right and wrong), but it does build up human capital, combat superstition with science, and give additional support to society's normative constraint.

Yet, despite these desirable social benefits which result from popular education, the division of labour and the existence of a prosperous commercial economy cause the masses more and more to neglect schooling:

> In rich and commercial nations the division of labour, having reduced all trades to very simple operations, affords an opportunity of employing children very young. In this country,[68] indeed, where the division of labour is not far advanced, even the meanest porter can read and write, because the price of education is cheap, and a parent can employ his child in no other way at six or seven years of age. This, however, is not the case in the commercial parts of England. A boy of six or seven years of age at Birmingham can gain his threepence or sixpence a day, and parents find it to be their interest to set them soon to work; thus their education is neglected.[69]

In a commercial society, workers might be more able to pay the direct costs of education and yet be less willing to cover the opportunity cost of sending their children to school rather than to work. After all, in a commercial society material values are on the ascendant. Perhaps Smith felt parents would treat expenditure on education as an investment in human capital: a skilled man, he points out, is analogous to an 'expensive machine'[70] and receives a superior reward on top of his wage which is not a rent to a scarce factor (all men being potentially similar in ability[71]) but 'a reasonable compensation for the time and labour which must be spent'[72] in acquiring the skill. The working classes, however, are not noted for their prudence in weighing future income against present satisfactions, and in any case there is the problem of maintenance if children of poor families stay on at school: 'Their parents can scarce afford to maintain them even in infancy. As soon as they are able to work, they must apply to some trade by which they can earn their subsistence.'[73]

Smith advocated state aid to education (although not complete state provision of schooling, lest there be insufficient competition among schools and schoolmasters), and believed that school-fees should not be beyond the pocket even of a common labourer. Yet this by itself would be inadequate to force upon the masses an expenditure which their material situation caused them not to make, and of which the opportunity and maintenance costs were prohibitive. Smith could have proposed scholarships as a means of dealing with such cases, and a compulsory school-leaving age as a means of dealing with recalcitrant parents,[74] but, in this, as in so many other things, he preferred to leave as much scope as possible to the invisible hand of enlightened self-interest.

II. Value, Distribution and Solidarity

Milton Myers has argued that Smith was writing in the tradition of those seventeenth- and eighteenth-century thinkers who believed social cohesion to be an unintended outcome of the division of labour. Economic exchange would lead to economic interdependence, improving man's material well-being, and to social solidarity, satisfying man's basic need for a life in society: 'Men know how to specialize and then to trade the products of their specializations. For Smith the division of labour creates mutual need and, therefore, social cohesion.'[1] Dr West, similarly, has asserted that 'Smith's whole emphasis was upon the claim that the emerging free market economy provided a means for *mutual* gain . . . The effect was not to destabilize, but to "cordialize" society.'[2]

In this section we shall examine Smith's views on the relationship between commerce and cordiality, and specifically the nature of mutual dependence resulting from differentiation of economic functions. We shall conclude that Smith expected some sort of cohesion to arise from exchange and interdependence, both between nations and between individuals within a nation; but that he also expected an element of social conflict once the division of labour ceased to be merely horizontal (between different tradesmen) and became vertical (a division between social classes).

Smith did not believe commerce should breed 'discord and

animosity': rather, he felt, it 'ought naturally to be, among nations, as among individuals, a bond of union and friendship'.[3] Among nations this means (in contrast to mercantilist doctrine) that national interests are complementary, not competitive, and that trade is not a form of warfare. It is advantageous to both parties if nations are able 'to relieve one another's wants, to increase one another's enjoyments, and to encourage one another's industry'.[4] A wider market is a great incentive to the division of labour,[5] and the economies of scale thereby realised benefit the domestic as well as the foreign consumer. Moreover, the international division of labour means a greater choice of commodities for the consumer, since nations can specialise on those goods in the production of which they have some special advantage.[6] Trade also means greater security, since there is greater probability of obtaining supplies quickly and reliably in time of shortage: a surplus in one country can relieve a dearth in another and politically independent states come to resemble 'the different provinces of a great empire'.[7] Finally, since rich countries (say, France and England) are the natural markets for one another's products,[8] there is no economic case for imperialism: 'Rich and civilized nations can always exchange to a much greater value with one another, than with savages and barbarians.'[9]

Of course, in wartime such interdependence could prove dangerous, and for this reason laissez-faire and the freedom of trade should not be extended to strategic materials;[10] but it is more probable that the equalising effects of trade on wealth will create a balance of power among nations which in turn will be the guarantor of international peace. In his discussion of the discovery of America, Smith comments:

> Hereafter, perhaps, the natives of those countries may grow stronger, or those of Europe may grow weaker, and the inhabitants of all the different quarters of the world may arrive at that equality of courage and force which, by inspiring mutual fear, can alone overawe the injustice of independent nations into some sort of respect for the rights of one another. But nothing seems more likely to establish this equality of force than that mutual communication of knowledge and of all sorts of improvements which an extensive commerce from all countries to all countries naturally, or rather necessarily, carries along with it.[11]

Among individuals within a nation, the effects of commerce are similar. First of all, interdependence is the source of an increasing pool of material satisfactions. As a result of the division of labour, men find they are 'of use to one another'[12] and 'in need of the assistance of one

another'.[13] Consequently they act in 'concert'.[14] When a customer
buys a coat, he is buying 'the produce of the joint labour of a great
multitude of workmen. The shepherd, the sorter of the wool, the wool-
comber or carder, the dyer, the scribbler, the spinner, the weaver, the
fuller, the dresser, with many others, must all join their different arts in
order to complete even this homely production.'[15] Men have a natural
propensity to 'truck, barter and exchange'[16] which causes them to
specialise and thus makes them dependent on one another, the services
performed being complementary: 'The porter is of use in carrying
burdens for the philosopher, and in his turn he burns his coals cheaper
by the philosopher's invention of the fire machine.'[17] In modern
society, the living standards of even 'the very meanest person' depend
on 'the assistance and co-operation of many thousands'.[18] Mutual
dependence is vital to the health of all individuals in society. As Herbert
Spencer was later to put it,

> We cannot cut a mammal in two without causing immediate death.
> Twisting off the head of a fowl is fatal . . . If in high societies the
> effect of mutilation is less than in high animals, still it is great.
> Middlesex separated from its surroundings would in a few days have
> all its social processes stopped by lack of supplies. Cut off the
> cotton-district from Liverpool and other ports, and there would
> come arrest of its industry followed by mortality of its people.[19]

The greater the separateness of functions, Spencer believed, the greater
their union, and there is clearly evidence that Smith took a similar view.
    Secondly, commerce leads to a domestic balance of power. The
establishment of a market economy means that the power of the old
magnates, the aristocracy and clergy, comes to be counterbalanced by
the power of the rising middle classes. The artificer comes to be
employed by a large number of customers and is dependent on none of
them for a substantial percentage of his income;[20] while the customer
buying a commodity finds he has contributed to the maintenance of
myriads of unknown workmen (the number often 'exceeds all
computation'[21]), each one employed for a very short time. Instead of
the old abuse of personal dependence, the workman is dependent only
on the market mechanism, the anonymity of which is underlined by the
role of money: 'The butcher seldom carries his beef or his mutton to
the baker, or the brewer, in order to exchange them for bread or for
beer; but he carries them to the market, where he exchanges them for
money, and afterwards exchanges that money for bread and for beer.'[22]
In a market economy, no magnate can dictate exchange ratios, which

are set impartially by the interaction of all sellers and all buyers of a commodity.

Reciprocal satisfaction of wants may, however, be inadequate to ensure social solidarity once exchange between independent craftsmen has been replaced by the dual system in industry, whereby some supply capital and others supply labour. In such a case interdependence, which does not preclude exploitation, might be unable to prevent conflict over relative shares.

Central to Smith's views on the objective existence of exploitation is the labour theory of value. It is possible that Smith was simply using labour as a stable measure of value, not as an explanation of its source; and that his labour theory is only a primitive approach to the problem of index-numbers. It is also possible, however, that the theory identifies labour as the unique creator of value, with the implication that the profit of the capitalist and the rent of the landowner reflect not compensation for value added but position in the power-structure. The sociological implications of these two interpretations are clearly very different, and will have to be examined in succession.

Smith argued that labour is a universal and accurate measure of value since its own value (unlike that of the precious metals, as the discoveries of the sixteenth century demonstrated[23]) is stable and constant: 'Equal quantities of labour, at all times and places, may be said to be of equal value to the labourer. In his ordinary state of health, strength and spirits; in the ordinary degree of his skill and dexterity, he must always lay down the same portion of his ease, his liberty, and his happiness.'[24]

In other words, labour, 'never varying in its own value, is alone the ultimate and real standard by which the value of all commodities can at all times and places be estimated and compared'.[25] This index can even be used to measure factor shares: 'Labour measures the value not only of that part of price which resolves itself into labour, but of that which resolves itself into rent, and of that which resolves itself into profit.'[26] The source of value and relative size of factor-incomes are left unexplained, and there is no implication of exploitation. The value of a commodity to its owner may be 'equal to the quantity of labour which it enables him to purchase or command',[27] but there is no hint of domination of one class by another: the labour-index ('the real measure of the exchangeable value of all commodities'[28]) simply indicates how much labour-value the labourer, capitalist or landowner can command once he has received his income, and all classes have the opportunity to exercise this command.

Once the division of labour has taken place, 'the real price of every thing, what every thing really costs to the man who wants to acquire it,

is the toil and trouble of acquiring it';[29] and in a market economy this
'toil and trouble' is measured by an impersonal cash value. Professor
Meek has suggested that Smith turned to the labour theory precisely
because he wanted to emphasise the basic social relationships between
man and man that underlie the exchange of goods and which were
increasingly being hidden by this monetary estimation, this veil of
money-price. As Meek says: 'The exchange of commodities is in essence
the exchange of social activities. The value relationship which manifests
itself in the act of exchange is in essence the reflection of a relationship
between men as producers.'[30] The true measure of value cannot be a
piece of paper or a lump of metal; it can only be the amount of my
'toil and trouble' that exchanges for a particular amount of your 'toil
and trouble'. Once again we have evidence of Smith's humanism and his
anthropocentrism: economics must be about people, not about things.

If labour is to be used as the index of value, however, then it is first
necessary to construct an index of labour. Labour-time by itself is an
incorrect measure of exchange value since 'there may be more labour in
an hour's hard work than in two hours easy business'.[31] An adequate
index of labour would have to take into account varying amounts of
responsibility, hardship, unpleasantness, status, constancy of employment, risk of failure, length and cost of training associated with
different occupations, in order to arrive at an abstract index representing
equality of sacrifice. Moreover, this index is not purely objective, since
it depends on the subjective evaluation of the situation as it is seen
through the eyes of each actor. It is difficult to see how the scholar
could, starting from first principles, construct such an index, even with
the most modern statistical techniques, and in practice Smith takes
long-run equilibrium factor rewards as established by the freely-
operating market mechanism to be his proxy for the index of labour-
value. As Professor Douglas explains: 'Smith believed he had established
the fact that equal units of labor in the sense of disutility were at any
one time compensated for by equal amounts of money wages. The
market, according to Smith, thus does reduce the various elements
composing labor to a common measure.'[32]

Of course, scarcity can, in the short run, cause the reward of a
particular grade of labour to rise above the 'ordinary or average rate'[33]
prevailing locally; but, in the long run, assuming mobility of labour,
new entry into the trade will cause wages to fall to their 'natural' level
once again. Speaking of the high earnings of colliers and coal-heavers,
for example, Smith says: 'How extravagant soever those earnings may
appear, if they were more than sufficient to compensate all the disagreeable circumstances of the business, there would soon be so great a

number of competitors as, in a trade which has no exclusive privilege, would quickly reduce them to a lower rate.'[34] The test of time is the proof that these earnings are the true measure of the value of labour.

Such an index may be criticised on several grounds. For one thing, earnings are only a measure of the value of labour in a perfectly competitive labour market with no information costs and no occupational or geographical obstacles to mobility. In other words, market imperfections such as those resulting from the laws of settlement and statutes of apprenticeship must be eliminated before the index can become operative. Moreover, even then it may be frustrated by the fact that not all men are money-motivated: Smith makes no mention of a residual element in his labour-index due to inertia or the disutility of changing jobs or towns, and yet admits in one of his more candid moments that 'a man is of all sorts of luggage the most difficult to be transported'.[35]

A second criticism relates to Smith's belief that labour is a constant standard of value 'at all times and places'.[36] If the value of labour is to be approximated by the equilibrium wage-structure, then this is in direct contradiction to Smith's assertion that there had been a secular rise in the natural wage in Britain over the previous century, associated with economic growth and the rising demand for labour.[37] Such a rise in *per capita* wages biases the national income figures upwards, giving the impression of an increase in quantity where there may only have been an increase in the price of the commodity-*numéraire*. A similar distortion of the national income can operate in the opposite direction. As Barber has pointed out, Smith's labour-index of value

> could not conveniently deal with the case in which the productivity of labour increased (i.e. when the same amount of labour input produced a larger volume of output). In this situation the total wage bill required for the production of a targeted level of output would be smaller than had formerly been the case, even if wage rates were constant. Should a reduction in the price of outputs then follow (not unlikely in such circumstances), the command-over-labour measurement would convey the impression that total output had shrunk when, in fact, it had grown.[38]

Moreover, and this is a third criticism of Smith's use of the equilibrium wage-structure as a measure of the value of labour, it is possible that there may be a surplus or rent element in observed long-run wage levels, due not to the existence of permanently scarce skills (in practice, Smith believed, all men have very similar potential at the start of life's race[39]), but because of the formidable entry barriers to skilled occupations imposed by education. These barriers are likely to remain,[40] and indeed are functionally of the greatest importance: they ensure a scarcity of professionals, keep the income and conspicuous consumption of such groups high, and guarantee thereby that such groups will command the respect of their clientele. As Smith says: 'We trust our health to the physician; our fortune and sometimes our life and reputation to the lawyer and attorney. Such confidence could not safely be reposed in people of a very mean or low condition. Their reward must be such, therefore, as may give them that rank in the society which so important a trust requires.'[41]

In any case, if supply of and demand for labour in the market-place can adequately measure the value of labour, there is no economic reason why supply of and demand for goods cannot adequately measure the value of goods. This being so, the whole labour-standard theory of value seems to be superfluous. As Joan Robinson puts it, value 'has no operational content. It is just a word.'[42] The sociological significance of the distinction between value and price should not, however, be forgotten.

Up to now we have been speaking of Smith's labour-commanded theory of the *measure* of value. In places, however, he also wrote as if he had a labour-embodied theory of the *source* of value. Naturally, this apparent contradiction may be explained by reference to Smith's keen sense of time and place. Labour may account for all of value in some situations and not in others. It is crucial to remember that he introduces his labour-embodied theory of value in *The Wealth of Nations* by stating the conditions in which it is obviously true, namely where labour is the only factor of production:

> In that early and rude state of society which precedes both the accumulation of stock and the appropriation of land, the proportion between the quantities of labour necessary for acquiring different objects seems to be the only circumstance which can afford any rule for exchanging them for one another. If among a nation of hunters, for example, it usually costs twice the labour to kill a beaver which it does to kill a deer, one beaver should naturally exchange for or be worth two deer. It is natural that what is usually the produce of two days or two hours labour, should be worth double of what is usually the produce of one day's or one hour's labour.[43]

Thus, in a civilised society it is reasonable to assume that labour-cost will be joined by land-cost and capital-cost in constituting a total-cost theory of value.[44] Certainly there are instances where Smith argues that all three factors are responsible for the generation of value. For example: 'Wages, profit, and rent, are the three original sources of all revenue as well as of all exchangeable value.'[45] And elsewhere: 'In a civilized country there are but few commodities of which the exchangeable value arises from labour only, rent and profit contributing largely to that of the far greater part of them.'[46]

Yet in other places Smith seems to be arguing that, although exchangeable value in commercial society is in fact divided into three categories, it has a unique source, labour-embodied; and that, if goods exchange at their 'natural price' (the long-run cost of production where each factor receives a natural reward such that there is no movement into or out of the line of production), this can only mean that labour has had to share the value-added it produced. Thus, whereas in primitive society 'the whole produce of labour belongs to the labourer',[47] in civilised society 'he must in most cases *share it* with the owner of the stock which employs him'.[48] A productive labourer 'adds, generally, to the value of the materials which he works upon, that of his own maintenance, and of his master's profit'.[49] A capitalist accumulates capital and employs workers 'in order to make a profit by the sale of their work, or by what their labour adds to the value of the materials ... The value which the workmen add to the materials, therefore, resolves itself in this case into two parts, of which the one pays their wages, the other the profits of their employer'.[50] In short, Smith believed that labour could create a net surplus, whether it was employed in agriculture or in industry (here he differed with the Physiocrats), and also seems to have believed that this surplus had to be shared with sterile groups: the 'whole annual produce, if we except the spontaneous productions of the earth', he asserted, is 'the effect of productive labour',[51] while profit and rent are 'deducation'[52] from that product of labour.

Of course, profit and rent may be necessary to reward the capitalist and landowner for some non-productive but essential service they perform (such as abstinence and accumulation). Moreover, these unique class-incomes are the price of a pluralist society and the maintenance of the *status quo*.[53] The anatomy of civil society is to be found in political economy, and in every civilised society labourers, capitalists and landowners form the 'three great, original and constituent orders'.[54] The failure to transfer income to capitalists and landowners, even if they are not productive of value-added, might lead to a society run exclusively by the productive; and this, as we shall see in Chapter 7, was to Smith tantamount to political suicide. Redistribution of income from the poor to the rich might be necessary simply to ensure stability and prevent the collapse of order.

In interpreting Smith's labour theory of value as implying an exploitation theory of distribution, the scholar would be following such distinguished commentators as the Earl of Lauderdale, who wrote: 'The Author of the Wealth of Nations appears to consider the profit of stock, as paid out of, and therefore derived from, the value added by the workman to the raw material.'[55] More recently, Professor Douglas has argued, along similar lines, that Smith intended the labour-embodied theory of value and exchange to apply in commercial as well as primitive society, and that thus the Ricardian Socialists may 'better be termed the Smithian Socialists, since they derive their inspiration from Smith rather than from Ricardo . . . Smith's formulation of the problems of exchange value and of the distribution of the national product among the factors of production was such as almost inevitably gave rise to the doctrines of the post-Ricardian socialists and to the labor theory of value and the exploitation theory of Karl Marx.'[56] And Professor Bowley says Smith believed that 'capital as such has . . . no claim to a special share of the product once the indirect labour[57] is paid for, and derives its income simply from exploitation'.[58]

It may be, however, that Smith did not have an exploitation theory of distribution at all, and that he did in fact identify profit and rent as proper compensation to the capitalist and the landowner for some productive service they rendered.

Consider first the case of the capitalist, and here Smith indicates three closely related functions which give rise to the factor income of profits:

Firstly, the capitalist may be an entrepreneur, receiving a surplus related directly to his willingness to innovate and to his managerial skill. Smith describes how he substitutes capital for labour when wages are rising (possibly in an attempt to maintain his profit-margins[59]), and even improves on technology to increase the surplus produced by the workers: 'The person who employs his stock in maintaining labour, necessarily wishes to employ it in such a manner as to produce as great a quantity of work as possible. He endeavours, therefore, both to make among his workmen the most proper distribution of employment, and to furnish them with the best machines which he can either invent or afford to purchase.'[60] Such 'new divisions of labour and new improvements of art'[61] may be defensive as well as offensive: the capitalist may have to be an entrepreneur, not in order to raise profits, but simply to prevent profits from falling abnormally in the face of an onslaught from new competitors.

Capitalistic profits can be earned in the country as well as the town. Smith speaks as follows about an improved farm: 'It requires . . . a more attentive and skilful management. Hence a greater profit becomes due to the farmer.'[62] The small proprietor of land (or the improving landlord with a capitalistic mentality) might become an innovator in order to raise profit-margins, and such profit is clearly qualitatively different from the reward to a bailiff or manager: no overseer would have been so attentive to the maximisation of productivity or the optimal combination of inputs as no overseer has a share in profits.[63] A peculiar and unique kind of efficiency exists when an entrepreneur is managing his own capital.

At the same time, however, Smith was insistent that profit is not merely the 'wages of superintendence' of a capitalist-manager. Often the owner of capital prefers to hire 'some principal clerk' to carry out the 'labour of inspection and direction' on his behalf, so that he may be 'discharged of almost all labour';[64] and in such cases he nonetheless continues to receive his profits despite the absence of any actual participation of his own in the production process. In other words, because of the separation of owner and overseer, profits 'bear no proportion to the quantity, the hardship, or the ingenuity of this supposed labour of inspection and direction'.[65] The 'profits of stock' is evidently more than 'only a different name for the wages of a particular sort of labour'.[66] The entrepreneur may be rewarded with profits; but profits may also accrue without entrepreneurship.

Secondly, whether or not he is an entrepreneur, the capitalist is continually putting his capital at risk, and without the incentive of profit would not 'hazard his stock'.[67] He is, after all, necessarily and prudently a risk-averter (unlike some young people who, in search of adventure, may be risk-lovers;[68] and unlike lawyers who, because of their inordinate vanity, gamble that they will win in a lottery where most lose[69]). Net profit is his 'compensation, and in most cases it is no more than a very moderate compensation, for the risk and trouble of employing the stock'.[70] Profit is analogous to insurance in that, the higher the risk, the greater the expected compensation (the greater the amount of insurance) one needs: in the real world, 'the ordinary rate of profit always rises more or less with the risk'.[71]

Thus, to attract a capitalist into a new and uncertain venture, he must be offered the opportunity of making super-normal profits (possibly maintained at artificially high levels by patents and temporary incorporation; or, for that matter, by the remission of taxes and tythes, which are disincentives to bear risk[72]). There is, after all, the possibility too that he will make no profits, or even make losses: 'The establishment of any new manufacture, of any new branch of commerce, or of any new practice in agriculture, is always a speculation, from which the projector promises himself extraordinary profits.'[73] Once the new trade has become established, however, and abnormal risk has been eliminated, then the rate of profit there falls to the normal, competitive rate for the whole economy.

Thirdly, the capitalist performs an important allocative function: if he earns abnormally low profits in one trade, he will be induced by the invisible hand of self-interest to withdraw his capital from that employment and transfer it to another where the rate of return (allowing for non-pecuniary considerations) is higher.[74] Thus, assuming profit-maximisation, perfect knowledge of alternative investment opportunities, and mobility of all factors, a long-run equilibrium rate of profit is established where no investor can obtain a higher return by switching his capital into an alternative employment. This 'ordinary rate of profit' (which will be established *ceteris paribus* in all trades if there is 'perfect liberty' of entry and exit and perfect competition) is a necessary cost and must be included in the 'natural price of commodities'. Capital is mobile and if, say, a farmer is not earning ordinary profits ('the smallest share with which the tenant can content himself without being a loser'[75]), he will be tempted to shift his resources to a higher-return employment. Ordinary profit, in other words, is an opportunity cost; and the capitalist's compensation is a reward for rationality in the allocation of scarce factors between alternative uses.

It is precisely because of this rationality that the market mechanism can be relied on in most cases to maximise national welfare in the long run. Suppose, for example, that the threat of a war, blockade or famine causes a sudden rise in the demand for a commodity. Clearly, since its supply is unchanged, scarcity will cause its market price to rise, as desperate bidders compete for limited supplies of the good: 'Rather than want it altogether, some of them will be willing to give more. A competition will immediately begin among them, and the market price will rise more or less above the natural price, according as either the greatness of the deficiency, or the wealth and wanton luxury of the competitors, happen to animate more or less the eagerness of the competition.'[76] In other words, rationing by price when quantity demanded exceeds quantity supplied means a short-run windfall for the capitalist, who thereby earns super-normal profits over and above the minimum inducement necessary to retain him in a particular trade. Consider the effect of a public mourning on the profits of a merchant with a stock of black cloth in his warehouse: 'A public mourning raises the price of black cloth (with which the market is almost always under-stocked upon such occasions), and augments the profits of the merchants who possess any considerable quantity of it. It has no effect upon the wages of the weavers. The market is under-stocked with commodities, not with labour.'[77]

Goods which are abundant tend to be cheap while goods which are scarce tend to be expensive. In the *Lectures* Smith writes: 'It is only on account of the plenty of water that it is so cheap as to be got for the lifting; and on account of the scarcity of diamonds . . . that they are so dear.'[78] And in *The Wealth of Nations* he reminds the reader that 'a produce of which the value is principally derived from its scarcity, is necessarily degraded by its abundance'.[79] Thus a capitalist might artificially reduce supplies of a good to the market in order, provided that he is the exclusive supplier and that the market demand curve is inelastic, substantially to raise his profits: this would be the case, for example, with a monopolist controlling supplies of a necessity such as corn.[80] The possibility of making such super-normal profits is less, of course, if there exist close substitutes for the good (say, wood for coal[81]), or if the good is a luxury rather than a necessity (in which case high prices could dispose consumers 'either to moderate, or to refrain altogether from the use of superfluities which they can no longer easily afford'[82]), or, most important, if the market is perfectly competitive.

It is the allocative function of the competitive capitalist which guarantees that, at least in the long run, windfall profits disappear: desiring to maximise the rate of return on his capital, he will shift it into that branch of trade where abnormal gains are to be made, thereby increasing the quantity supplied of the good, reducing its scarcity, and causing both price and profit to fall to their natural levels. The natural price (the 'price of free competition') is 'the lowest which can be taken, not upon every occasion indeed, but for any considerable time altogether . . . the lowest which the sellers can commonly afford to take, and at the same time continue their business'.[83] Assuming mobility of factors (no trade secrets, legal barriers, or sentimental attachment of tradesmen to a particular calling), the natural price is 'the central price, to which the prices of all commodities are continually gravitating'.[84] Once reached, such an equilibrium price is a 'center of repose and continuance'.[85] All three factors receive their natural rewards and industry is in a state of 'natural balance'.[86] In brief, effective demand and the utility-functions of consumers, operating through the profit-motive and the market-mechanism, ensure optimal economic welfare of the society.

Smith, then, saw the capitalist as performing three essential and closely-related functions: the capitalist may be an entrepreneur, he takes risks, and he most efficiently allocates the national stock of capital. None of these three functions need necessarily mean, however, that the capitalist is actually productive of wealth, or that profit is not a transfer payment analogous to that made to non-productive (but useful) labourers such a civil servants, school-teachers and actors.[87]

Moreover, the transfer might be too large, and the capitalist might be willing to perform his three essential services at a lower rate of compensation. Smith was aware that profits in his own time were often substantially more than adequate:

Our merchants frequently complain of the high wages of British labour as the cause of their manufactures being undersold in foreign markets; but they are silent about the high profits of stock. They complain of the extravagant gain of other people; but they say nothing of their own. The high profits of British stock, however, may contribute towards raising the price of British manufactures in many cases as much, and in some perhaps more, than the high wages of British labour.[88]

Naturally the capitalist has a reserve price for his capital: 'He could have no interest to employ (labourers), unless he expected from the sale of their work something more than what was sufficient to replace his stock to him.'[89] Yet clearly a surplus over and above that minimum inducement exists, and this interest-component could be taxed away by the government without having any effect on the supply of the factor. Perfect competition, resulting from the suppression of restrictive practices, has an analogous effect in paring down profit-margins to the bare minimum; and this method of reducing the surplus is particularly desirable as it favours the consumer directly.

A low rate of profit in one trade causes capital to move to another trade, and a low rate of profit in one country *ceteris paribus* causes capital to move abroad (the capitalist, like the philosopher, is 'a citizen of the world'[90]). It is very unlikely, however, for all the reasons discussed in Chapter 3, that a low rate of profit would drive capital out of productive employment altogether: in Holland, for example, where the rate of interest on government debt (a measure of the rate of profit, since to Smith the rate of interest is determined by real, not monetary forces) had fallen to 2 per cent, capitalists had shown no signs of substituting luxury and expense for abstinence and accumulation.[91] Indeed, as we have seen, they would have been more likely to do so at very high rates of interest.[92] One should thus not be unduly alarmed by the observable secular decline in the rate of profit over time: there is no threat in the foreseeable future that the capitalist's compensation for his three basic functions will be less than adequate to induce him to fulfil them.

Consider now the landlord and the factor-income of rent. The land itself is unquestionably productive: in agriculture, 'nature labours along with man; and though her labour costs no expence, its produce has its value, as well as that of the most expensive workmen'.[93] Yet since the land cannot be rewarded directly, her non-productive servant, the landowner, acts as her representative and accepts the prize on her behalf: thus 'rent may be considered as the produce of those powers of nature, the use of which the landlord lends to the farmer'.[94] In other words, nature produces a product (the residual 'after deducting or compensating every thing which can be regarded as the work of man'[95]); and the landowner, having engrossed land ('a great evil'[96]) early in feudal times and made it his private property, is able to 'demand a rent even for its natural produce'.[97] He acts, as it were, in *loco naturae*.

Locke had argued that appropriation by labour of nature's gifts is the source of a natural right to retain them: whatsoever a man 'removes out of the state that nature hath provided and left it in, he hath mixed his labour with it, and joined to it something that is his own, and thereby makes it his property'.[98] Smith recognised, however, more realistically, that land is not held in common but has itself been appropriated, and that the landowner would insist on a part of whatever natural gifts were found on his estates: 'As soon as land becomes private property, the landlord demands a share of almost all the produce which the labourer can either raise, or collect from it. His rent makes the first deduction from the produce of the labour which is employed upon land.'[99] The factor-income of rent is thus closely related to private property, social stratification and the power-structure.

In short, the land is productive but the landowner *qua* landowner is not. He may, of course, also be an entrepreneur or risk-taker, as in the case of the improving landlord who invests in 'clearing, draining, enclosing, manuring'[100] schemes, or the landlord who operates his own coal-mine on marginal land.[101] But such investments, like any other, are rewarded with profit. Pure rent is a reward neither for entrepreneurship nor for risk-taking: the landlords' income costs them 'neither labour nor care, but comes to them, as it were, of its own accord, and independent of any plan or project of their own'.[102] Perhaps this is just as well: although landlords 'love to reap where they never sowed',[103] in practice they are indolent and ignorant.[104]

The landlord obtains rent not in exchange for some productive service he performs but because he is able to play 'the part of a monopolist'[105] (and Smith was no friend of monopoly[106]): 'The rent of land, therefore, considered as the price paid for the use of the land, is naturally a monopoly price. It is not at all proportioned to what the landlord may have laid out upon the improvement of the land, or to what he can afford to take; but to what the farmer can afford to give.'[107] For this reason rent is an eminently suitable subject for taxation: 'A tax upon ground-rents would not raise the rents of houses. It would fall altogether upon the owner of the ground-rent, who acts always as a monopolist, and exacts the greatest rent which can be got for the use of his ground . . . without any care or attention of his own.'[108] There is clearly a surplus element in rent since, although a tax may be imposed on it, 'no discouragement will thereby be given to any sort of industry'.[109]

Indeed, it could be argued that the whole of rent is a surplus. It is neither a functional reward aimed at encouraging the landlord to improve his land nor even an inducement to him to supply it. After all, whereas labour and capital are mobile and can be shifted from a low-return to a high-return employment, land is not; so that, if minimum factor rewards are measured by opportunity cost, pure rent is zero. Rent is a remainder: 'High or low wages and profit, are the causes of high or low price; high or low rent is the effect of it.'[110] Indeed, if the price of agricultural produce is so low that only ordinary wages and ordinary profits can be covered, then no rent at all will be paid;[111] and yet, since the only alternative to renting out land is not renting it out (sale being out of the question for reasons of primogeniture and entailing) and since landownership in any case yields substantial non-economic benefits (in the form of social status and political power), there are no grounds for thinking the landlord will reduce the quantity supplied of his factor to zero or, indeed, at all.

Although it appears that rent is a transfer, a deduction from value-added which exists because the landowner exists and owns the land, it nonetheless has an important allocative function. Because it is differential rent, it equalises rates of return on different capitals and helps to establish a single rate of ordinary profit *ceteris paribus* throughout the economy:[112]

The rent of land not only varies with its fertility, whatever be its produce, but with its situation, whatever be its fertility. Land in the neighbourhood of a town gives a greater rent than land equally fertile in a distant part of the country. Though it may cost no more labour to cultivate the one than the other, it must always cost more to bring the produce of the distant land to market.[113]

Yet, in the same way that rent does not precisely measure the value of nature's gifts, so the landlord is not personally responsible, as a residual-income recipient, for this process of allocation: he simply pockets whatever income (if any) farmers can afford to pay him. It is therefore difficult to believe that Smith seriously considered the landlord's contribution to be value-generating (as would have been the case had he had a cost-of-production theory of value-creation). Of course, Smith knew that rents could not be abolished without abolishing the land-owning classes; and such a course of action would have been highly undesirable to a social philosopher who favoured both continuity and diversity in the social structure. In that sense rent was an essential (if social rather than economic) cost.

We have up to now in this section been dealing with the exploitation of productive by non-productive economic classes. Let us, in concluding our discussion of objective reasons for social conflict, also note Smith's dynamic view, that all classes do not benefit equally from the process of economic growth. The interest of the landowners (high rents) and of the workers (high wages) is 'strictly and inseparably connected with the general interest of the society';[114] that of the capitalist is not, since the rate of profit shows a secular tendency to fall as the economy grows (albeit the mass of profit continues to grow with the mass of capital).

Rents rise due to an increasing demand for foodstuffs from a growing population and for raw materials from a growing economy. Wages rise due to an expanding capital-stock and the resultant competition among employers for labour. Meanwhile, Smith says, rising wages and falling prices (both resulting from industrial expansion and intensified competition[115]) squeeze profit-margins and victimise those same frugal, parsimonious entrepreneurs upon whose accumulation future economic growth depends.

Fortunately, the social conflict implicit in a situation where high wages mean low profits and high profits mean low wages may be more apparent than real. For one thing, high wages lead the worker to increase his effort and thus to raise his productivity. Moreover, in a growing economy the capitalist himself invents machinery and reorganises production processes in order to get more output per unit of input. In this way, the same cause 'which raises the wages of labour, the increase of stock, tends to increase its productive powers, and to make a smaller quantity of labour produce a greater quantity of work'.

Clearly high wages can exist side by side with high profits, and the
worker and the capitalist need not be adversaries.

Again, rising wages do not mean falling profits if the capitalist is able
to pass the increase on to the consumer in the form of higher prices:
'The increase in the wages of labour necessarily increases the price of
many commodities, by increasing that part of it which resolves itself
into wages.'[116] Of course, the effectiveness of a policy to keep profit-
margins constant and pass on any wage-increase to the consumer
depends on the elasticity of demand: obviously the higher price of
goods 'tends to diminish their consumption both at home and
abroad',[117] and capitalists want maximum returns, not maximum
prices. Consider the example of the coal industry, where the highest
possible price (with respect to substitutes) is never charged: at such a
price 'a small quantity only could be sold, and the coal masters and coal
proprietors find it more for their interest to sell a great quantity at a
price somewhat above the lowest, than a small quantity at the
highest'.[118]

Finally, the capitalist may be able to compensate himself for the
burden of higher wages by reducing the burden of the rent he pays to
the landlord. Thus a tax on necessaries is automatically reflected in
higher wages but its long-run incidence is clear: 'Taxes upon necessaries,
so far as they affect the labouring poor, are finally paid, partly by landlords in the diminished rent of their lands, and partly by rich consumers,
whether landlords or others, in the advanced price of manufactured
goods; and always with a considerable over-charge.'[119] The rich, if they
were fully aware of their own interest, would oppose taxes on subsistence goods and militate for their reduction: such taxes 'fall heaviest
upon the landlords, who always pay in a double capacity; in that of
landlords, by the reduction of their rent; and in that of rich consumers,
by the increase of their expence'.[120] Since subsistence to Smith means
social as well as physical subsistence, there is clearly a wide range of
tax increases that can be passed on to rent-earners (those very classes,
coincidentally, with a high propensity to waste capital and a low
propensity to employ it prudently and productively).

In any case, Smith offers an alternative explanation of the tendency
of the profit rate to fall, expressed not in terms of rising wages and
falling profits, but in terms of an increasing scarcity of desirable investment opportunities:

As capitals increase in any country, the profits which can be made
by employing them necessarily diminish. It becomes gradually more
and more difficult to find within the country a profitable method of

employing any new capital. There arises in consequence a competition between different capitals, the owner of one endeavouring to get possession of that employment which is occupied by another. But upon most occasions he can hope to justle that other out of this employment, by no other means but by dealing upon more reasonable terms. He must not only sell what he deals in somewhat cheaper, but in order to get it to sell, he must sometimes too buy it dearer.[121]

Yet even here Smith counsels hope: the 'acquisition of new territory, or of new branches of trade'[122] will reduce competition between capitals employed in existing trades and maintain profit-rates at reasonable levels. Theoretically, of course, there exists the feared stationary state when a country has acquired 'that full complement of riches which the nature of its soil and climate, and its situation with respect to other countries, allowed it to acquire'.[123] But there is no need for alarm: in practice 'no country has ever yet arrived at this degree of opulence'[124] where further expansion and diversification were impossible.

III. The Sense of Exploitation

In Section II we discussed the nature of interdependence of function in the three-class economy Smith was analysing, and concluded that, objectively speaking, it is possible there was some exploitation arising from the method in which value is added and then distributed, some conflict over relative shares.

While Smith's views on the objective existence of exploitation of the labourer by the capitalist and the landowner may be ambiguous, there can be no doubt, however, that he expected the labourer to have a subjective sense of exploitation. Clearly, the feeling that exploitation is taking place can be as destructive of social solidarity as the actual existence of exploitation, and for this reason society may not after all be cordialised by commerce. It is with these subjective perceptions that we shall be concerned in this section.

As Durkheim reminds us, co-operation and adaptation of function, even where they exist, are not by themselves morally binding or socially integrative. Organic solidarity in a society is a subjective phenomenon, an awareness of the state of dependence of each upon all: a man needs to see himself not just as an individual but as a social function, 'as part of a whole, the organ of an organism',[1] and to appreciate that 'he is working for everybody and everybody is working for him'.[2] It is this common spirit, this spontaneous sense of togetherness, which is conspicuously lacking in the rather anomic world of labour and capital as depicted by Adam Smith.

For example, it is easy to argue objectively that self-love, via the 'higgling and bargaining of the market', establishes a 'rough equality'[3] of value in exchange: after all, the market mechanism is unquestionably impartial and is not manipulated at the whim of tyrannical lords, superstitious priests, despotic monarchs or inefficient bureaucrats. In the labour market this means that a 'natural' wage will automatically be established by the inexorable and impersonal forces of supply and demand in competitive conditions. And yet, despite this unquestionable fairness of the market mechanism, the worker might still refuse to look upon his employer as his brother. Instead he might insist on perceiving society as a Hobbesian jungle in which relative shares depend not on (marginal) productivity or some other absolute criterion, but simply on power. He might come to the conclusion that, the greater is the power of the capitalists, the higher are profits and the lower are wages. All trade is 'a species of warfare',[4] and the compromise represented by the wage-bargain (however 'natural' and fair) may be inadequate to cordialise society or repress antagonisms: 'What are the common wages of labour, depends every where upon the contract usually made by those two parties, whose interests are by no means the same. The workmen desire to get as much, the masters to give as little as possible.'[5]

In the course of the struggle competition breaks down: coalitions of workers are formed (to raise wages) and confront coalitions of employers (whose common interest it is to reduce wages and raise prices). Thus 'masters are always and every where in a sort of tacit, but constant and uniform combination, not to raise the wages of labour above their actual rate',[6] and 'people of the same trade seldom meet together, even for merriment and diversion, but the conversation ends in a conspiracy against the public, or in some contrivance to raise prices'.[7]

The advantage in wage-bargaining clearly lies with the urban capitalist. The situation of inland corn-dealers approximates to perfect competition since they are numerous and 'their dispersed situation renders it altogether impossible for them to enter into any general combination'.[8] Manufacturers, however, 'collected together in numerous bodies in all great cities, easily can'.[9] Employers are fewer in number than workers, and can thus enter more smoothly into oligopsonistic collusion. Moreover, the law 'authorises, or at least does not prohibit their combinations, while it prohibits those of the workmen. We have no acts of parliament against combining to lower the price of work; but many against combining to raise it.'[10] Finally, the capitalist can hold out longer than the worker in any industrial dispute. The capitalist has capital: 'A landlord, a farmer, a master manufacturer, or merchant . . . could generally live a year or two upon the stocks which they have already acquired.'[11] The worker, on the other hand, 'has nothing but his labour to live by'.[12] In the domestic system it was at least possible to be 'a country weaver, who likewise cultivates a small farm'.[13] Once the worker had given up his plot of land, moved to the towns, and become a full-time factory operative, however, he became dependent for his subsistence on the continued sale of his labour-power: 'Many workmen could not subsist a week, few could subsist a month, and scarce any a year without employment.'[14]

There are, of course, reasons to be hopeful about the future. For one thing, competition replaces 'the wretched spirit of monopoly'[15] in a growing economy. An increasing supply of capital leads to competition for a given supply of labour, and thus to the breakdown of cartels and to higher wages: 'The scarcity of hands occasions a competition among masters, who bid against one another, in order to get workmen, and thus voluntarily break through the natural combination of masters not to raise wages.'[16] Furthermore, the state might in future cease to intervene in and distort the labour market, withdrawing obstacles to mobility (such as statutes of apprenticeship and laws of settlement) and ending the privileges of exclusive bodies such as corporations. Yet although both the breakdown of cartels and political laissez-faire will improve the material position of the labourer, neither will eliminate the basic conflict of interest subjectively perceived by the lower classes each time a wage-bargain is made. Neither will be adequate to eliminate the socially divisive sensation that exploitation is taking place.

Put in its simplest form, the problem is that the awareness of having to share his product with capitalist and landowner makes the worker feel anything but cordial towards them: 'A poor independent workman will generally be more industrious than even a journeyman who works by the piece. The one enjoys the whole produce of his own industry; the other shares it with his master.'[17] Similarly, a colonist will work harder and produce more than an ordinary labourer, since the land he tills is his very own: 'No landlord shares with him in its produce . . . He has every motive to render as great as possible a produce, which is thus to be almost entirely his own.'[18] Compare this with the indigence of the slave: 'A person who can acquire no property, can have no other interest but to eat as much, and to labour as little as possible.'[19] Or even with the semi-independent sharecropper: 'It could never . . . be the interest even of this last species of cultivators to lay out, in the further improvement of the land, any part of the little stock which they might save from their own share of the produce, because the lord, who laid out nothing, was to get one-half of whatever it produced.'[20]

The problem seems not to be one of shares but of sharing: men desire independence and are most productive of capital and output when they are working for themselves. The effect of democratisation of landownership on incentives is hence one of the main reasons why Smith opposed primogeniture: 'A small proprietor . . . who knows every part of his little territory, who views it all with the affection which property, especially small property, naturally inspires . . . is generally of all improvers the most industrious, the most intelligent, and the most successful.'[21] In ancient Greece and Rome, the important benefits accruing to the owner of land were a source of class conflict: 'The people became clamorous to get land, and the rich and the great, we may believe, were perfectly determined not to give them any part of theirs. To satisfy them in some measure, therefore, they frequently proposed to send out a new colony.'[22] And in North America the artificer seems to desire independence not only from his employer but from his customers as well, since he eagerly purchases land despite the high wages he could elsewhere earn:

> From artificer he becomes planter, and neither the large wages nor the easy subsistence which that country affords to artificers, can bribe him rather to work for other people than for himself. He feels that an artificer is the servant of his customers, from whom he derives his subsistence; but that a planter who cultivates his own land, and derives his necessary subsistence from the labour of his own family, is really a master, and independent of all the world.[23]

In modern society, 'for one very rich man, there must be at least five hundred poor';[24] and, whatever the fairness of this arrangement and despite the natural respect which the 'great mob of mankind' have for wealth and greatness, the Machtapparat of the state becomes necessary to police the 'sacred rights of private property'.[25] If the masses do encroach on these sacred rights, they may do so because they are 'driven by want' (absolute deprivation, which can be dealt with by an improvement in living standards), but they may also do so when 'prompted by envy'[26] (relative deprivation, which can only be dealt with by doing away with magnates worth envying). It might therefore be possible to extend Smith's dictum 'Wherever there is great property, there is great inequality'[27] to say that wherever there is great inequality, there is great resentment. Whatever the fairness of the market mechanism in determining factor-shares, so long as there are rich and poor commerce need not mean cohesion, community and cordiality.

IV. Employment and Standards of Living

In this section we shall try to show that capital accumulation occupies a central place in Adam Smith's thought for sociological as well as for purely economic reasons. Specifically, its importance lies not mainly in its function of increasing the supply of 'trinkets and baubles' *per capita*, but in setting to work previously unemployed labourers and in improving the living standards of the lower classes, since these are desirable goals in themselves.

Capital is of two kinds, circulating and fixed. Circulating capital is used to buy raw materials or labour-power: the capitalist employs 'industrious people' and supplies them 'with materials and subsistence, in order to make a profit by the sale of their work, or by what their labour adds to the value of the materials'.[1] The capitalist advances food and raw materials to the worker at the beginning of the period and receives in return the whole product of labour at the end. Clearly such accumulation of stock is necessarily antecedent to the division of labour and the specialisation of the labourer: 'A stock of goods of different kinds . . . must be stored up somewhere sufficient to maintain him, and to supply him with the materials and tools of his work'.[2]

The worker himself is seldom able to store up this stock of goods, and it is his inability to save enough in one period to advance himself food and materials in the next which makes him dependent on the company store' function of the capitalist with a wages-fund at the ready: 'It sometimes happens, indeed, that a single independent workman has stock sufficient both to purchase the materials of his work, and to maintain himself till it be completed . . . Such cases, however, are not very frequent, and in every part of Europe, twenty workmen serve under a master for one that is independent.'[3] Independence is nonetheless possible, even if not typical: fortunes can be made 'in consequence of a long life of industry, frugality, and attention',[4] and even in this imperfect world 'every virtue naturally meets with its proper reward'.[5] Smith was clearly an optimist concerning social mobility: 'We see every day the most splendid fortunes that have been acquired in the course of a single life by trade and manufactures, frequently from a very small capital, sometimes from no capital.'[6] Yet his economic arguments do not lend support to his optimism. The need to acquire a wages fund in advance is a formidable entry barrier to the capitalist class, and in fact 'the greater part of the labouring poor in all countries'[7] are dependent for their incomes on the sale of their labour-power alone: 'The patrimony of a poor man lies in the strength and dexterity of his hands.'[8] Virtually the best a

poor man can hope for is a good harvest: the cheapness of grain allows
him to leave his master and possibly even employ a few journeymen of
his own.[9] Yet as soon as there is a bad harvest he, no longer able to
store up a stock of food and materials in advance, loses his independence
and must go to work for another, more opulent capitalist.[10] His
progress is thus cyclical: from rags to riches and then back to rags again.

Fixed capital is comprised of four parts: machines 'which facilitate
and abridge labour', factories, warehouses and other 'profitable
buildings which are the means of procuring a revenue', investment made
in the improvement of land, and human capital such as is embodied in
acquired skills.[11] While Smith believed circulating capital to be by far
the most important type of capital at the time, he recognised that some
industries could not help but be fixed-capital intensive: 'In a great iron-
work, for example, the furnace for melting the ore, the forge, the slitt-
mill, are instruments of trade which cannot be erected without a very
great expence. In coal-works, and mines of every kind, the machinery
necessary both for drawing out the water and for other purposes, is
frequently still more expensive.'[12] The operator of an iron-forge
employs a large capital 'in erecting his forge and smelting-house, his
work-houses and warehouses, the dwelling-houses of his workmen,
etc.'; while the undertaker of a mine must invest heavily 'in sinking his
shafts, in erecting engines for drawing out the water, in making roads
and waggon-ways, etc.'.[13] Similarly, there is fixed investment in the silk
industry (in the form of 'workhouses' and 'instruments of trade',[14] a
rigidity which must be reckoned with when import restrictions on
silken goods are eased) and even in the famous pin-factory (where there
are tools as well as wire and the wages-fund[15]). Some industries employ
the steam-engine[16] (although there is no mention of an industrial
revolution in the textiles industry), and a machine-making industry
already exists[17] (and is presumably fixed-capital intensive itself).
Moreover, much fixed capital is employed on the land, by the farmer or
by an improving landlord: consider 'the capital which the person who
undertakes to improve land employs in clearing, draining, enclosing,
manuring, and ploughing waste and uncultivated fields, in building
farm-houses, with all their necessary appendages of stables, granaries,
etc.'.[18]

Capital is essential to the health of society for two reasons: First,
because in an economy with a large pool of unemployed or underemployed labour, an increase in capital means an increase in jobs; and,
second, because as the point of full employment is approached, an
increase in capital comes to mean an increase in wages and a redistribution of the national income in favour of the wage-earning classes. Let us

examine these two possibilities more closely.

The first case is the proto-Keynesian situation where labour is abundant, and where an increase in demand for goods is met not by rising prices and wages but by increased employment and output. Free trade, for example, by enriching farmers and aristocrats, means they 'would buy more goods . . . and would employ more labour';[19] and economies of scale in the holding of idle money-balances would, by raising aggregate demand, 'give constant employment to a greater number of industrious people'.[20] Supplies of potentially productive labourers are clearly at times abundant, while capital is scarce; and employment 'can never be much increased, but in consequence of an increase of capital, or of the funds destined for maintaining them'.[21] Not only does the demand for labour necessarily rise 'with the increase of the revenue and stock of every country', but it 'cannot possibly increase without it'.[22]

Capital means employment:

> As a merchant who has a hundred and ten thousand pounds worth of wine in his cellar, is a richer man than he who has only a hundred thousand pounds worth of tobacco in his warehouse, so is he likewise a richer man than he who has only a hundred thousand pounds worth of gold in his coffers. He can put into motion a greater quantity of industry, and give revenue, maintenance, and employment, to a greater number of people than either of the other two.[23]

The employment of the poor is a far better argument for economic growth and capital accumulation than a mere increase in the consumption of 'trinkets and baubles'. Such goods yield satisfaction to a philosopher such as Smith largely because jobs are created in order to produce them.

Because capital means employment, it must not be wasted. Condemning the mercantilist preoccupation with idle stocks of bullion, Smith says: 'The expence of purchasing an unnecessary quantity of gold and silver must, in every country . . . necessarily diminish the wealth which feeds, clothes, and lodges, which maintains and employs the people.'[24] Similarly, since the optimal allocation of capital through the free market mechanism can be depended upon to give 'maintenance and employment to great multitudes',[25] taxation should not be allowed to distort that natural equilibrium. Nor should customs duties:

> The industry of the society can augment only in proportion as its

capital augments, and its capital can augment only in proportion to
what can be gradually saved out of its revenue. But the immediate
effect of every such regulation is to diminish its revenue, and what
diminishes its revenue is certainly not very likely to augment its
capital faster than it would have been augmented of its own accord,
had both capital and industry been left to find out their natural
employments.[26]

Again, speaking of the 'manifest absurdity' of concentration on
inefficient lines of production (such as the growing of grapes in
Scotland), Smith makes clear that he is concerned with the waste of
'capital and industry'[27] resulting from this misallocation of resources,
not with lost consumption opportunities. His hostility to the government is not unrelated to its wasteful 'profusion';[28] and he attacks
monopoly both because, in the absence of competition, it is 'a great
enemy to good management'[29] and because high profits cause the
merchant or manufacturer to substitute 'superfluous luxury' for the
discipline of capital accumulation.[30]

In at least one situation, however, the free market mechanism fails
to maximise capital accumulation and the employment of labour. This
occurs when the consumer employs an unproductive labourer (say, a
menial servant or an actor) whose labour 'perishes in the very instant
of its production' without leaving 'any trace or value. . . for which an
equal quantity of service could afterwards be procured'.[31] A productive
labourer, on the other hand, both produces a material object and gives
rise to a surplus which becomes the basis for further accumulation by
the capitalist and increased employment of labour in the next period.
Such savings by the capitalist are clearly like 'a public workhouse',[32]
and this result has substantial class implications: since the upper classes
tend to maintain unproductive labour while the middle classes employ
labourers who reproduce and augment the capital, redistribution of
income towards the middle classes would increase the employment of
the lower classes. The middle classes have a high propensity to save and
accumulate. Agreeing with the Physiocrats, Smith says: 'If merchants,
artificers and manufacturers are . . . naturally more inclined to
parsimony and saving than proprietors and cultivators, they are, so far,
more likely to augment the quantity of useful labour employed within
their society, and consequently to increase its real revenue, the annual
produce of its land and labour.'[33] The justification for the usury laws
is that they prevent wealthy prodigals from squandering capital that
prudent businessmen would have used to provide perpetual employment
for the poor: 'Stock cultivates land; stock employs labour.'[34] A burden-

some tax on profits would only drive capital from the country and reduce the employment of productive labourers at home, to the benefit of productive labourers abroad.

Consider now the second case where, in a growing economy, the position is reversed: capital becomes relatively abundant and labour relatively scarce. In this situation, as the economy approaches full employment cartels break down, employers compete with one another for workers, and wages rise: 'Those masters . . . who want more workmen, bid against one another, in order to get them, which sometimes raises both the real and the money price of their labour.'[35] The growth of the supply of capital (a function of growth of the national product) relative to the supply of labour (a constant in the short run) improves labour's bargaining position and raises its 'natural wage': 'The wages of the labourer . . . are never so high as when the demand for labour is continually rising, or when the quantity employed is every year increasing considerably.'[36]

Clearly, the 'natural wage' is not always high: it is no more than the equilibrium price of labour-power as set by the competitive tug-of-war of the market mechanism, and different conditions generate different equilibria. This can be shown by comparing the state of the labour market in three economies, Bengal, China and North America.

In Bengal, a declining economy with a shrinking capital-stock, there was surplus population and 'want, famine, and mortality'. This would continue 'till the number of inhabitants in the country was reduced to what could easily be maintained by the revenue and stock which remained in it'.[37]

In China, a stationary economy with a stationary capital stock, competition among the unemployed for jobs forced wages down to the subsistence level (the long-run supply price of labour). The masses were reduced to eating 'any carrion, the carcase of a dead dog or cat, for example',[38] and when population rose, infanticide became rife. In China 'the poverty of the lower ranks of people . . . far surpasses that of the most beggarly nations in Europe',[39] and yet China was in absolute terms wealthier.[40] The problem was one of distribution: wealth was owned mainly by 'grandees' who used it to purchase and hoard gold and silver rather than to set to work productive labourers,[41] with the result that the market price of gold and silver was extremely high while the market price of food was extremely low. Moreover, in an economy where labour is in surplus relative to capital, workmen become 'humble and dependent',[42] and employers see no need to treat them with 'generosity and humanity'.[43] The result is: 'Rent and profit eat up wages, and the two superior orders of people oppress the inferior

one.'[44] The solution, as we saw in Chapter 4, is to alter this repugnant
state of the market mechanism through economic growth and the redistribution of income it will cause; but here there is the obstacle of
oppressive 'laws and institutions'. In China the state protected owners
of considerable fortunes, but proprietors of small capitals enjoyed
hardly any security. They were 'liable, under the pretence of justice, to
be pillaged and plundered at any time by the inferior mandarines'.[45]
There was thus no incentive to investment and enterprise, the economy
remained stationary, and the vicious circle of poverty remained un-
broken.

In North America, however, a growing economy with a growing
capital stock, the lower classes were prosperous. Although the absolute
stock of capital was smaller than in Britain, its rate of increase relative
to the supply of labour was more rapid, and this meant that wages were
higher in the Colonies than in the home country:[46] workmen being
scarce, the employer does not 'dispute about wages, but is willing to
employ labour at any price'.[47] Whereas in China infanticide was
practised to destroy excessive population, in America children clearly
count 'as a sort of fortune':

> We cannot, therefore, wonder that the people in North America
> should generally marry very young. Notwithstanding the great
> increase occasioned by such early marriages, there is a continual
> complaint of the scarcity of hands in North America. The demand
> for labourers, the funds destined for maintaining them, increase, it
> seems, still faster than they can find labourers to employ.[48]

Britain too was a growing economy: 'The real quantities of the
necessaries and conveniencies of life which are given to the labourer,
has increased considerably during the course of the present century',[49]
and the reason clearly had been 'an increase in the demand for labour
in Great Britain, arising from the great, and almost universal prosperity
of the country'. Wages had been for some time unquestionaly above
the subsistence minimum necessary for physical survival and reproduc-
tion: 'In Great Britain the wages of labour seem, in the present times,
to be evidently more than what is precisely necessary to enable the
labourer to bring up a family . . . There are many plain symptoms that
the wages of labour are nowhere in this country regulated by this
lowest rate which is consistent with common humanity.'[51] This suggests
a more or less fully employed economy: if there was unemployment, it
was likely to have been the result of impediments to mobility, either
geographical (such as the laws of settlement[52]) or occu-

pational (such as long apprenticeships or the lack of educa-tion[53]) rather than to any deficiency in the aggregate demand for labour.

In short, there need be no reserve army of the unemployed and no absolute impoverishment of the masses in a capitalist economy. On the contrary, an increase in the stock of capital resulting from economic growth improves the bargaining power of the labourer *vis-à-vis* the employer as the point of full employment is reached, and has the effect of an incomes policy to favour the 'inferior ranks of people':

> It is in the progressive state, while the society is advancing to the further acquisition, rather than when it has acquired its full comple-ment of riches, that the condition of the labouring poor, of the great body of the people, seems to be the happiest and the most comfort-able. It is hard in the stationary, and miserable in the declining state. The progressive state is in reality the cheerful and the hearty state to all the different orders of the society. The stationary is dull; the declining melancholy.[54]

Unlike his mercantilist predecessors (who had feared that high wages would lead to voluntary idleness, or would price British goods out of world markets[55]), Smith clearly welcomed the rising real wage rates that resulted from economic growth. Partly his reasons were humanistic:

> Servants, labourers and workmen of different kinds, make up the far greater part of every great political society. But what improves the circumstances of the greater part can never be regarded as an incon-veniency to the whole. No society can surely be flourishing and happy, of which the far greater part of the members are poor and miserable. It is but equity, besides, that they who feed, cloath and lodge the whole body of the people, should have such a share of the produce of their own labour as to be themselves tolerably well fed, cloathed and lodged.[56]

Partly, however, his reasons were tied up with his general equilibrium view of economy and society: labour is the source of value, and high wages increase both the numbers of workmen and the intensity of their application.

Consider first the effect of high wages on the quantity of labourers. Smith's basic maxim in microeconomics is 'The quantity of every commodity which human industry can either purchase or produce, naturally regulates itself in every country according to the effectual

demand',[57] and this he applies to the labour market by arguing that
wages above the subsistence level will lead to a net increase in the
population: 'It is in this manner that the demand for men, like that for
any other commodity, necessarily regulates the production of ment.'[58]
The mechanism is not so much earlier marriage or a higher birth rate as
it is a decrease in infantile mortality due to improved standards of living.
Of course, the eventual and inevitable expansion in the labour force
may cause wages to fall towards subsistence levels and those standards
of living to be reduced; but in practice this will only happen if the rate
of growth of the stock of capital fails to keep pace with the rate of
growth of the labouring population. In other words, the index of the
welfare of the lower classes is not the level of national income but the
ratio between the increase in demand for, and in supply of, labour: 'It
is not the actual greatness of national wealth, but its continual increase,
which occasions a rise in the wages of labour. It is not, accordingly, in
the richest countries, but in the most thriving, or in those which are
growing rich the fastest, that the wages of labour are highest.'[59]

A growing economy is characterised by high real wages, a rising
population, more labour, more value, more growth, more capital, and
thus sustained high wages: 'The liberal reward of labour . . . as it is the
effect of increasing wealth, so it is the cause of increasing population.
To complain of it, is to lament over the necessary effect and cause of
the greatest public prosperity.'[60] The lower classes enjoy higher wages
and the country benefits from a greater labouring population. Moreover,
the increase in population moderates the *per capita* standards of
living[61] of the lower classes and prevents them from attaining the
wasteful opulence of a consumer society built around 'trinkets and
baubles'. Nonetheless, in aggregate terms, just as the lower classes
contribute most to production, so, on the other side of the circular
flow, their consumption provides the greatest market for that output:
'Though the expence of those inferior ranks of people . . . taking them
individually, is very small, yet the whole mass of it, taking them
collectively, amounts always to by much the largest portion of the
whole expence of the society.'[62] Since the division of labour is a
function of the extent of the market, the worker as consumer clearly
plays an important role in stimulating improved productivity; but since
Smith believed in Say's Law that supply creates its own demand[63] and
chose to neglect the possibility that a deficiency in aggregate demand
could place a ceiling on economic growth, he would not also have
argued that the worker as consumer could not be replaced by some
other source of demand. For the same reason he would not have
believed that high wages might be necessary in some circumstances to

create a market for output that would otherwise be unsaleable.

Let us now consider the effect of high wages on the intensity of application of the labour-force. Smith believed that the supply curve of industry and effort was unambiguously upward-sloping, and that high wages would stimulate diligence:

> The liberal reward of labour, as it encourages the propagation, so it increases the industry of the common people. The wages of labour are the encouragement of industry, which, like every other human quality, improves in proportion to the encouragement it receives ... Where wages are high, accordingly, we shall always find the workmen more active, diligent, and expeditious, than where they are low.[64]

The fact is that 'a plentiful subsistence increases the bodily strength of the labourer',[65] and a man who is well fed and in good health is able to work harder and produce more. Nor should the psychological state of mind of the workman be neglected: 'The comfortable hope of bettering his condition, and of ending his days perhaps in ease and plenty, animates him to exert that strength to the utmost.'[66] Indeed, so great is the substitution effect (as wages rise, a man substitutes work for leisure) relative to the income effect (as wages rise, he can afford more leisure without a fall in his standard of living) that high wages are more likely to lead to voluntary overwork than to voluntary unemployment: some workmen, 'when they can earn in four days what will maintain them through the week, will be idle on the other three. This, however, is by no means the case with the greater part. Workmen, on the contrary, when they are liberally paid by the piece, are very apt to over-work themselves, and to ruin their health and constitution in a few years.'[67] In practice, 'in civilized nations, the inferior ranks of people have very little leisure'.[68]

The more tempting the bait, the more the worker will be prepared to substitute the pleasure or utility of commodity-consumption for the pain or 'toil and trouble' of labour: the greater the 'enjoyments' offered, the greater the 'industry' of the labourer.[69] Work is by definition a burden; if it were not, there would be no need to compensate the worker for sacrificing a 'portion of his ease, his liberty, and his happiness',[70] and in the limiting case people might even pay for the privilege of taking part (the position of hunting and fishing in a civilised society[71]). In every profession, 'the exertion of the greater part of those who exercise it, is always in proportion to the necessity they are under of making that exertion'.[72] Payment independent of results makes bureaucrats negligent in the absence of incentives[73] and causes Oxford dons to give up 'even the pretence of teaching':[74] it is clearly not just among the lower classes that we find 'the hatred of labour and the love of present ease and enjoyment'.[75] Moreover, because society is consumption-orientated (men work to earn money to buy goods) rather than production-orientated (where men would work because they took pleasure in being creative), the quality of production as well as its quantity becomes a function of remuneration. In a dairy, if prices are high the enterprise is 'worthy of the farmer's attention', but if prices are low 'he will be likely to manage his dairy in a very slovenly and dirty manner . . . This inferiority of quality is, perhaps, rather the effect of this lowness of price than the cause of it'.[76] Commodity-utility is clearly the motive for action. The greater the opportunities men have of sharing in the pleasures of the affluent society, the more they will exert themselves.

The conclusions we have so far reached in this section are that an increase in capital will have beneficial consequences for society as a whole, both in raising the level of employment and in improving the standards of living of the working classes. Yet because of Smith's vagueness as to the allocation of the total supply of capital between its two component parts, there remains the possibility of a case where an increase in capital need not lead to full employment and prosperity, namely the case where the increase in the total is accompanied by a rise in the proportion of fixed to circulating capital. Put in its simplest form, the problem is that rapidly rising wages as the point of full employment is approached might cause capitalists to substitute new kinds of machinery for human labour: in such a situation, 'though, in consequence of the flourishing circumstances of the society, the real price of labour should rise very considerably, yet the great diminution of the quantity will generally much more than compensate the greatest rise which can happen in the price'.[77]

It is doubtful, however, if Smith actually regarded machinery as a threat to the employment and prosperity of the lower classes. For one thing, a man displaced by fixed capital in one trade could, in a growing and buoyant economy like Britain, always find employment elsewhere: more than a hundred thousand men had been released from the army and navy at the end of the Seven Years War, 'all accustomed to the use of arms, and many of them to rapine and plunder', and yet 'the number of vagrants was scarce any-where sensibly increased by it, even the wages of labour were not reduced by it in any occupation . . . except in that of seamen in the merchant-service'.[78] So long as there is capital in the country, labour will be employed; if not in one trade, then in another.

Mechanisation could at most create frictional unemployment.

Moreover, Smith seems to have seen fixed capital as complementary to circulating capital, not as a substitute for it; and to have envisaged machinery principally as a means for raising the productivity of a given labour-force, not as taking its place. There need be no competition between machines and men: 'The intention of the fixed capital is to increase the productive powers of labour, or to enable the same number of labourers to perform a much greater quantity of work.'[79] In general, 'the productive powers of the same number of labourers cannot be increased, but in consequence either of some addition and improvement to those machines and instruments which facilitate and abridge labour; or of a more proper division and distribution of employment'.[80] Thus, in manufacturing, it is evident that 'the same number of hands, assisted with the best machinery, will work up a much greater quantity of goods than with more imperfect instruments of trade'.[81] the 'exchange of the rock and spindle for the spinning-wheel', for example, meant that 'the same quantity of labour' was now able to 'perform more than double the quantity of work'.[82] An identical result obtains in agriculture: 'An improved farm may very justly be regarded in the same light as those useful machines which facilitate and abridge labour, and by means of which, an equal circulating capital can afford a much greater revenue to its employer'.[83] In none of these cases is the stock of circulating capital reduced or employed labour displaced. Simply, as the division of labour advances, 'in order to give constant employment to an equal number of workmen, an equal stock of provisions, and a greater stock of materials and tools than what would have been necessary in a ruder state of things, must be accumulated beforehand'.[84]

This leaves the problem of the unquestioned coincidence of rising wages and the introduction of labour-saving technology. Professor Hollander has, however, convincingly argued that the relationship is not causal (where the employer moves upwards along a downward-sloping demand curve, meeting higher prices of the input by reducing the quantity of it he employs), and that both phenomena are the resultants of a third phenomenon, economic expansion.[85] In such a situation, wages are rising due to increased demand for scarce supplies of labour, and economies of large scale (due to mechanisation, innovation and improved division of labour) are simultaneously becoming possible in industry which break the labour bottleneck and enable each worker to produce more output. No labour is displaced; rather, labour is regarded by the entrepreneur as a fixed cost to be rendered more efficient and economical by being employed with more fixed capital.

In support of this view that Smith believed substantial potential economies to exist which would be tapped only when the scale of operation rose, the following argument may be cited: the capitalist, Smith says, necessarily wishes to employ his capital

> in such a manner as to produce as great a quantity of work as possible. He endeavours, therefore, both to make among his workmen the most proper distribution of employment, and to furnish them with the best machines which he can either invent or afford to purchase. His abilities in both these respects are generally in proportion to the extent of his stock, or to the number of people whom it can employ. The quantity of industry, therefore, not only increases in every country with the increase of the stock which employs it, but, in consequence of that increase, the same quantity of industry produces a much greater quantity of work.[86]

Such improved efficiency of labour in a growing economy benefits the consumer: 'It is the natural effect of improvement . . . to diminish gradually the real price of almost all manufactures.'[87] Not only is there full employment and a high level of money wages, but real wages are rising due to the fall in goods prices that naturally accompanies economies of large scale in the division of labour and the use of capital. Of course, the division of labour means 'mental mutilation' for the factory operative, and capital accumulation may lead to class conflict (objectively or subjectively perceived) and overwork. Progress is not an unmixed blessing, but Smith was never adverse to a reasonable compromise. Commerce, after all, means that each benefit has its price. Smith wanted the benefit. He was prepared to pay the price.

7 THE STATE

It is well known that Adam Smith believed in the beneficial effect on the economy of competition, the profit motive and the free market mechanism:

> The natural effort of every individual to better his own condition, when suffered to exert itself with freedom and security, is so powerful a principle, that it is alone, and without any assistance, not only capable of carrying on the society to wealth and prosperity, but of surmounting a hundred impertinent obstructions with which the folly of human laws too often incumbers its operations.[1]

Yet Smith was the supreme eclectic. His goal was not simply to create a suitable environment for business but to use business as an instrument of economic and social progress; and his recommendations were delimited by time (the early stages of the industrial revolution) and place (Great Britain). To Adam Smith, no recommendation could be eternally and universally valid, and different situations were bound to need different policies. Our aim in this chapter is to examine those features of the British situation in the late eighteenth century which led Smith to favour private enterprise and disparage state intervention.

In Section I we shall examine evidence of policy-distortions resulting from the influence of vested interests. Pressure-groups had forced the state into misguided policies (such as mercantilism, the class-doctrine of merchants and manufacturers) which had misallocated resources, retarded growth, and sacrificed justice by favouring one group at the expense of another. To neutralise these vested interests there should be a balance of powers, first, between executive, judiciary and legislative branches of government, and, second, between social classes and orders. Thus Smith hoped that the power of the middle classes would come to counterbalance that of the upper classes and the king (and that the masses, being stupid and ignorant, would remain without any power at all). He was aware that the army and the sinister brotherhood of politicians represented potential threats to the balance of powers, but believed that checks and balances to their influence could be found.

In Section II we shall argue that, as far as Smith was concerned, government power needed not simply to be dispersed but had to be reduced:

First of all, the state was more often than not ignorant of trade, and had selected false policy-goals (such as maximisation of treasure) while neglecting goals more clearly in the national interest (such as full employment and rising standards of living). It had selected policy instruments which were wasteful of capital and whose results often were perverse. Moreover, market realities are too diverse and complex for the state to be able to impose controls such as wage and price norms, partly because of the lack of reliable statistics, but primarily because there *is* no 'correct' wage or price independent of what, in a free market situation, each buyer is willing to give and each seller willing to take.

Secondly, the state was wasteful of capital. Monarchs had wasted precious capital on luxury and extravagance, employed unproductive labourers, and in general set a bad example of idleness rather than industry.

Thirdly, the civil service was negligent, corrupt, careless and arrogant. Bureaucrats on fixed salaries are not properly motivated to run a business properly since they do not share in its profits; and while this was a problem of large-scale corporate enterprise (such as the South Sea Company or East India Company) as well as of the state, Smith was confident that the collapse of mercantilism would reverse the managerial revolution. The reduction of state influence and the consequent decline of the corporation would return business decisions to their natural locus, the capitalist entrepreneur, the owner-operator, whose private interest was the same as that of the firm and of the nation.

Fourthly, arbitrary laws which ignored the natural motion of phenomena, could generally be evaded or avoided; while, fifthly, if markets were allowed to find their own level based on the natural motion of phenomena, then state direction would simply not be necessary. State intervention in economic matters is as superfluous as state intervention to make the body thrive. The welfare of the body is the unintended outcome of the circulation of the blood, and the welfare of the economy is the unintended outcome of individual self-interest: 'Every individual is continually exerting himself to find out the most advantageous employment for whatever capital he can command. It is his own advantage, indeed, and not that of the society which he has in view. But the study of his own advantage naturally, or rather necessarily leads him to prefer that employment which is most advantageous to the society.'[2] It is as if he were led by an invisible hand to promote group-interests while aspiring only to promote his own, an optimistic view of the harmony between individual self-love and the common good that had been shared, among others, by Shaftesbury, Mandeville, Montesquieu and Pope. Montesquieu wrote: 'The individual's self-interest is always to be found in the common interest.'[3] And Pope made the same point in poetry: 'Thus God and Nature linked the general frame/And bade Self-Love and Social be the same.'[4] In Smith's opinion, the health of the economy, like that of the biological organism, depends on 'natural inclinations' rather than 'human institutions',[5] on 'the obvious and simple system of natural liberty' rather than 'preference' and 'restraint'.[6] The result is opulence and 'a natural balance of industry, or a disposition in the people to apply to each species of work precisely in proportion to the demand for that work'.[7] National opulence is clearly not the aim of the businessman, any more than the wheels of a watch have the conscious aim of telling the time. When we observe, however, how 'the wheels of the watch are all admirably adjusted to the end for which it was made',[8] we do not attribute this perfection to the 'desire and intention' of the wheels but to the skill of the watchmaker; and, as we saw in Chapter 3, a similar case may be made out for identifying divine beneficence in God's Works without needing to refer to God's Word or even to the explicit personal goals of the individual marionette.

In Section III we shall examine the positive functions Smith assigned to the state. It was to maintain a standing army for defence (a popular militia was not practical because of the debilitating effects of the division of labour on the masses), ensure justice (the *sine qua non* of a mercantile society) and undertake certain public works (particularly where social benefits exceed private benefits). It should also have certain regulatory functions through the discriminatory use of interest rates and taxation. State enterprise had been successful abroad (for example, in Amsterdam and Geneva), but the British Government had not yet acquired the necessary mercantile virtues of parsimony and industry and should refrain from such activity.

This chapter, like all others in this book, is an essay in the history of ideas. It is an attempt to understand the reasoning which led a highly intelligent and sensitive thinker like Adam Smith to make the recommendations he did on the scope for state action. At the same time, we must remember that these recommendations refer to a situation very different from our own. In modern Britain the working classes have been enfranchised, while the aristocracy, clergy and monarchy play a greatly reduced role in the political process. Compared with the eighteenth century, there has been an increase in the power of politicians to impose their own schemes on the nation, and political pluralism has increasingly come to be understood as the countervailing power of groups of politicians rather than a triangle of forces between clearly-defined economic classes. Politicians are probably less open to pressure from vested interests, partly because of the existence of a well-educated electorate kept constantly in touch with politics by the mass media, and partly because greater sophistication of economic and sociological intelligence has made them less dependent on interested parties for advice. Meanwhile, in the economy the small business is overshadowed in many spheres by the large corporation on the one hand, and the large trade union on the other, and whereas the profit-maximising owner-operator in a perfectly competitive market could be counted on to allocate resources in the most efficient manner, the same cannot be said of large organisations. The goals of the corporate bureaucrats are not known (but may resemble those of the state bureaucrats or of salaried trade union officials) and oligopolistic market structures may lead to waste and misallocation. In any case, the similarity of background of political and industrial leaders may have caused the state to have developed those virtues of parsimony and industry (rather than luxury and extravagance) that Smith so much admired in the governments of foreign 'republics'. Finally, even if the free market mechanism does establish the 'natural' order, a society may consciously select another order which fulfils some higher social purpose. Thus a rich society may waste capital, misallocate resources and sacrifice consumption opportunities in the interests of, say, equality of wealth or the 'quality of life'. The natural need not be the desirable order: all too often 'violence and artifice prevail over sincerity and justice'[9] and the widow and orphan are left with no other consolation than 'the belief of a future state'.[10] In such cases, apparently, God's Works fail to establish natural harmony, and conscious action, as we saw in Chapter 3, may be preferable to the natural functioning of the social organism: 'Man is by nature directed to correct, in some measure, that distribution of things which she herself would otherwise have made.'[11] Evil is no part of the Divine pattern, and man has a natural inclination to reverse those unintended outcomes which, although natural, he finds unacceptable. The social welfare function depends on time and place, and no 'end' (such as maximisation of commodity-consumption) is more 'natural' than another. Intervention to replace one unintended outcome by another is perfectly justifiable, but only if the transplant is done skilfully and respects the natural motion inherent in matter. One can divert the course of a river but not command it to stand still.

Fortunately, since this chapter is a study in the history of ideas, we do not need to examine how far Smith's recommendations on the scope for state action are relevant to the rich industrial democracies of modern Europe and North America, or to the developing countries experiencing their own industrial revolutions. Smith's recommendations refer to the conditions of Great Britain in the late eighteenth century, and must be accepted as such. It is the height of intellectual arrogance to interpret past thinkers in terms of present needs.

I. Balance of Interest and Balance of Power

Adam Smith was convinced that the state should be impartial as between groups of citizens: 'To hurt in any degree the interest of any one order of citizens, for no other purpose but to promote that of some other, is evidently contrary to that justice and equality of treatment which the sovereign owes to all the different orders of his subjects.'[1]

Equally, however, Smith was convinced that the state had not been impartial, and remained subject to the influence of interest-groups. Government had arisen in the first place, after all, out of social division and the need to protect one group against another: 'Civil government, so far as it is instituted for the security of property, is in reality instituted for the defence of the rich against the poor, or of those who have some property against those who have none at all.'[2] Possibly the 'sacred rights of private property'[3] have their 'original foundation'[4] in the labour a man chooses to embody in an object, as Locke said it did:[5] if I take possession 'of what formerly belonged to nobody', if 'I have gathered some wild fruit, it will appear reasonable to the spectator that I should dispose of it as I please'.[6] But this Lockean justification of private property in terms of labour-embodied ceases to apply in a developed society, where the *raison d'être* of private property seems to be simply its own existence and the proper sympathy that it thereby attracts. In a developed society, the justification for private property is to be found in social convention and group experience, not in utility, natural rights or labour-embodied: nowadays the spectator sympathises with private property because of the aesthetically satisfying propriety of habitual associations ('when a man has a right to one thing in consequence of another, as of a horse's shoes along with the horse'[7]), because of long-standing and uninterrupted possession, because of the sanctity of inheritance, or because of the justice implicit in a fair exchange of assets. In short, in a developed society property rights are legitimated *ex post*. The idea is that the masses sympathise with men of wealth and admire the suitability of great property as the means to attain great happiness.[8] The ownership of property generates sympathy, posterior to the acquisition of property but still its justification; and where this sympathy is insufficient (as it very often appears to be), the state undertakes to defend property-owners, not because of their natural rights but simply because of their vested interests.

Other social groups too had succeeded in using the state to foster
their interests. Thus in 1688 Parliament was persuaded to grant a
bounty on the export of corn:

> The country gentlemen, who then composed a still greater proportion
> of the legislature than they do at present, had felt that the money
> price of corn was falling . . . The government of King William was not
> then fully settled. It was in no condition to refuse any thing to the
> country gentlemen, from whom it was at that very time soliciting
> the first establishment of the annual land-tax.[9]

Economic interest on both sides was thus responsible for these
concessions. To make matters worse, the country gentlemen, whom
Smith did not credit with much intelligence at the best of times,[10]
turned out to have acted without 'that complete comprehension of
their own interest which commonly directs the conduct of those two
other orders of people . . . They discouraged, in some degree, the
general industry of the country, and, instead of advancing, retarded
more or less the improvement of their own lands.'[11] Not only were
their class-interests allowed to take precedence over the interests of
other orders in the nation, but they were even mistaken as to what
their true class-interests were.

The middle classes at least had a better knowledge of their own
interest.[12] The mercantile system arose because merchants and manufacturers had succeeded in persuading the government that their class-
interest was the national interest. This was, of course, not the case:
'It cannot be very difficult to determine who have been the contrivers
of this whole mercantile system; not the consumers, we may believe,
whose interest has been entirely neglected; but the producers, whose
interest has been so carefully attended to.'[13]

The mercantile lobby was thus able to convince the government that
the welfare of the nation lay in the protection of trade. The idea of
founding an Empire in order to have a monopoly of trade with it is a
devious, wasteful and expensive means of expanding commerce. It is
'a project altogether unfit for a nation of shopkeepers; but extremely
fit for a nation whose government is influenced by shopkeepers'.[14]
After all, the state bears the cost and the merchants reap the benefits.
Public cost exceeds public benefit but private benefit exceeds private
cost, and greediness is 'natural to man'.[15]

Similarly, the manufacturers of capital goods were able to persuade
the state to prohibit the importation of machinery from abroad. Such

importation 'would interfere too much with the interest of those manufactures'.[16] And in wage-bargaining, there were laws to repress combination among workers or to fix maximum wages. The interests of workers and masters were not the same, but the state had on all occasions favoured 'the rich and the powerful' rather than 'the poor and the indigent':[17] 'Whenever the legislature attempts to regulate the differences between masters and their workmen, its counsellors are always the masters.'[18] The state has thus received biased advice, for the employers 'are silent with regard to the pernicious effects of their own gains. They complain only of those of other people.'[19] Wealth leads to influence, and justice is sacrificed to interest.

French mercantilists were just as persistent as their English counterparts, and even the wise Colbert seems 'to have been imposed upon by the sophistry of merchants and manufacturers, who are always demanding a monopoly against their countrymen'.[20] Yet in England, while on the one hand merchants and manufacturers had 'extorted from the legislature'[21] very severe penalties for illegal importation and exportation, in order to strengthen 'their own absurd and oppressive monopolies',[22] on the other hand even smugglers were a successful pressure group. Sir Robert Walpole was forced to drop his excise scheme at least partly because of their lobby.[23] The government was thus drawn in different directions by different pressure groups, and was unable even to act consistently because of them.

Each group seems to have entered into the scramble for influence. Some were rewarded, others not. For example: 'Our tanners . . . have not been quite so successful as our clothiers, in convincing the wisdom of the nation, that the safety of the commonwealth depends upon the prosperity of their particular manufacture. They have accordingly been much less favoured.'[24] The Bank of England lobby, however, was successful in obtaining laws favouring itself, and in having them made 'perpetual',[25] and politicians had gone ahead with public works for their own glory and convenience.[26]

Particularism and influence were not purely a problem of national government. At the local level, merchants and manufacturers in towns corporate had combined to restrict output and raise prices. This upset the social and economic balance between town and country, and turned the domestic terms of trade against the landed interest:

The government of towns corporate was altogether in the hands of traders and artificers; and it was the manifest interest of every particular class of them, to prevent the market from being over-stocked, as they commonly express it, with their own particular

species of industry; which is in reality to keep it always under-
stocked . . . (Such measures) give the traders and artificers in the
town an advantage over the landlords, farmers, and labourers in the
country, and break down that natural equality which would otherwise take place in the commerce which is carried on between
them.[27]

After all, combination in towns is easier to bring about than in the
countryside, where the population is scattered and there is less specialisation or scope for restrictive practices such as apprenticeship. Smith,
however, was disturbed by the lack of fairness in the exchange of goods
between town and country that resulted from such combination: 'The
whole annual produce of the labour of the society is annually divided
between those two different sets of people. By means of those regulations a greater share of it is given to the inhabitants of the town than
would otherwise fall to them; and a less to those of the country.'[28]
It is interesting to note his use of personification in the preceding
passages. Rather than speaking of impersonal units such as 'the town'
and 'the country' he speaks of 'the traders and artificers in the town'
and 'the landlords, farmers, and labourers in the country'. This avoidance of reification is a common feature of his work, and reminds us
again that he was at all times more concerned with relationships
between persons than with relationships between things.

  In general, any one interest group can 'tyrannize the government'
and 'warp the positive laws of the country from what natural justice
would prescribe';[29] and in Britain such groups had clearly been all too
successful. Smith was obsessed with 'the passionate confidence of
interested falsehood',[30] which had prevented the state from showing
exemplary fairness to all citizens. The solution seemed to lie in a
separation of powers and set of checks and balances: a mixed constitution, as most eighteenth-century social thinkers would have agreed,
is 'a happy mixture of all the different forms of government properly
restrained, and a perfect security to liberty and property'.[31] The
'balance of the constitution' is preferable to increasing 'either the
influence of the crown on the one hand, or the force of the democracy on the other',[32] and means that one leader or group of leaders
would have the power unchecked to use the state as their own creature.
Here Smith was arguing in the tradition of Locke, who had called for
separation of executive and legislative powers on the grounds that 'it
may be too great temptation to human frailty, apt to grasp at power,
for the same persons who have the power of making laws, to have also
in their hands the power to execute them'.[33]

Even more than by Locke, however, Smith was influenced by Montesquieu, who, of course, had advocated the separation of executive, legislative *and* judiciary branches of government, and whose views on the British political order[34] were to have so great an influence on the fathers of the American constitution. Montesquieu wrote:

> Constant experience shows us that every man invested with power is apt to abuse it, and to carry his authority as far as it will go. Is it not strange, though true, to say that virtue itself has need of limits? . . . There would be an end of everything, were the same man or the same body, whether of the nobles or of the people, to exercise those three powers, that of enacting laws, that of executing the public resolutions, and of trying the causes of individuals.[35]

In practical terms, Smith had in mind the system which (as we saw in Chapter 5) he believed to be already evolving in Britain. He was anxious that the king should remain chief executive, but that judges should be appointed for life and be independent of that ececutive power.[36] He believed that there should be habeas corpus[37] and a jury system (proof that the law is 'the friend of liberty'[38]). Moreover, he welcomed the idea of a bi-cameral legislature, where finance bills originated in the lower house[39] (in Britain, the House of Commons, which coincidentally also contained the greatest number of middle class members).

Such a system seems to be characteristic of a 'republic'. Thus in his discussion of the American colonies Smith points out that the colonial assemblies, although 'not always a very equal representation of the people, yet . . . approach more nearly to that character'.[40] There is no taxation without representation.[41] There is security, guaranteed to all by the check the elected assembly exercises over the executive: 'The authority of this assembly over-awes the executive power, and neither the meanest nor the most obnoxious colonist, as long as he obeys the law, has any thing to fear from the resentment, either of the governor, or of any other civil or military officer in the province.'[42] There is not a single hereditary aristocrat with 'privileges by which he can be troublesome to his neighbours',[43] and although there are some old colonial families with great fortunes, in general there is more equality of wealth than in Britain. Members of upper houses in the colonial legislature are even sometimes selected by the lower houses, by the 'representatives of the people'.[44] Such a climate has understandably been very congenial to economic progress.[45]

Again, in Holland, industry and trade have flourished because of good government, despite an unusually low return on capital:

The republican form of government seems to be the principal
support of the present grandeur of Holland. The owners of great
capitals, the great mercantile families, have generally either some
direct share, or some indirect influence, in the administration of that
government. For the sake of the respect and authority which they
derive from this situation, they are willing to live in a country where
their capital, if they employ it themselves, will bring them less profit
. . . than in any other part of Europe.[46]

In short, prestige, security, the law of contract, the ability to participate
in government, all induced Dutch businessmen to keep their capitals at
home despite the low rate of profit. This does not appear to Smith a
misallocation of resources since, although pecuniary returns are low,
non-pecuniary benefits are high. It is clear, however, that Dutch prosperity depends on the continuance of the republican form of
government. A *coup d'état* by either military or aristocracy would
terminate that form of government and anihilate the political power of
the merchants. This in turn would create uncertainty about property
and contracts, and moreover 'would soon render it disagreeable to them
to live in a country where they were no longer likely to be much
respected'.[47] The merchants would remove themselves and their
capitals to some other country, and the Dutch economy would stagnate.

Elsewhere, Smith praises good government in other 'republics' such
as Geneva, Berne, Hamburg and Venice. All these republics had one
thing in common, that the merchants and manufacturers had considerable say in the process of government. The state guaranteed the security
of property and the enforcement of contracts, and placed no
discriminatory restrictions on industry and trade. It is certainly
tempting to see Smith's ideal as a 'bourgeois state', governing in the
interests of the 'bourgeois class'. It is here, however, that we encounter
the second strand of Smith's theory of the separation of powers,
namely his belief in a parallelogram of forces between orders and social
classes. In other words, Smith was thinking not only in terms of a
constitution where different branches of government counterbalance
one another, but of a society where different classes and social groups
neutralise and offset each other. On the international scene, peace and
security depend on 'that equality of courage and force which, by
inspiring mutual fear, can alone overawe the injustice of independent
nations into some sort of respect for the rights of one another'.[48] The
same balance must come to prevail domestically.

Smith's theory of social action is so often couched in the language of
individualism that one tends to forget its corporatist overtones. But

Smith was in no doubt that society is an aggregate of groups, not simply an amorphous agglomeration of discrete and isolated individuals. A state is in reality a vast network of smaller collectivities each with its corresponding set of group loyalties and group solidarities:

> Every independent state is divided into many different orders and societies, each of which has its own particular powers, privileges, and immunities. Every individual is naturally more attached to his own particular order or society than to any other. His own interest, his own vanity, the interest and vanity of many of his friends and companions, are commonly a good deal connected with it: he is ambitious to extend its privileges and immunities – he is zealous to defend them against the encroachments of every other order or society.[49]

Group solidarity results when men have common interests, as they share the same problems and fear the same enemies: in truth, 'in order to live comfortably in the world, it is upon all occasions as necessary to defend our dignity and rank, as it is to defend our life or our fortune.'[50] Moreover, men with common interests more often than not have similar patterns of conduct and character and similar life styles, giving them a further sense of solidarity. Whatever the reasons for group solidarity, it is a fact that the countervailing power of such groups is the precondition for a stable constitution: 'Upon the ability of each particular order or society to maintain its own powers, privileges, and immunities, against the encroachments of every other, depends the stability of that particular constitution.'[51]

Naturally, loyalty to one's order is secondary to loyalty to the state; but 'the love of our country' means a respect for its constitution, and that in turn means nothing more than respect for the existing balance of power and balance of social groupings. Preservation of the 'established balance among the different orders and societies into which the state is divided' is the basis for the 'stability and permanency' of the constitution;[52] and hence, by being sympathetic with and benevolent to the members of his order, a man simultaneously promotes the public interest. Smith, like Burke, was eager to defend the convection of interest-groups represented by the existing constitution and thus to defend a going concern, particularly against the hare-brained schemes of 'men of system' who often propose 'to new-model the constitution, and to alter in some of its most essential parts that system of government under which the subjects of a great empire have enjoyed, perhaps, peace, security, and even glory, during the course of several centuries together'.[53]

While distrusting revolutionaries who erect their own judgements 'into the supreme standard of right and wrong',[54] however, Smith did recognise the dynamic nature of reality: the fact is that economic growth itself, by raising up some classes (particularly the mercantile and manufacturing classes) and depressing others (notably the traditional upper classes), does, through the redistribution of property, cause a redistribution of power in the state. Nonetheless, whatever changes take place, some internal balance of power between orders and classes continues to exist, and such balance is vital since no one class is the natural repository of authority. The Smithian ideal is dispersion of political power, not its transference from one class to another.

Adam Smith was as critical of the middle classes as he was of other orders in society (such as the nobility and clergy, the masses, or the Crown). Thus, he warns against 'the sneaking arts of underling tradesmen'[55] and 'the mean rapacity, the monopolizing spirit of merchants and manufacturers, who neither are, nor ought to be, the rulers of mankind'.[56] The business classes are obsessed with restricting competition in order to raise prices. Clearly, 'their interest is, in this respect, directly opposite to that of the great body of the people':[57] they 'levy, for their own benefit, an absurd tax upon the rest of their fellow-citizens'.[58] Even in a landlord-dominated society, merchants and manufacturers had succeeded far too often in influencing government policy. They are 'an order of men, whose interest is never exactly the same with that of the public, who have generally an interest to deceive and even to oppress the public, and who accordingly have, upon many occasions, both deceived and oppressed it'.[59] Writing of the East India Company, he says: 'No two characters seem more inconsistent than those of trader and sovereign.'[60] The German Historical School was wrong to equate Smithianismus with Manchestertum: Smith was hardly the mere mouthpiece of the emergent bourgeoisie.

As for the aristocracy and clergy, Smith was far from putting complete faith in them. The landed classes as a whole were tyrannical, wasteful and ignorant; and the clergy had the further disadvantage of being factious and superstitious. Their political power needed to be substantially reduced.[61]

The political power of the masses, on the other hand, was to remain totally non-existent. Smith did not seriously consider the possibility of democracy. He praises the 'orderly, vigilant, and parsimonious administration of such aristocracies as those of Venice and Amsterdam'[62] (where meritocracy ruled alongside traditional aristocracy[63]), warns against the 'thoughtless extravagance'[64] of democracies, and reminds us that the masses want good government, not representative government: 'In Venice the people freely gave up the government, as they also did in Holland, because they could not support the trouble which it gave them.'[65]

Smith had an almost Shakespearean distrust of the masses, whom he felt to be 'incapable either of comprehending (the social) interest, or of understanding its connexion with their own'.[66] Confusion resulted in ancient Greece when vast bodies of citizens, rather than a single judge, constituted courts of justice, since the citizenry 'frequently decided almost at random, or as clamour, faction and party spirit happened to determine'.[67] And 'disorder and confusion'[68] resulted too when the followers of Calvin acquired the right to elect their own pastor. In wartime as in peacetime, the lower classes are unreliable and defend their country as soldiers only because they are more afraid of their officers than they are of the enemy: 'Gentlemen may carry on a war without much discipline, but this a mob can never do.'[69]

The common people are 'so jealous of their liberty', although 'never rightly understanding wherein it consists';[70] and for this reason a wise man should prefer the approbation of a single other wise man to 'all the noisy applauses of ten thousand ignorant though enthusiastic admirers'.[71] The masses are dazzled by 'the most ignorant quacks and imposters, both civil and religious',[72] and may easily be misled by braggarts and men of 'excessive self-estimation'[73] (since men of 'no more than ordinary discernment' tend to judge a man by appearances, and may mistake pretence for real superiority). Men are particularly likely to be led by their employers, and in a mercantile society the worker appears to be their tool in politics as well as in trade: 'In the public deliberations . . . his voice is little heard and less regarded, except upon some particular occasions, when his clamour is animated, set on, and supported by his employers, not for his, but for their own particular purposes.'[74] Enfranchisement of the masses would only strengthen the political power of the bosses, who would exploit the servility and stupidity of the workers to make them the Trojan Horse of capitalism. Disenfranchisement of the lower classes is the only way to protect them from themselves, to prevent them from being to the modern era what private armies were to feudalism.

The factory operative is unusually dull because of the routine work he performs, far duller than the agricultural worker who is challenged by a variety of tasks. Concentration on one or two simple processes makes the intellect into a vestigial organ, causes the mind to fall into 'drowsy stupidity',[75] and renders the worker particularly ill-equipped

to play any part in the political process: 'The torpor of his mind
renders him, not only incapable of relishing or bearing a part in any
rational conversation, but of conceiving any generous, noble, or tender
sentiment . . . Of the great and extensive interests of his country he is
altogether incapable of judging.'[76] Since character is primarily the result
of the work-function, there is little that education can do to combat
this intellectual decay, especially professionally-orientated education of
the type Smith envisaged. The masses are thus not intrinsically unfit
for democracy, but are made so by the division of labour, particularly
in an industrial society. Men are born equal; it is 'alienation' at the
place of work that more than any other factor converts good citizens
into the 'Pöbel', the 'canaille', the 'mob' that Voltaire, Diderot, even
Holbach feared as much as Smith.

Of course, historically speaking, the masses have not always been so
debased as to be incapable of judging the vital interests of their society.
In primitive society, for example, hunters were not unable to take an
intelligent part in political deliberations; nor were they unwilling to put
the interests of the community before their own private interest.[77]
Thus democracy once (albeit only among savages in a propertyless,
unstratified, non-industrial society anterior to the division of labour)
was more than an abstraction. In present-day conditions, however, the
masses are no longer suited for such democracy;[78] and in any case have
natural sympathy with men of wealth and greatness, which makes them
consent to their own exclusion from the councils of state and inspires
them to delegate power to those classes able to make better use of it.
Admiration of success in a stratified society is the means by which 'we
are taught to submit more easily to those superiors whom the course
of human affairs may assign to us'.[79] It is the guarantor of political
stability and, no less important, of that Stoic apathy which makes the
inevitable tolerable (and even agreeable).

Smith dismissed without any discussion schemes (such as those of
More and Harrington) for a communistic society, although Hutcheson
and Hume had treated these 'systems of community' to a more detailed
analysis;[80] and he used the terms 'Utopia' and 'Oceana' as synonyms for
'useless' and 'chimerical'.[81] Basically, he felt, the masses desire full
employment and a rising standard of living. This means division of
labour and capital accumulation, for which the precondition is security
of property and political stability, which in turn are only possible if
the mercantile classes are allowed to share in government (their
'rapacity' having been checked by the countervailing vices of aristocracy, clergy and monarchy), and if the lower classes are protected
from their own dullness and fickleness by being kept far from the

reins of power.

We have discussed the role in the political process that Smith assigned to the middle classes, the upper classes, and the lower classes. It is important to remember, however, that in Smith's ideal republic the king too had a role to play. The fact that Smith wanted to curb the powers of the monarch does not mean that he wanted to abolish him. After all, the hereditary principle ensured continuity in government. It is for this reason that Smith defended so warmly the principle of primogeniture in the royal succession: 'That the power, and consequently the security of the monarchy, may not be weakened by division, it must descend entire to one of the children. To which of them so important a preference shall be given, must be determined by some general rule, founded not upon the doubtful distinctions of personal merit, but upon some plain and evident difference which can admit of no dispute.'[82]

Smith recognised that 'all constitutions of government . . . are valued only in proportion as they tend to promote the happiness of those who live under them'[83] and that no authority can be without limit. Once that limit is reached, considerations of utility may justify a revolution: 'It is hard to determine what a monarch may or may not do. But when the *summa potestas* is divided as it is in Britain, if the king do anything which ought to be consented to by the parliament, without their permission, they have a right to oppose him . . . Thus King James, on account of his encroachments on the body politic, was with all justice and equity in the world opposed and rejected.'[84] Rulers are responsible to their subjects and there can be no legitimate government without the voluntary if tacit consent of the governed. Like Locke, Smith believed that political power is in the last analysis fiduciary, and that the people retains the right to rebel (a right which it exercised with perfect propriety in 1688). Revolution is particularly justifiable if the government has failed to maintain tranquillity or prevent disorder.[85] Yet innovation can be dangerous: 'In Turkey eight or ten years seldom pass without a change of government.'[86] Revolution becomes perpetual and the principle of continuity is sacrificed.

Smith was aware of the danger of a 'general insurrection', a threat which must be taken into account in formulating policy.[87] He advised the sovereign to have a strong standing army at the ready in case of need before he releases the iron grip of tyranny and allows any individual freedom whatever. A standing army is favourable to liberty: the existence of law and order gives the sovereign security, and makes it possible for him to allow freedom of speech. Otherwise, 'where a small tumult is capable of bringing about in a few hours a great revolution, the whole authority of government must be employed to suppress and punish every murmur and complaint against it.'[88]

Yet 'popular discontent' is not the only potential cause of revolution. The standing army itself may seize power, as happened in the time of Caesar or Cromwell. Here again, however, the solution is institutional, to make sure the leaders of the army are chosen from those classes which have most to lose if revolution does take place:

> Where the sovereign is himself the general, and the principal nobility and gentry of the country the chief officers of the army; where the military force is placed under the command of those who have the greatest interest in the support of the civil authority, because they have themselves the greatest share of that authority, a standing army can never be dangerous to liberty.[89]

Thus, there is a set of checks and balances: the standing army checks the power of the people and a set of officers sharing the sovereign's vested interests checks any threat from the army.[90]

The monarch is, furthermore, a counterbalancing factor to the ambitions of politicians. Such men, like any other zealots, have little respect for the truth: 'A true party-man hates and despises candour: and, in reality, there is no vice which could so effectually disqualify him for the trade of a party-man as that single virtue. The real, revered, and impartial spectator, therefore, is upon no occasion at a greater distance than amidst the violence and rage of contending parties.'[91] The politician is, almost by definition, an 'insidious and crafty animal',[92] preoccupied with his own aggrandisement and power. Political office is a 'method of acquiring importance', a 'dazzling object of ambition';[93] and 'men desire to have some share in the management of public affairs chiefly on account of the importance which it gives them'.[94] In America, men felt a 'proportionable rise in their own importance' as soon as they entered the council chamber: 'From shopkeepers, tradesmen, and attornies, they are become statesmen and legislators, and are employed in contriving a new form of government for a extensive empire, which, they flatter themselves, will become . . . one of the greatest and most formidable that ever was in the world.'[95]

Such men are doubly dangerous. First of all, politicians may turn out to be demogogic 'men of system' who exploit the fanaticism of their followers in order to gain power. The more ignorant of those followers are 'intoxicated with the imaginary beauty of this ideal system, of which they have no experience',[96] while the more practical know that politicians can exert considerable patronage through their 'disposal of many places of trust and profit'.[97] In practice, ideal schemes are doomed to fail if inappropriate to the conditions of the real world, and can create considerable disorder.

Secondly, politicians tend to form into rival factions. The capital is the 'principal seat of the great scramble of faction and ambition',[98] and one social upheaval might follow another if the monarch did not exist to preserve continuity of the executive. The position of the monarch is unquestionable. He is at the apex of the pyramid of rank, which is maintained intact by the natural sympathy of the masses with greatness. As the greatest of the great, the king commands the most sympathy: 'The traitor who conspires against the life of his monarch, is thought a greater monster than any other murderer.'[99] The very existence of the monarchy is a psychological obstacle to revolution. The middle classes, however, are very far down the pyramid. Merchants, for example, cannot really be taken seriously. They exercise 'a profession no doubt extremely respectable, but which in no country in the world carries along with it that sort of authority which naturally over-awes the people, and without force commands their willing obedience'.[100] On the other hand, the people have considerable veneration for 'ancient greatness',[101] and the principle of birth proves a necessary delusion which, via the mechanism of sympathy, can contribute to stability and tranquillity without undue recourse to repression and force.

Stability of the social order was to Smith of the utmost importance: 'The peace and order of society is of more importance than even the relief of the miserable.'[102] It is sometimes better for a public-spirited man to acquiesce in the existing social order and to content himself with 'moderating, what he often cannot annihilate without great violence'[103] than for him to make a revolution which would upset the functioning of the whole social organism. Political revolutions are violent and unpleasant, and the cure may be worse than the disease. Smith makes clear that, provided the government has shown itself capable of maintaining justice and security, then the support of the established government is 'the best expedient for maintaining the safe, respectable, and happy situation of our fellow-citizens'.[104]

In conclusion, we have argued in this section that Smith did not put complete faith in any single social group, and seems to have distrusted most classes equally (except for the masses, whom he distrusted slightly more). One of the reasons for Smith's instantaneous popularity as a theorist must surely have been his evident impartiality, his detached objectivity, his advocacy of balance rather than interest. His rule of thumb appears to have been: 'Such, it seems, is the natural insolence of man, that he almost always disdains to use the good instrument, except when he cannot or dare not use the bad one.'[105] In a growing economy, however, dispersion of fortunes would lead to dispersion of power, and no group would be able to use the 'bad instrument' unchecked. The manufacturers and merchants would come to counterbalance the aristocracy and clergy, while the aristocracy and clergy would act as a brake on the rapacity of the industrial and mercantile classes. Both upper and middle classes, supported by the impartial administration of justice, would keep the king from becoming a despot, as had happened to even the best monarchs of ancient times:[106] since 'one man is more apt to fall into imprudent measures than a number',[107] a parliamentary system is highly desirable. And the king, by acting as a check on the politicians and as the apex of the hierarchy of wealth, power and sympathy, serves as the guarantor of social continuity, particularly if he enlists the military on his side.

A revolution by means of economic growth means a gradual dispersion of powers, whereas a political revolution of the French type tends to mean their sudden transfer from one set of rulers to another. An industrial revolution does not break the link with the past, and actors from the past do not become redundant. Their role changes, however, due to the appearance of new actors with whom they must share the stage.

II. The Case Against the State

Governmental powers were not simply to be shared. They were to be reduced. The state had consistently been misguided in its policies, and government itself was wasteful of capital. Civil servants were corrupt and inefficient. Moreover, laws that went against the motion inherent in matter simply could not be enforced; while laws that did not related to natural equilibria and enforced themselves. In this section we shall discuss these five reasons which Smith gave for reducing the influence of the state in economy and society.

1. The state was ignorant of trade (and, indeed, unreformed parliaments in the past had often been 'conscious to themselves that they knew nothing about the matter'[1]). As a result, it had often chosen false policy-goals, neglected goals truly in the national interest, and selected policy-instruments unsuitable for attaining the end sought.

Thus Smith felt the encouragement of export by means of bounties had been an improper objective of policy since it misallocated resources: 'The effect of bounties, like that of all the other expedients of the mercantile system, can only be to force the trade of a country into a channel much less advantageous than that in which it would naturally run of its own accord.'[2] By artificially attracting precious capital to otherwise unattractive trades, bounties distorted the natural 'balance of industry'.[3] They caused the farmer to employ his capital wastefully in producing a commodity he would otherwise have found unprofitable to produce,[4] and prevented him from shifting his capital to alternative employments which in real terms would have been more productive of growth. Bounties raised the price of corn in the home market, and as a result the consumer had been obliged to pay higher food prices. Not only might this reduction in his welfare be translated into a reduction in his industry or in the rate of population growth, but it might also mean unemployment if higher food prices were matched by higher wages, since the capitalist would then be able to support less labour with a given wage-fund.[5]

In any case, government intervention in the economy can have quite unexpected results. The higher price of provisions caused by the export bounty for grain made British manufactures more expensive and thus less competitive abroad, while the availability from Britain of cheap grain at subsidised prices enabled Dutch manufacturers to keep wages low, thereby rendering their own goods more competitive. It thus gave them a double advantage over British producers.[6] And bounties, by ensuring unnaturally high profits to entrepreneurs in the herring fisheries, had sometimes encouraged the wrong sort of new entrants: 'The usual effect of such bounties is to encourage rash undertakers to adventure in a business which they do not understand, and what they lose by their own negligence and ignorance, more than compensates all that they can gain by the utmost liberality of government.'[7] The aim was to catch not fish but the bounty,[8] and this was easy to do as the bounty was proportional to the size of the ship, not the size of the catch. Government money and national resources were wasted, and fishing was not substantially encouraged as a result.

The effects of governmental policies can actually be perverse. The state on one occasion hoped to make grain supplies cheaper by passing laws against the middle-man. Yet the disappearance of specialist intermediaries meant the farmer had to tie up part of his capital in storing grain, rather than employing the whole of it in cultivation. Grain prices rose rather than fell,[9] and there was more of a chance of a dearth turning into a famine.[10]

To Smith, the whole mercantile system was a case of false priorities served by improper means. It falsely identified prosperity with 'money' (a veil and no more) rather than 'money's worth'[11] (real wealth, commodities produced by industry and agriculture), and favoured the vested interests of merchants and manufacturers at the expense of consumers and labourers. For example, since the capital of foreigners was deliberately excluded by the Navigation Laws from trade with

British colonies, the colonial market was undersupplied with goods, and British merchants were able to make windfall profits by selling at inflated prices.[12] Similarly, the interests of a regulated trading company are by no means those of the consumer: 'The constant view of such companies is always to raise the rate of their own profit as high as they can; to keep the market, both for the goods which they export, and for those which they import, as much understocked as they can.'[13] The only case in which such a company would be justified is along the lines of the infant industries argument: a temporary monopoly might be granted in order to open up a new branch of trade.[14] But it must be temporary.

As well as the consumer, the mercantile system also victimised the labourer. It diverted capital into channels where it would not otherwise have gone,[15] and misallocation means waste. Yet full employment and rising standards of living are dependent on rapid capital accumulation. Thus the Navigation Acts artificially drew capital into trade with the colonies where its turnover was sluggish. This meant the effective quantity of capital available to support labour at any given time was less than if the gestation period of the scheme were shorter: 'A British capital of a thousand pounds, for example, which is returned to Great Britain only once in five years, can keep in constant employment only one-fifth part of the British industry which it could maintain if the whole was returned once in the year.'[16]

State intervention to regulate the labour market had been particularly unfortunate. Settlement laws and statutes of apprenticeship restricted the mobility of labour (both geographical and occupational) and retarded economic growth by misallocating workers, while maximum wage laws and charters granted to corporations and guilds restrained competition and prevented the market from establishing a natural equilibrium wage. In setting wages, the state is liable to err since its advisers are partial (the masters), and since the labour market is not only highly complex but ever changing: state intervention thus runs the risk of ossifying obsolete social conditions in the form of law, so that a maximum wage of, say, two shillings might represent past conditions, not present ones. The collection of statistics was in its infancy, but the argument against regulation of wages goes beyond a mere information gap: supply and demand alone ('perfect liberty') and not law can determine how much labour should be employed, where, in what trades, and at what price. In any case, even if the state were to set a maximum wage, collusion among employers might force workers to accept less (especially where that collusion is sanctioned by the privileges of incorporation); and, indeed, some employers might secretly be willing to pay more, depending on the abilities of the workers and their own 'easiness or hardness'.[17]

In the interests of both producer and consumer, there should be free trade in the labour market. The abolition of apprenticeship, for example, would increase competition and 'the public would be a gainer, the work of all artificers coming in this way much cheaper to market'.[18] Such free trade should even extend to the professions. Smith saw little difference between the privileges of graduates and those of skilled tradesmen who had served an apprenticeship:[19] both sets of privileges had prevented new entry and mobility of labour, and kept returns artificially high while not guaranteeing standards of workmanship.[20] Licensing by degree or title is only a sophisticated form of restrictive practice, and hence he recommended that even doctors should be freed from the obligation to have formal qualifications in medicine.[21] For doctors, as for butchers and coal-heavers, entry into the trade is to be governed solely by ability to do the job, as estimated by the sovereign consumer. Here as elsewhere the rule is 'caveat emptor'.

In summary, therefore, it is clear that Smith (unlike, for example, his contemporary, Sir James Steuart) saw little scope for the wise policies of enlightened rulers precisely because those policies had seldom been wise and those rulers rarely enlightened. If history is a museum, then recent British economic history was to Smith a chamber of horrors, displaying how ignorant aristocrats had been influenced by special pleading (notably by merchants and manufacturers despite their modest active participation in government) to pursue bizarre objectives (such as a huge trade surplus and the accumulation of gold and silver) rather than objectives truly in the national interest (such as the optimal allocation of resources and maximal accumulation of capital, which would lead to full employment and a rising standard of living). Not all countries can simultaneously enjoy a balance of payments surplus, and hence trade had become war, whereas it ought to be 'a bond of union and friendship'[22] among nations; and should actual war break out, the state had introduced policies which actually threatened security as well as misallocating resources (for example, the concentration of capital in the colonial trades, which made a sea-war an economic catastrophe to the nation as well as a political threat[23]). Finally, through its interventionist policies the state had redistributed the national income away from the 'natural equilibrium' that would otherwise have obtained,[24] and in so doing had needlessly sacrificed the notion of fair play to all its subjects. The state had behaved like a bull in a china shop, where it was as out of place as a sow in a drawing-room.

2. Smith further sought to reduce the influence of the state because governments tend to be wasteful of capital. Britain was a monarchy, and courts are notorious for their love of luxury and extravagance. He compares ostentatious expenditure at the court of the Viceroy of Peru to a tax, both particular (levied to support the cost of a given celebration such as the reception of a new Viceroy) and perpetual (the effect on the economy of setting an example of vanity and prodigality rather than parsimony and hard work).[25] In trading and industrial nations, rather than absorbing the new middle class virtues of application and self-denial, the sovereign is found to be particularly extravagant in his pursuit of 'gaudy finery'. After all, he can always raise more funds effortlessly, by levying a new tax (unless there are checks and balances to his power). Moreover, he follows 'the mode of the times', which in a rich nation is nothing less than 'extravagant vanity': 'The insignificant pageantry of (the) court becomes every day more brilliant, and the expense of it not only prevents accumulation, but frequently encroaches upon the funds destined for more necessary expences.'[26]

In other words, the behaviour patterns of the king resemble those of the great landed proprietors rather than those of the middle classes; and even in the government of republics, that parsimony which fosters the accumulation of capital was hardly more to be found than in monarchies.[27] It is no surprise that Smith sought to minimise the role of the executive: 'Public prodigality and misconduct'[28] far more than private extravagance, is the cause of national impoverishment. Consider the case of England, which,

> as it has never been blessed with a very parsimonious government, so parsimony has at no time been the characteristical virtue of its inhabitants. It is the highest impertinence and presumption, therefore, in kings and ministers, to pretend to watch over the oeconomy of private people, and to restrain their expence, either by sumptuary laws, or by prohibiting the importation of foreign luxuries. They are themselves always, and without any exception, the greatest spendthrifts in the society. Let them look well after their own expence, and they may safely trust private people with theirs. If their own extravagance does not ruin the state, that of their subjects never will.[29]

The merchant sets an example of parsimony and industry; the court sets an example of idleness and imprudence,[30] of 'dissolution of manners'.[31] Clearly, 'the profusion of government must, undoubtedly, have retarded the natural progress of England towards wealth and improvement'.[32]

Qualitatively as well as quantitatively, the expenditure of the executive is reprehensible. The merchant has a propensity to employ productive labourers, and thereby to enrich the nation; while the court has a propensity to spend on luxury rather than to accumulate, and specifically to employ unproductive servants and retainers. The executive has no incentive to employ labourers whose work embodies itself in any 'permanent subject, or vendible commodity, which endures after that labour is past', [33] and instead employs actors, orators, musicians (or, for that matter, clergymen, politicians and lawyers) whose work 'perishes in the very instant of its production'.[34] Such services are not morally reprehensible, and may indeed be highly honourable; but if the goal is economic growth, then such orders are a brake on progress, since they live off the capital reproduced by productive labour and do not replace it. They produce nothing 'for which an equal quantity of service could afterwards be procured'.[35] The excessive employment of unproductive labourers could even arrest economic growth completely (although fortunately this had not been the case in Great Britain); and (since civil servants and politicians are no less unproductive than actors and domestic servants) the danger would be present in a government made up of shopkeepers as well as in an absolute monarchy. Waste of capital and governmental activity seem inextricably linked. In the interests of economic growth and social progress, both must be reduced.

3. The state, like any other large organisation, is dependent on a network of bureaucrats, and such a network cannot but prove inefficient and negligent: 'The agents of a prince regard the wealth of their master as inexhaustible; are careless at what price they buy; are careless at what price they sell.'[36] After all, they have no incentive to be prudent, since payment is not related to results. It is a fault of the institutional arrangements that the interest of the parts is in conflict with the interest of the whole. One of the reasons for reducing the number of functions in the state sector is this lack of motivation on the part of civil servants on fixed salaries: 'Public services are never better performed than when their reward comes only in consequence of their being performed, and is proportioned to the diligence employed in performing them.'[37]

The state is no more successful as a landlord than it is in trade. The crown lands 'do not at present afford the fourth part of the rent, which could probably be drawn from them if they were the property of private persons. If the crown lands were more extensive, it is probable they would be still worse managed.'[38] The problem once again is management, the 'abusive management' of 'idle and profligate bailiffs',[39] the 'negligent, expensive, and oppressive management' of 'factors and agents'.[40] The reward of the Crown's salaried agents is fixed and independent of the rent of the land, and civil servants have no incentive to maximise revenues in which they do not share. Moreover, bailiffs and agents are known not just for their 'neglect' but for their 'fraud' and 'depredation' as well.[41] Mismanagement wastes capital and means inefficient allocation of resources.[42] The problems of neglect, corruption and waste are, of course, common to all absentee landlords, but the Crown is particularly vulnerable because of the huge size of its estates: 'The servants of the most careless private persons are, perhaps, more under the eye of their master than those of the most careful prince.'[43] Economic growth would be encouraged by releasing the Crown lands from the public sector: 'When the Crown lands had become private property, they would, in the course of a few years, become well-improved and well-cultivated.'[44] Negligent bureaucrats would be replaced by industrious farmers, whose private interest is the same as the national interest.

Mismanagement and negligence are no less characteristic of salaried bureaucracies in the private sector, and for this among other reasons Smith did not see any future for the large joint-stock company. The South Sea Company, for example, had suffered from the burden of 'the loss occasioned by the negligence, profusion, and malversation of the servants of the company'.[45] The problem arose because the Company had an 'immense capital divided among an immense number of proprietors',[46] few of whom understood the Company's business, and all of whom were willing simply to 'receive contentedly such half yearly or yearly dividend, as the directors think proper to make to them'.[47] The shareholders did not exert the necessary 'vigilance and attention' that would have stopped the 'folly . . . profusion and depredations' of their 'factors and agents; some of whom are said to have acquired great fortunes even in one year'.[48] Managers were responsible for 'wasting', 'embezzling', and 'disorderly conduct'.[49] Smith, however, was never quick to reproach a man for acting in his own interest:

> The directors of such companies . . . being the managers rather of other people's money than of their own, it cannot well be expected, that they should watch over it with the same anxious vigilance with which the partners in a private copartnery frequently watch over their own. Like the stewards of a rich man, they are apt to consider attention to small matters as not for their master's honour, and very easily give themselves a dispensation from having it. Negligence and

profusion, therefore, must always prevail, more or less, in the management of the affairs of such a company.[50]

Inefficiency is thus not the fault of the managers but of their situation: 'It is the system of government, the situation in which they are placed, that I mean to censure; not the character of those who have acted in it. They acted as their situation naturally directed.'[51] It is not their fault that 'the real interest of the servants is by no means the same with that of the country'.[52] The private entrepreneur has an incentive to seek efficiency, since he has a share in the company's profits. The manager does not. Yer business is 'a species of warfare of which the operations are continually changing, and which can scarce ever be conducted successfully, without such an unremitting exertion of vigilance and attention, as cannot long be expected from the directors of a joint stock company'.[53] It is no surprise that 'joint stock companies for foreign trade have seldom been able to maintain the competition against private adventurers'.[54] Such commercial monopolies, artificially created by charter, have considerable diseconomies due to the indifference of managers. Large-scale private enterprise, like the national civil service, may be criticised on the grounds that it does not enlist men's self-interest, their desire to 'better their condition', on the side of progress. Business is too complicated to be left to bureaucrats, and hence the managerial revolution must be reversed: if efficiency is to be attained, large-scale corporate capitalism must give way to the small firm with its owner-operator.

A secondary objection that Smith makes to bureaucrats (public or private) is that, apart from being inefficient, they are oppressive and arbitrary. The American colonists were well governed since local parliaments kept a careful eye on civil servants,[55] and in Spain and Portugal the 'inferior officers' of the Crown dared not pervert the course of justice in the capital, the seat of the monarch. Such officers, however, in those parts of the Empire far removed from the king, and 'from whence the complaints of the people are less likely to reach him', could 'exercise their tyranny with much more safety'.[56] And in India, a country governed by the corporate civil service of the East India Company, the situation was worst of all: the managers were responsible to no one but themselves, and moreover had as little personal interest in good government for India as in maximum profit for their shareholders.[57]

Tax collectors too can be abusive, especially if taxes are not certain, allowing discretion to the individual civil servant: 'The uncertainty of taxation encourages the insolence and favours the corruption of an order of men who are naturally unpopular, even where they are neither insolent nor corrupt.'[58] Assessment of a man's total fortune, should it be made the basis for taxation, would give scope for further 'insolence of office',[59] since such an assessment 'must in most cases depend upon the good or bad humour of his assessors, and must, therefore, be altogether arbitrary and uncertain'.[60]

Similarly, educational inspectors can be arrogant. Their power is 'arbitrary and discretionary', and they thus have scope to use it 'ignorantly and capriciously'.[61] Possibly unacquainted with the subject taught, and unable to attend the course itself to form an impression of the teacher's merit, they may still choose 'to censure or deprive (the teacher) of his office wantonly, and without any just cause'.[62] Originality is penalised, and a teacher comes to acquire merit 'not by ability or diligence in his profession, but by obsequiousness to the will of his superiors'.[63]

4. Arbitrary laws which do not respect the natural momentum of phenomena will prove difficult or impossible to enforce. Thus import duties have been evaded by smuggling: 'Smugglers are now the principal importers, either of British goods into France, or of French goods into Great Britain.'[64] Draconian penalties are simply not effective: the price-differential 'presents such a temptation to smuggling, that all the rigour of the law cannot prevent it'.[65] The solution is not to repress men's urge to 'better their condition', but to enlist it on the side of the national interest. The smuggler is 'a person, who, though no doubt highly blameable for violating the laws of his country, is frequently incapable of violating those of natural justice, and would have been, in every respect, an excellent citizen, had not the laws of his country made that a crime which nature never meant to be so'.[66] By violating bad laws he helps to re-establish the natural order. The criminal, by applying Newtonian mechanics to the study of importing and exporting, turns out to be a man of God.

Again, when the government sought artificially to maintain the mint price of gold below the bullion price, there was a flourishing clandestine trade in melting down gold coin and re-selling it to the mint as bullion. The government could have destroyed this trade at a stroke by allowing the mint price to float and to find its true value, based on supply of and demand for gold. It was unable, however, to destroy the trade by even the most severe penalties. Evasion made a mockery of government policy: 'The operations of the mint were, upon this account, somewhat like the web of Penelope; the work that was done in the day was undone in the night.'[67]

As well as evasion, the government must, in formulating policy, face the danger of avoidance. Burdensome taxation and the insolence of assessors might cause a merchant or manufacturer to deprive the home country of industry and employment by sending his capital abroad: after all, 'the proprietor of stock is properly a citizen of the world'.[68]

5. As a materialist, Smith felt that reformers cannot simply impose ideal solutions without regard to the momentum inherent in the material conditions themselves: 'In the great chess-board of human society, every single piece has a principle of motion of its own, altogether different from that which the legislature might choose to impress upon it.'[69] Of course, these two principles might coincide, as when enlightened rulers try to make positive laws that correspond to the laws of nature; but what is more likely is that the sovereign will 'be exposed to innumerable delusions' in the execution of a duty 'for the proper performance of which no human wisdom or knowledge could ever be sufficient; the duty of superintending the industry of private people, and of directing it towards the employments most suitable to the interest of the society'.[70] The only way to ensure the 'natural division and distribution of labour in the society',[71] coupled with the 'natural and most advantageous distribution of stock',[72] is to let the market find its own level: 'Open the flood-gates, and there will presently be less water above, and more below, the dam-head, and it will soon come to a level in both places.'[73]

The rules for 'the game of human society' should not be imposed arbitrarily by the state but should arise naturally from the situation:

> All systems either of preference or of restraint, therefore, being thus completely taken away, the obvious and simple system of natural liberty establishes itself of its own accord. Every man, as long as he does not violate the laws of justice, is left perfectly free to pursue his own interest his own way, and to bring both his industry and capital into competition with those of any other man, or order of men.[74]

Men are better judges of the imperatives of their own 'local situations' than any legislator can ever be, and for this reason 'the law ought always to trust people with the care of their own interest'.[75]

Of course, the businessman is motivated solely by considerations of 'his own private profit'.[76] The interests of society 'never enter into his thoughts'.[77] Yet he is led by an 'invisible hand' to promote the ends of society, although this is seldom his intention: 'By pursuing his own interest he frequently promotes that of the society more effectually than when he really intends to promote it. I have never known much good done by those who affected to trade for the public good.'[78]

By pursuing their own interests in economic matters, therefore, men further the social interest. The 'automatic adjustment' and 'perfect liberty' of the market mechanism ensure that goods and factor services will be allocated with the greatest sensitivity to conditions of demand, and optimal allocation of resources maximises output per unit of input and leads to a growth in the 'riches and power'[79] of the nation.

Suppose, for example, that there is an increase in the demand for a commodity, causing its price to rise. Because the rate of profit is now higher in one trade than another, and 'without any intervention of law',[80] capital is redistributed and more of the commodity is produced. The profit motive induces businessmen automatically to alter a 'faulty distribution' of capital and 'to turn their stock towards the employments which in ordinary cases are most advantageous to the society'.[81] Moreover, new entry into a lucrative trade and the resultant competition among rival producers leads to 'new divisions of labour and new improvements of art, which might never otherwise have been thought of',[82] as businessmen struggle to undersell one another. An increase in demand is met with an increase in supply, windfall profits disappear, and prices fall again

Or consider the case of the speculator, who stores grain and gambles that its price will have risen by the time he comes to sell it: by spreading supplies more evenly over the period, he helps to moderate fluctuations in grain prices, and to prevent a dearth from turning into a famine.[83] It is very much in his interest to guess future price-movements correctly, since an error costs him his own profit and possibly his capital.[84] Here as elsewhere, 'the study of his own advantage naturally, or rather necessarily leads him to prefer that employment which is most advantageous to the society'.[85] Society benefits, but this outcome is totally unintended by the speculator.

Thus, competition and self-interest could, through the market mechanism, be depended upon to establish natural solutions to economic problems, and thus to foster the social interest. Adam Smith believed that 'the progressive state, while the society in advancing to the further acquisition . . . of riches . . . is in reality the cheerful and the hearty state to all the different orders of the society'.[86] He also believed that the best way for the government to encourage such continued economic growth was for it to pass responsibility in economic affairs to private enterprise. The 'liberal plan of equality, liberty and justice'[87] (also known as 'perfect justice, perfect liberty and perfect equality'[88]) is 'the very simple secret which most effectually secures the highest degree of prosperity to all the three classes'.[89]

Smith is postulating perfect competition. His model remains inland dealers in corn whose 'dispersed situation renders it altogether impossible for them to enter into any general combination',[90] and who are so numerous that no one dealer can affect the market-price of grain. He was aware of collusion and cartels[91] to raise prices or keep wages low, but felt these would break down in a dynamic economy, while the large firm would crumble into a large number of small firms as soon as 'preference and restraint' on the part of the government ended: it is important to remember that economic growth and the wealth of nations result from competition, not simply private enterprise. Smith may be criticised for neglecting the threat to 'perfect liberty' that could develop from economies of large-scale operation and the resultant market structure of oligopoly, but such neglect is consistent with his general approach of not looking too far into the future. He was concerned simply with the problem of replacing mercantilism by atomistic competition. If he considered the possibility at all that atomistic competition would one day be replaced by whatever represented the next stage in economic evolution, he probably dismissed such considerations as excessively speculative: no one knows what the future might bring and anyway, no recommendation can be valid in all circumstances. If the situation were to change, future generations of thinkers would have to make new recommendations.

Smith is also postulating rationality, which in economic affairs means the pursuit of utility and profit. Naturally, it is not unheard of for people to act without 'that complete comprehension of their own interest'[92] which the market mechanism presupposes for efficient allocation; or to suffer from 'attachment to old customs'.[93] But such men tend to be on the fringes of the capitalist system (for example, the landowner[94]), and are moreover increasingly becoming conscious of the new set of norms (as when landowners grant long leases to maximise rents, in order to maximise their commodity consumption;[95] or when they divert their great wealth to experimentation and to agricultural improvements such as clearing and drainage schemes[96]). A rational approach to land ownership would be stimulated by the abolition of the law of primogeniture and the practice of entailing, as this would both allow smaller plots of land to be sold and encourage the development of a new class of landowner interested in treating the land as he would any other investment.

Other groups too which had hitherto been leading a sheltered existence would have to be put in a situation such as to stimulate their rationality. For example, since 'it is the interest of every man to live as much at his ease as he can',[97] the spur of 'rivalship'[98] might be necessary for efficiency even in university teaching. And, most important, the revolution in management following the abandonment of mercantilist restriction would replace sleepy managers by wide-awake capitalist owner-operators, by men who are particularly eager to discover those employments of labour and capital which are most profitable to themselves (and incidentally too most advantageous to society as a whole).

III. The Scope for Intervention

The state was not to wither away, but its influence was to be reduced. Smith recommended that in future the state should limit itself to the performance of three clearly defined and relatively modest functions: defence, the enforcement of justice, and the provision of certain public works.[1]

1. Opulence makes a country more liable to aggression from its jealous neighbours. It also makes a country better able to wage war, since wars are costly, particularly if fought abroad.[2] Opulence thus is necessary for defence, while defence (by offering protection from violence and invasion) encourages industry and trade and is the precondition for opulence. Smith goes further and states categorically: 'Defence . . . is of much more importance than opulence.'[3] This is why, despite his otherwise unrelenting opposition to mercantilism, he favours the Navigation Acts and describes them as 'perhaps, the wisest of all the commercial regulations of England'.[4] After all, merchant shipping is a nursery for seamen who in wartime can be enlisted in the Navy, and hence it must be protected. Similarly, bounties are justifiable to encourage the production at home of strategic commodities (such as sail-cloth or gunpowder) which would otherwise have been imported, despite the obvious abuse that some industries are being taxed while others are subsidised.[5]

A wealthy country will need a full-time professional standing army. In the process of industrialisation, men become less warlike, martial virtues decay, and 'the natural habits of the people render them altogether incapable of defending themselves'.[6] If they are to be defended, the state will have to defend them through a mercenary army, precisely because the division of labour makes industrial workers more mercenary in their own way, less willing to sacrifice paid labour for patriotic service. Military exercises, vital to the martial prowess of a nation, are abandoned for lack of interest or time (shepherds, hunters and farmers have much more leisure than the factory operative[7]). The habit of obedience to authority, so great in a nation of shepherds or farmers, decays as dependence becomes impersonal (through the market mechanism) and authority becomes diffuse. In any case, the art of war requires specialisation as much as any other trade, and becomes a profession in its own right.[8] A militia is no substitute for a standing army because of the fact that men's employments largely determine their characters: 'In a militia, the character of the labourer, artificer, or tradesman, predominates over that of the soldier: in a standing army, that of the soldier predominates over every other character.'[9]

The citizens of a wealthy country are less able to defend themselves but more able to pay others to defend them. Whereas 'our ancestors were brave and warlike', and 'their minds were not enervated by cultivating arts and commerce',[10] the 'commercial spirit' makes men 'effeminate and dastardly', preoccupied with their individual interests and indifferent to the fate of the group. No people could have been less emotionally involved in the fate of their country than the prosperous Dutch: 'In the beginning of this century the standing army of the Dutch was beat in the field, and the rest of the inhabitants, instead of rising in arms to defend themselves, formed a design of deserting their country, and settling in the East Indies.'[11] A standing army may thus not be sufficient for the defence of an opulent country, but it is certainly necessary.

2. The state should also attempt to prevent aggression at home through 'an exact administration of justice'.[12] Smith defines justice negatively as the abstention from harming others rather than positively as an obligation to promote their happiness, since a society can exist without benevolence but not if there is no security of person and property. Such security is the precondition for economic activity, and indeed is 'alone sufficient to make any country flourish.'[13]

The danger of fraud is a disincentive to bear the risks of economic activity; and since fraud can be public as well as private (for example, the sovereign's unjust debasement of the coinage[14]), there must be a separation of the judiciary from the executive to ensure the impartiality and independence of the courts. All groups in society are thus to be equal before the law. In Britain, the 'equal and impartial administration of justice . . . renders the rights of the meanest British subject respectable to the greatest'.[15] Contracts are enforceable, a man is sure of having 'the fruits of his own industry', and self-love is set free to work for economic growth.

3. The state should also undertake certain public works (for example, the construction and maintenance of roads, bridges, canals and harbours) provided that it can be shown in each case that the project is 'in the highest degree advantageous to a great society', but that 'the profit could never repay the expence to any individual or small number of individuals'.[16]

In general, an individual should pay for an undertaking in proportion to the benefit he derives or expects to derive from it. If, however,
social benefits exceed private benefits, then the government should bear
a part of the cost on behalf of society. For example: 'The expence of
the institutions for education and religious instruction is . . . no doubt,
beneficial to the whole society, and may, therefore, without injustice,
be defrayed by the general contribution of the whole society.'[17] This
is particularly important as education, which holds a very important
place in Smith's social welfare function, might not be demanded at all
if the consumer had to bear the whole expense. The division of labour
makes the masses 'stupid and ignorant' and indifferent to education.
The philosopher, however, is free to disagree with the verdict of the
market mechanism and to warn that without education 'all the nobler
parts of the human character may be, in a great measure, obliterated
and extinguished in the great body of the people'.[18] Smith seems to be
speaking on behalf of the General Will, and to be pleading for the state
to provide a service which society desires even if each individual in it
does not.

Of course, government aid to education may lead to substantial dis-
tortions in the market for human capital. A considerable number of
people had been trained as teachers at public expense, and as a result
the pay of teachers was abnormally low compared with that of other
professionals and with what it otherwise would have been. The philosopher, however, does not regret this interference with the market: 'The
cheapness of literary education is surely an advantage which greatly
over-balances this trifling inconveniency.'[19] Everyone knows that knowledge is bliss, even if they are stupid enough not to vote for education
in the market-place.

The state should contribute to the costs of education (because of
the spill-over benefit to society as a whole, and because education
would otherwise probably be neglected); but it should not cover the
full cost. Moreover, there should be competition among schoolmasters:
they would become careless if their earnings were not in some way
related to their effort, as estimated by their customers.[20] Competition
in the education industry is thus more important than whether or not it
is nationalised.

In general, the charge levied on the user of a public utility should be
'exactly in proportion to his gain'.[21] State enterprise should not mean a
hidden subsidy, and taxation should be as local as the benefit expected:
'It is unjust that the whole society should contribute towards an
expence of which the benefit is confined to a part of the society.'[22]
User-charges are ideal since the tax is raised from the persons using the

facilities provided, and from no others: 'It seems impossible to imagine a more equitable method of raising a tax.'[23] Similarly, local public utilities such as street-lighting should be paid for out of local rates, not out of national revenues.[24] The equation of costs and benefits is also the basis of his first maxim of taxation: 'The expence of government to the individuals of a great nation, is like the expence of management to the joint tenants of a great estate, who are all obliged to contribute in proportion to their respective interests in the estate.'[25]

State enterprise has its disadvantages. For one thing, the state may come under pressure from vested interests to indulge in wasteful and uneconomic schemes that a commercially-minded entrepreneur would never have considered. A highway might be constructed in a deserted area where there is no traffic 'merely because it happens to lead to the country villa of the intendant of the province, or to that of some great lord to whom the intendant finds it convenient to make his court'.[26] Moreover, civil servants have nothing personally to gain from keeping a canal or road in good repair and may allow it to go to ruin. But proper upkeep is a problem in the private sector as well: so long as a road is usable, so long as tolls are being collected, the proprietors might feel their duty is done and restrict their outlay, no matter how neglected the condition of the road. Canals can safely be left to private enterprise since if their maintenance is neglected, they become impassable and cease to be productive of tolls for their operators. Roads, however, may have to be publicly operated.[27] Furthermore, since private enterprise is motivated by the desire for utilitarian results rather than by the desire to conform to a more absolute normative standard of workmanship, it will be particularly negligent where it has a natural monopoly. After all, the consumer has no choice but to use the services of the monopolist: 'At many turnpikes, it has been said, the money levied is more than double of what is necessary for executing, in the completest manner, the work which is often executed in a very slovenly manner, and sometimes not executed at all.'[28]

Thus, despite his criticism of state action and his admiration of the market mechanism, Smith nonetheless saw a role for state enterprise, where social benefits exceeded private benefits or where private enterprise had insufficient incentive satisfactorily to perform a particular function.

Similarly, despite his apparent advocacy of laissez-faire, it is striking how far Smith was prepared to go in advocating state regulation of the economic life of the nation.[29] Thus, although it is unquestionably a violation of a banker's natural liberty for the state to regulate banking, he believed that such controls are in the greater interest of society as a whole:

> Those exertions of the natural liberty of a few individuals, which
> might endanger the security of the whole society, are, and ought to
> be, restrained by the laws of all governments; of the most free, as
> well as of the most despotical. The obligation of building party walls,
> in order to prevent the communication of fire, is a violation of
> natural liberty, exactly of the same kind with the regulations of the
> banking trade which are here proposed.[30]

Excess currency would never have been issued if banks had understood
their own interest properly,[31] but they had not, and financial instability
was the result.

Again, Smith supported the retention of the usury laws, hoping to
use government policy to foster growth by keeping money out of the
hands of 'prodigals and projectors'.[32] Since only spendthrifts and
speculators could afford to pay high rates of interest, there should be
a ceiling beyond which those rates should not be allowed to rise.
Smith's liberalism was clearly more guarded than Bentham's.

Elsewhere, Smith advocates the use of the tax system to tailor
society. Thus rents in kind should be taxed more heavily than money
rents to wean landlords from 'a practice which is hurtful to the whole
community;[33] and for the same reason, landlords who specify a particular succession of crops to their tenants should also be taxed at a discriminatory rate.[34] On the other hand, an improving landlord who
farms part of his own land (thereby putting some of his wealth to
productive use as capital) should get tax relief.[35] The state should not
be afraid to make indirect taxation progressive, since the rich squander
considerable money on luxury and vanity, while the poorer classes 'find
it difficult to get food'.[36] Thus a tax on house-rents, falling as it would
most heavily on the rich, is quite acceptable.[37] And highway tolls
ought to be levied at a higher rate on luxury carriages than on freight
waggons (which, after all, carry the food of the poor): 'When the toll
upon carriages of luxury, upon coaches, post-chaises, etc. is made
somewhat higher in proportion to their weight, than upon carriages of
necessary use, such as carts, waggons, etc. the indolence and vanity of
the rich is made to contribute in a very easy manner to the relief of the
poor.'[38] This reminds us that, although Smith felt the government
should work *through* the market mechanism, he was not adverse to
interfering with the variables contained in supply and demand functions.
Indeed, he felt the state had a positive duty to do so.

Smith favoured the use of a state-run Post Office as a source of revenue for the government. It is easy to operate, and returns are certain and immediate. There is minimum opportunity for carelessness on the part of civil servants and minimum risk.[39] He was certainly not opposed to such state activities. Abroad they had been very successful. The government of Berne does a flourishing trade in making loans to other states, while in Hamburg (admittedly 'a small republic, where the people have entire confidence in their magistrates'[40]) it runs a public pawnshop, wine-cellar, apothecary and bank.[41] Similar banks are operated by the governments of Pennsylvania, Venice and Amsterdam, and perhaps one day even the British Government would be efficient and honest enough to do so as well. Until that day comes, however, business dealings should be left to businessmen:

> The orderly, vigilant, and parsimonious administration of such aristocracies as those of Venice and Amsterdam, is extremly proper, it appears from experience, for the management of a mercantile project of this kind. But whether such a government as that of England; which, whatever may be its virtues, has never been famous for good oeconomy; which, in time of peace has generally conducted itself with the slothful and negligent profusion that is perhaps natural to monarchies; and in time of war has constantly acted with all the thoughtless extravagance that democracies are apt to fall into; could be safely trusted with the management of such a project, must at least be a good deal more doubtful.[42]

NOTES

CHAPTER 1 INTRODUCTION

1. J. S. Mill, *Essays on Some Unsettled Questions of Political Economy* (London: John W. Parker, 1844), p. 120.
2. L. Robbins, *An Essay on the Nature and Significance of Economic Science* (London: Macmillan, 1952), p. 16.
3. A. Marshall, *Principles of Economics*, 8th ed. (London: Macmillan, 1947), p. 1. Even Robbins seems to feel that in practice the economist should apply his peculiar state of mind mainly to material commodities and services. Thus in his discussion of the Reformation he points out the features of interest to the economist as 'chiefly changes in the distribution of property, changes in the channels of trade, changes in the demand for fish, changes in the supply of indulgences, changes in the incidence of taxes' (Robbins, *op. cit.*, p. 40). And the invention of the steam-engine is economically significant because 'it affected the supply of and the demand for certain products and certain factors of production, because it affected the price and income structures of

the communities where it was adopted' (*ibid.*, p. 41).

4. R.A. Nisbet, *The Sociological Tradition* (London: Heinemann, 1967), p. vii.

5. Article in the *Revue Philosophique* (1886), reprinted in A. Giddens (ed. and trans.), *Emile Durkheim: Selected Writings* (Cambridge: the University Press, 1972), pp. 56-7.

6. T. Parsons, *The Structure of Social Action* (New York: The Free Press, 1968), pp. 264-8, 607-8.

7. See, for example, T. Parsons and N. Smelser, *Economy and Society: A Study in the Integration of Economic and Social Theory* (London: Routledge and Kegan Paul Ltd, 1956).

8. J.W. Burrow, *Evolution and Society* (Cambridge: the University Press, 1970), pp. xxiii, xxii.

9. N. Hampson, *The Enlightenment* (Harmondsworth: Penguin Books, 1968), p. 11.

10. J.K. Galbraith, 'Adam Smith: Then and Now', unpublished paper read at the Adam Smith Commemorative Symposium, Kirkcaldy, on 6 June 1973.

11. The view of the Rev. Dr R. Selby Wright in his booklet 'Our Club and Panmure House', written to commemorate the conversion of Panmure House, Edinburgh, where Adam Smith died in 1790, into a Youth Club on 6 October 1957.

12. The word 'historicism' is here being used, following Troeltsch and Mannheim, to refer to the recognition that all actions, values and ideas are subject to historical change, and must be seen not as permanent and fixed but as involved in a developmental process.

13. J.K. Galbraith, *American Capitalism* (Harmondsworth: Penguin Books, 1967), p. 93.

14. L. Kolakowski, *Positivist Philosophy* (Harmondsworth: Penguin Books, 1972), p. 244.

15. C. Wright Mills, *The Sociological Imagination* (Harmondsworth: Penguin Books, 1970), p. 193.

16. Smith wrote on many subjects; what is striking is his consistency of outlook. In this book we will treat his work as an organic whole; and assume, except where expressly indicated otherwise, that there is no internal contradiction within that whole.

17. G. Lukács, *History and Class Consciousness*, trans. by R. Livingstone (London: Merlin Press, 1971), p. 225.

18. K. Marx, 'Economic Studies from Marx's Notebooks' (1844-5), quoted in T.B. Bottomore and M. Rubel (eds.), *Karl Marx: Selected Writings in Sociology and Social Philosophy* (Harmondsworth: Penguin Books, 1961), p. 179.

19. E.J. Mishan, *The Costs of Economic Growth* (Harmondsworth: Penguin Books, 1969), p. 32.

20. A. Small, *Adam Smith and Modern Sociology* (Chicago: University of Chicago Press, 1907), p. 4.

CHAPTER 2 METHODOLOGY

Introduction

1. *MS*, p. 265.

2. *MS*, p. 110.

I. Epistemology

1. J. Locke, *An Essay Concerning Human Understanding* (1690) (Oxford: Clarendon Press, 1894), vol. I, p. 121.

2. *ibid.*, p. 141.

3. D. Hume, *An Enquiry Concerning Human Understanding* (1748) (Oxford: Clarendon Press, 1966), p. 62.
4. *WN*, II, p. 311.
5. Hume, *op. cit.*, p. 165.
6. *ibid.*, p. 110.
7. 'ES', p. 185.
8. 'ES', pp. 191-2.
9. Locke, *op.cit.*, p. 173.
10. *ibid.*, p. 175.
11. *id.*
12. 'ES', p. 192.
13. 'ES', p. 193.
14. 'ES', p. 193.
15. Hume, *op. cit.*, p. 78.
16. *MS*, pp. 248, 500; 'Considerations', p. 231.
17. 'Considerations', pp. 231, 233; 'ALM', p. 130.
18. *MS*, p. 3.
19. 'HAL', pp. 125-6; 'ES', p. 208.
20. *MS*, pp. 3, 5.
21. *MS*, p. 18.
22. *LRBL*, p. 66.
23. *LRBL*, p. 63.
24. *LRBL*, p. 63.
25. *MS*, p. 234.
26. 'ES', pp. 205-6.
27. 'ES', p. 218.
28. *MS*, pp. 191-2.
29. 'ES', p. 208.
30. 'ALM', p. 124.
31. 'ALM', p. 123.
32. 'ALM', p. 128.
33. 'ALM', p. 123.
34. 'HA', p. 57.
35. 'HA', p. 58.
36. 'HA', p. 30.
37. 'HA', p. 33.
38. 'HA', p. 32.
39. 'HA', p. 33.
40. 'HA', p. 32.
41. 'HA', p. 30.
42. 'HA', pp. 37-8.
43. 'HA', p. 38.
44. 'HA', p. 61.
45. *LRBL*, p. 39.
46. *LRBL*, p. 100.
47. 'HA', p. 71. See also p. 53.
48. *LRBL*, p. 100.
49. *LRBL*, p. 80. See also *WN*, II, pp. 290-1. But occasionally Smith does seem to lose patience with people who insist on admiring the useless and thus wasting the scientists' time on trivia. Speaking of the distant stars, for example, he says: 'The most precise knowledge of the relative situation of such objects could be of no other use to us than to satisfy the most unnecessary curiosity.' ('ES', p. 204.)
50. 'HA', p. 46.
51. 'HA', p. 45.

52. 'HA', p. 50.
53. 'HA', pp. 42, 67, 81-2; *LRBL*, p. 133.
54. *LJ*, pp. 167-8; *WN*, I, pp. 13-4.
55. *WN*, I, p. 14.
56. 'HA', p. 44.
57. 'HA', p. 68.
58. 'HA', p. 70.
59. 'HA', p. 107; see also p. 99.
60. 'HA', p. 106.
61. 'Letter', p. 18.
62. *MS*, p. 459; see also *LRBL*, p. 140.
63. 'HA', p. 65.
64. 'ES', p. 190.
65. *WN*, II, p. 293.
66. 'ALM', p. 129.
67. 'ALM', p. 126.
68. 'ALM', p. 130.
69. *WN*, II, p. 293.
70. 'ES', p. 189.
71. 'ES', pp. 189-90.
72. *MS*, p. 428; see also pp. 401-2.
73. 'HA', p. 67; see also p. 65.
74. 'HA', p. 83.
75. 'HA', p. 76.
76. J.K. Galbraith, *The Affluent Society*, 2nd edn (Harmondsworth: Penguin Books, 1970), p. 32.
77. *WN*, I, p. 17.
78. *LJ*, p. 171.
79. *LJ*, p. 169.
80. *MS*, p. 110
81. *MS*, pp. 74-6, 84.
82. *MS*, p. 230.
83. *WN*, I, p. 371.
84. *MS*, pp. 446 f. See also pp. 27-8.
85. *LJ*, p. 169.
86. *WN*, I, p. 478. See also II, p. 208.
87. *MS*, p. 110.
88. *WN*, I, pp. 362-3.
89. *MS*, p. 263.
90. *MS*, p. 170.
91. *MS*, p. 470.
92. *MS*, p. 224.
93. *WN*, II, p. 471.
94. *WN*, II, p. 42. See also I, p. 87.
95. *LJ*, p. 224.
96. *WN*, I, p. 492.
97. *WN*, II, p. 405.
98. *WN*, I, pp. 179-80.
99. *WN*, I, p. 94.
100. *WN*, I, pp. 8-9.
101. *MS*, p. 224.
102. *MS*, p. 501.
103. *MS*, p. 109. Italics mine.
104. *LRBL*, p. 37.
105. *MS*, p. 348.

II. Scientific Method

1. D. Stewart, 'Account of the Life and Writings of Adam Smith, LL.D.' (1793), printed as an Introduction to A. Smith, *Essays on Philosophical Subjects* (London: T. Cadell Jun. and W. Davies and W. Creech, 1795), pp. lxxxi-ii.
2. Quoted in W.C. Lehmann, *John Millar of Glasgow 1735-1801* (Cambridge: the University Press, 1960), p. 363f.
3. 'HA', p. 45.
4. 'ALM', p. 124.
5. *WN*, II, p. 292.
6. *MS*, p. 191.
7. 'HA', p. 46; *LJ*, p. 168.
8. 'HA', pp. 108-9.
9. M. Weber, *The Theory of Social and Economic Organization,* ed. T. Parsons (New York: The Free Press, 1964), p. 88.
10. 'HA', pp. 74-5.
11. 'HAP', p. 110.
12. 'HA', p. 36.
13. 'Considerations', p. 227.
14. *WN*, II, p. 291. See also *MS*, p. 459
15. 'HA', pp. 39-40. See also pp. 64, 93-4.
16. For example, *MS*, p. 126.
17. *MS*, p. 463.
18. *MS*, p. 265.
19. *MS*, p. 126. See also p. 259.
20. See P. Gay, *The Enlightenment: An Interpretation* (London: Weidenfeld and Nicholson, 1970), vol. II, pp. 12-17. See also *WN*, II, p. 194.
21. See J.D.Y. Peel, *Herbert Spencer: The Evolution of a Sociologist* (London: Heinemann, 1971), ch. 7.
22. 'HA', p. 108. Italics mine.
23. 'HA', p. 66. Italics mine. Elsewhere he says: 'To render, therefore, this lower part of the great theatre of nature a coherent spectacle to the imagination, *it became necessary to suppose . . .*' ('HAP', p. 110. Italics mine.) See also 'HA', p. 39.
24. 'HA', p. 108. See also p. 99.
25. 'HA', p. 67.
26. 'HA', p. 66.
27. 'HA', pp. 58-9.
28. A. Pope, 'Epitaph Intended for Sir Isaac Newton', in *Poetical Works,* ed. H. Davis (London: Oxford University Press, 1966), p. 651.
29. 'HA', p. 100. See also 'Considerations', pp. 226-7.
30. 'HA', p. 108.
31. 'HA', p. 107.
32. 'HA', p. 106.
33. *WN*, I, p. 65. See also pp. 157, 277, 344; II, pp. 37, 48, 90, 169, 208.
34. *WN*, I, p. 402. See also p. 405
35. *WN*, II, p. 208.
36. *MS*, p. 438.
37. 'A Letter', p. 18.
38. J.A. Schumpeter, *History of Economic Analysis* (London: George Allen and Unwin Ltd, 1954), p. 185.
39. 'HA', pp. 45-6.
40. 'HA', p. 61.
41. 'HA', p. 46.
42. 'HAP', pp. 110-11.

43. 'HA', p. 108.
44. 'HA', p. 108. See also p. 88.
45. 'HA', pp. 73-4.
46. 'HA', p. 85.
47. 'HA', p. 75. See also p. 83.
48. 'HA', p. 46.
49. 'HA', p. 88.
50. 'HA', p. 91.
51. 'HA', p. 91.
52. 'HA', p. 91.
53. *MS*, p. 43.
54. 'HA', p. 56.
55. *MS*, p. 272.
56. 'HA', p. 87.
57. 'HA', p. 87.
58. 'HA', p. 88.

III. Aesthetics

1. *LRBL*, p. 140. See 'IA', p. 136.
2. *LRBL*, p. 116.
3. *LRBL*, p. 101.
4. *LRBL*, p. 118.
5. *LRBL*, p. 119.
6. Stewart, *op. cit.*, p. lix.
7. *WN*, II, p. 291. See also 'HA', pp. 62, 64.
8. *LJ*, p. 159.
9. 'Considerations', p. 234.
10. 'Considerations', p. 234.
11. 'IA', p. 146.
12. 'IA', p. 168.
13. 'IA', p. 155. See also *MS*, p. 49; 'OES', pp. 222-3. In passages such as these, it is difficult to avoid the suspicion that Smith was indulging in wishful thinking. They are, however, perfectly consistent with his general view that it is easier to sympathise with 'the affections which tend to unite men in society' (such as kindness) than with those (such as hatred) which 'drive men from one another'. *MS*, p. 357.
14. *LRBL*, pp. 66-7. See also 'IA', p. 150.
15. *LRBL*, p. 68.
16. *LRBL*, p. 73. See also pp. 6, 27.
17. *LRBL*, p. 117. A tragi-comedy is 'a monstrous production': rather than the parts uniting to form a unique whole, the tragic elements contradict the comic leaving the audience confused and unsatisfied.
18. Quoted in W.R. Scott, *Francis Hutcheson* (Cambridge: the University Press, 1900), p. 187.
19. *LRBL*, p. 29.
20. *LRBL*, p. 51. See also p. 15.
21. *LRBL*, p. 36.
22. *LRBL*, p. 6.
23. *LRBL*, p. 6.
24. *LRBL*, p. 30.
25. *LRBL*, p. 11, 'HA', p. 66.
26. *LRBL*, p. 5.
27. 'IA', p. 135. See also pp. 144, 146.
28. 'IA', p. 139.
29. *LRBL*, p. 38

30. *LJ*, p. 159.
31. *MS*, p. 287.
32. *MS*, p. 288. See also p. 163.
33. *MS*, p. 289.
34. *LRBL*, p. 62.
35. *MS*, p. 290.
36. *LRBL*, p. 1.
37. *MS*, p. 258.
38. *MS*, p. 463-4.
39. *MS*, pp. 265-6. See also p. 267.
40. *MS*, p. 257.
41. *MS*, p. 480.
42. Smith's Deism will be discussed in Chapter 3. Section II.
43. *MS*, p. 20.
44. *MS*, p. 46.
45. *MS*, p. 47.
46. *LRBL*, p. 40.
47. *LRBL*, pp. 40-1.
48. *MS*, p. 284.
49. *MS*, p. 271.
50. *MS*, p. 464.
51. *MS*, p. 262.
52. *LRBL*, p. 120. See also *MS*, p. 332.
53. *MS*, p. 284.
54. *MS*, p. 284.
55. *MS*, p. 282.
56. H. Bergson, *Le Rire,* in *Oeuvres* (Paris: Presses Universitaires de France, 1970), pp. 388-9.
57. *MS*, p. 281. Italics mine.
58. *LRBL*, pp. 22-3.
59. *LRBL*, p. 55.
60. *MS*, p. 352.
61. *WN*, II, p. 183.
62. *LRBL*, p. 2.
63. 'AEIV', p. 181.
64. *MS*, p. 285.
65. *LJ*, p. 248.
66. *LRBL*, pp. 13, 14
67. *LRBL*, p. 23.
68. *LRBL*, pp. 36-7.
69. *LRBL*, p. 52.
70. *LRBL*, p. 52. See also pp. 44, 49.
71. *LRBL*, p. 54.
72. *LRBL*, p. 55.
73. *LRBL*, p. 101.
74. *LRBL*, p. 107.
75. J.–P. Sartre, *Qu'est-ce que la littérature?* (Paris: Gallimard, 1948), p. 96.
76. *LRBL*, p. 37.
77. *LRBL*, p. 38.
78. *LRBL*, p. 32.
79. *LRBL*, p. 110.
80. *LRBL*, p. 108.
81. J.–P. Sartre, *op. cit.*, p. 122.
82. *ibid.*, p. 116.
83. *LRBL*, p. 144.

84. *LRBL*, p. 152.
85. *LRBL*, p. 155.

IV. Science and Social Science

1. Hume, *op. cit.*, p. 9.
2. D. Hume, *A Treatise of Human Nature* (1739-40), ed. E.C. Mossner
   (Harmondsworth: Penguin Books, 1969), p. 42.
3. 'HA', p. 47.
4. 'HAP', p. 117.
5. 'HA', p. 49.
6. 'HA', p. 51.
7. 'HA', pp. 49-50. See also p. 67.
8. *LRBL*, p. 132.
9. *LRBL*, p. 132.
10. D. Hume, 'Of Refinement in the Arts', in *Political Discourses* (1752),
    reprinted in E. Rotwein (ed.), *David Hume: Writings on Economics* (London:
    Nelson, 1955), p. 23.
11. *ibid.*, p. 22.
12. 'HA', p. 43. See also p. 44.
13. Hume, *Enquiry*, p. 45.
14. 'HA', p. 42.
15. *MS*, p. 365. See also pp. 30, 289.
16. *MS*, p. 364.
17. *MS*, p. 281.
18. 'IA', p. 136. See also pp. 139, 143.
19. *MS*, p. 395.
20. 'IA', p. 162.
21. The important relationship between Hegel and English political economy is
    examined in G. Lukács, *Der Junge Hegel: Ueber die Beziehungen von
    Dialektik und Oekonomie* (Zurich: Europa Verlag, 1948).
22. *LRBL*, p. 132. See also *LJ*, p. 160.
23. *WN*, II, p. 318. Smith clearly did not regard the theatre as 'the Devil's Home',
    a 'pavilion of Satan', a 'Temple of Belial', by the time he came to write *The
    Wealth of Nations*. A decade earlier, however, he had participated on a
    University committee to prevent the establishment of a playhouse in
    Glasgow. See W.R. Scott, *Adam Smith as Student and Professor*, (Glasgow:
    University of Glasgow Press, 1937), pp. 164-5.
24. *LRBL*, p. 86.
25. *LRBL*, p. 102. See also p. 85.
26. *LRBL*, p. 43.
27. *LRBL*, p. 132.
28. *WN*, II, p. 296.
29. *WN*, II, p. 296.
30. E. Durkheim, *Moral Education*, trans. E.K. Wilson and H. Schnurer (New
    York: The Free Press, 1961), p. 273.

CHAPTER 3. CONDUCT AND CHARACTER

Introduction

1. *LRBL*, p. 53. See also *MS*, pp. 463, 468.
2. *MS*, p. 127. See also *MS*, pp. 436-7.
3. *MS*, p. 127.
4. Man does not take refuge in society from some pre-existent state of nature. To
   begin with, there is nowadays no empirical basis for observation: 'It in
   reality serves no purpose to treat of the laws which would take place in a

state of nature . . . as there is no such state existing.' (LJ, p. 2.) Moreover, even if such a state did once exist, there is no reason to think men tried to escape from it by concluding a social contract: there is no historical evidence for such a contract, no discussion of it outside Britain although all countries have governments, no awareness of its existence among the masses who are nonetheless supposed to be bound by it, and no way to contract out save by emigration. In any case, the future ought not to be bound by an agreement made so long in the past. (LJ, pp. 11-12.) Here Smith's views resemble those expressed in Hume's essay 'Of the Original Contract'.

5. MS, p. 124.
6. MS, p. 127.
7. MS, p. 480.
8. MS, p. 56. See also p. 357.
9. MS, p. 52.
10. MS, p. 363.
11. MS, p. 204.
12. MS, p. 21. See also pp. 17, 100, 105, 134, 143.
13. MS, p. 184.
14. MS, p. 20.
15. MS, p. 16. See also p. 223.
16. MS, pp. 7-9.
17. E. Durkheim, The Division of Labor in Society, trans. G. Simpson (London: Collier-Macmillan Ltd., 1964), p. 32. See also The Rules of Sociological Method, trans. S.A. Solvay and J.H. Mueller (London: Collier-Macmillan Ltd, 1964), p. 23.
18. Durkheim, op. cit., p. 399.
19. For example, Durkheim, Moral Education, p. 85.
20. ibid., ch. 7.
21. ibid., p. 47.
22. ibid., p. 87.
23. ibid., p. 68.
24. ibid., p. 90.
25. ibid., p. 59.
26. Durkheim, Sociological Method, p. 6. See also p. 104.
27. MS, p. 83.
28. MS, pp. 27-8.
29. MS, p. 230.
30. MS, p. 231.
31. Quoted in L. Schneider (ed.), The Scottish Moralists on Human Nature and Society (Chicago: University of Chicago Press, 1967), p. 103. Lord Kames, another member of the Scottish Enlightenment (and an elder of the Church of Scotland) took a similar view. For example: 'The finger of God may be clearly traced in the provisions made for animal food for man.' Even light 'is intended by our Maker for action, and darkness for rest'. Quoted in W.C. Lehmann, Henry Home, Lord Kames, and the Scottish Enlightenment (The Hague: Martinus Nijhoff, 1971), p. 175.
32. Hampson, op. cit., p. 127. Even the great Newton himself (a devoutly religious man who attempted to discover from the Bible the exact plan of Solomon's Temple as a guide to the topography of Heaven, and believed that Moses had been aware of the principle of gravity) was convinced that there were defects in the fabric of the universe such as necessitated the direct and continuous intervention of God himself in order to regulate nature.
33. MS, pp. 153-4.
34. WN, II, p. 302.
35. P. Berger, Invitation to Sociology (Harmondsworth: Penguin Books, 1963), p. 128.

36. Smith himself, however, exercised the intellectual's prerogative to be a massive non-conformist and solved his own problem of freedom by withdrawal and detachment, preferring where possible to observe reality from the side-lines (for example, from the academic anonymity of a Chair in Glasgow, or from the isolation of Kirkcaldy).

37. *WN*, II, p. 188.

I. Conduct

1. *MS*, p. 23.
2. *MS*, p. 357.
3. *MS*, p. 4.
4. *MS*, p. 8.
5. *MS*, p. 466.
6. *MS*, p. 7.
7. *MS*, p. 23. See also pp. 61, 66.
8. *LRBL*, p. 51.
9. *MS*, p. 27. See also pp. 31, 58.
10. *MS*, p. 81. In his belief that morality is only possible in a society, that there can be no realisation of the 'good' independent of the well-being of the group, that man is a social animal who can only fulfil himself by participating in the life of the community, Smith clearly in many respects resembles Aristotle; and it is therefore no surprise that the 'middle course' should have been of such importance to both philosophers.
11. *MS*, p. 166. See also pp. 273-5.
12. *MS*, p. 429. See also pp. 16, 108, 222-3, 456.
13. *MS*, p. 123. See also pp. 171, 234.
14. *MS*, p. 207.
15. *MS*, p. 194.
16. *MS*, p. 167.
17. *MS*, p. 177.
18. *MS*, pp. 121-2. See also p. 173.
19. *MS*, p. 171. See also p. 194.
20. *MS*, p. 165.
21. *MS*, p. 347.
22. *MS*, p. 195.
23. *MS*, p. 346.
24. *MS*, p. 276. See also pp. 10, 53, 81, 351, 420, 452-6.
25. *MS*, p. 469. See also p. 248.
26. *MS*, pp. 162. See also pp. 301, 500.
27. A. Ferguson, *Principles of Moral and Political Science* (Edinburgh: A Strahan and T. Cadell and W. Creech, 1792), vol. II, p. 126.
28. *MS*, pp. 224-5.
29. *MS*, p. 162.
30. *MS*, p. 333. See also pp. 33, 110.
31. *MS*, p. 164. The relationship between the real and the impartial spectator in Smith's ethical theory is similar to his distinction, in discussing the theory of value, between the popular verdict on the value of a commodity (the market price) and the objective, stable standard of measurement (labour-embodied). Smith thus sought, in both his ethics and in his economics, to steer a middle course between total relativism and absolute, immutable, eternal standards. His approach seems to postulate a sort of moving absolute, unique for the moment but still delimited by time and place.
32. *MS*, p. 179.
33. *MS*, p. 180.
34. *MS*, p. 214. See also pp. 142, 177-8.

35. *MS*, p. 173. See also p. 52.
36. *MS*, p. 363.
37. *MS*, p. 460.
38. *MS*, p. 192.
39. *MS*, p. 460.
40. *MS*, p. 174.
41. *MS*, p. 172.
42. *MS*, p. 291.
43. *MS*, p. 359.
44. *WN*, II, p. 317.
45. *WN*, II, p. 303. See also I, p. 277.
46. *WN*, II, p. 188.
47. *MS*, p. 110. On the other hand, reciprocation of benefits does mean continuous, close contact, which may breed greater understanding among men (as it appears to do among nations).
48. *MS*, p. 229. See also p. 244.
49. *MS*, p. 171.
50. *MS*, p. 250. See also pp. 485, 488-9.
51. *MS*, p. 124.
52. *MS*, p. 124.

II. Benevolence and the Sacred

1. *MS*, p. 448. See also p. 441.
2. *MS*, p. 448.
3. *MS*, p. 446. See also p. 359.
4. *MS*, p. 311.
5. *MS*, p. 321. See also p. 119.
6. *MS*, p. 445.
7. *WN*, I, p. 91.
8. *MS*, pp. 262-3.
9. *MS*, p. 120.
10. *MS*, p. 247.
11. *WN*, I, p. 364.
12. *MS*, p. 446.
13. *WN*, I, p. 18.
14. *MS*, p. 325.
15. *MS*, p. 321.
16. *MS*, p. 329.
17. *MS*, p. 323.
18. *MS*, p. 326.
19. *MS*, pp. 325-6.
20. *MS*, p. 321.
21. *MS*, p. 321.
22. *MS*, p. 328.
23. *MS*, p. 331.
24. *MS*, p. 11. Thus we might want to foster the happiness of others, although we derive nothing from it except the pleasure of seeing others happy; and avoid causing sorrow to others because it would be painful to contemplate their misery. There is clearly more to self-satisfaction than pecuniary self-love. See *MS*, pp. 3, 338-9.
25. *MS*, p. 331.
26. *MS*, p. 452.
27. *MS*, p. 321. Men, though naturally sympathetic, always feel less strongly the passions of others than they do their own: 'We are always so much more deeply affected by whatever concerns ourselves than by whatever concerns

other men.' (*MS*, p. 193.) Every man is his own best friend; but this does not mean he has no other friends towards whom he also feels affectionate.

28. *MS*, p. 337.
29. *MS*, p. 334.
30. *MS*, p. 217.
31. *MS*, p. 192.
32. *MS*, p. 197.
33. *MS*, p. 197.
34. *MS*, p. 348. Thus, unlike the Stoics, Smith did not believe that a man should regard himself as a citizen of the world: the love of mankind in general is desirable but hardly practical as man's fantasy is limited and there is no intimacy of contact between himself and beings in more distant parts of the globe. Possibly Smith believed, however, that international trade, by bringing nations closer together, would eventually establish bonds of habitual sympathy between them.
35. *MS*, p. 27.
36. *MS*, p. 112.
37. *WN*, II, pp. 49-50. See also I, pp. 475-7; *MS*, pp. 264, 331
38. *MS*, p. 110.
39. *MS*, p. 124.
40. *MS*, p. 371. A similar statement is found in *WN*, II, p. 195.
41. *MS*, p. 235.
42. In the sixth edition of the *Moral Sentiments* the only reference to revelation was deleted. It had read: 'The doctrines of revelation coincide, in every respect, with those original anticipations of nature.' In its place Smith substituted: 'In every religion, and in every superstition that the world has ever beheld . . . there has been a Tartarus as well as an Elysium; a place provided for the punishment of the wicked, as well as one for the reward of the just.' See H.J. Bittermann, 'Adam Smith's Empiricism and the Law of Nature', *Journal of Political Economy*, 1940, p. 712. The change may have been made when Smith, at the end of his career, no longer needed to camouflage his views for fear of those accusations of blasphemy that had so seriously harmed Robert Simson, Francis Hutcheson, and his close friend David Hume. His occasional references to 'the great law of Christianity' (*MS*, p. 27), 'our Saviour' (*MS*, p. 253), or 'the inspired writers' (*MS*, p. 109) seem very much out of place, particularly as Smith is said to have been reluctant to open his lectures with the customary prayer or to take holy orders, although having been a Snell Scholar at Oxford. The Earl of Buchan, who had been his pupil, once said: 'Oh, venerable and worthy man, why was you not a Christian?' Quoted in J. Rae, *Life of Adam Smith* (1895) (New York: Augustus M. Kelley, 1965), p. 130.
43. *MS*, p. 235.
44. T.D. Campbell, *Adam Smith's Science of Morals* (London: George Allen and Unwin Ltd, 1971), p. 219.
45. *MS*, p. 447.
46. *MS*, p. 235.
47. *MS*, pp. 187-8. See also pp. 345-6.
48. *MS*, p. 132.
49. *MS*, p. 233.
50. *MS*, p. 234.
51. E. Durkheim, *The Elementary Forms of the Religious Life*, trans. J.W. Swain (London: George Allen and Unwin Ltd, 1971), p. 206. Of course, since Smith is dealing with advanced and not primitive religions, he refers to Gods and not to the images of totemic animals or plants in which the primitive tends to objectify the 'sacred'.

51. *MS*, p. 232. Both Smith and Durkheim were influenced by Montesquieu, who in 1721 daringly related religious beliefs to the social environment. Rica writes to Uzbek that in his opinion 'all our judgements are made with reference covertly to ourselves. I do not find it surprising that the negroes paint the devil sparkling white, and their gods black as coal . . . It has been well said that if triangles had a god, they would give him three sides.' (*Persian Letters*, trans. C.J. Betts (Harmondsworth: Penguin Books, 1973), p. 124.) From this argument Montesquieu draws two conclusions. First, there is a need for religious toleration, since different religious doctrines arise from and are relative to different sets of local conditions, while remaining nonetheless in essence very much the same: Uzbek in Paris is astonished to discover that 'I see Islam everywhere, though I cannot find Mohammed. Whatever you do, truth will always emerge.' (p. 89.) And second, religion can help to maximise social utility and human welfare, since the best way to please God is to live as a good citizen in society: 'Is it not the case that the chief concern of a religious man must be to please the Divinity who established the religion that he professes? But the surest way to achieve this is certainly to observe the rules of society, and the duties of humanity. For, whatever religion you may have, you must, immediately you suppose that there is a religion, suppose also that God loves mankind, since he founded a religion to make them happy; and if he loves mankind, you are certain to please him by loving them also; that is to say, in performing all the duties of charity and humanity towards them, and in not violating the laws under which they live.' (p. 101.)
53. *MS*, p. 238.
54. *MS*, p. 188.
55. *MS*, p. 239.
56. *MS*, p. 132.
57. *MS*, p. 176.
58. For example: 'Every part of nature, when attentively surveyed, equally demonstrates the providential care of its Author.' (*MS*, p. 153.) See also *MS*, pp. 346-8, 405, 422-3.
59. *MS*, p. 132. See also p. 427.

III. Character

1. *MS*, p. 296.
2. *MS*, p. 296.
3. *MS*, p. 303.
4. *MS*, p. 296.
5. *MS*, p. 292.
6. *MS*, p. 293. See also pp. 19-20; *WN*, I, pp. 108, 433
7. *MS*, p. 292.
8. *MS*, p. 292.
9. *WN*, II, p. 302.
10. *MS*, p. 414. So convinced was Smith of the importance of a man's profession that he even attributed physical characteristics to it. This is the case with the sailor's sense of sight. Sight, he argued, depends not just on man's natural endowments but 'seems frequently to arise altogether from the different customs and habits which (men's)respective occupations have led them to contract. Men of letters, who live much in their closets, and have seldom occasion to look at very distant objects, are seldom far-sighted. Mariners, on the contrary, almost always are; those especially who have made many distant voyages, in which they have been the great part of their time out of sight of land, and have in day-light been constantly looking out towards the horizon for the appearance of some ship, or of some distant shore.' ('ES', p. 204.)

11. *WN*, II, p. 431.
12. *MS*, p. 294. See also pp. 215, 361.
13. *MS*, p. 296.
14. *WN*, I, pp. 492-3.
15. *WN*, II, p. 158.
16. *MS*, p. 214.
17. *LJ*, p. 155.
18. *LJ*, p. 155.
19. *LJ*, pp. 155-6.
20. *LJ*, p. 256. See also *WN*, II, pp. 302-3. The question of the division of labour will be discussed more fully in Chapter 6, Section I.
21. *WN*, I, pp. 19-20. Smith's belief in the basic equality of men at birth, and his view that environment rather than heredity is responsible for differentiation of character, has three implications which may in this context be noted. Firstly, since there are no natural inequalities, there cannot be what Durkheim called the 'forced division of labour': a man cannot be forced into a job for which he is unsuited if he is naturally suited for all jobs. Secondly, there cannot be alienation from one's true identity: a man cannot be alienated from an essence he does not have, nor discover his 'true' self (since this true self would be different in a different material situation, and one true self cannot be more true than another). Thirdly, Smith seems to have believed that the horizontal division of labour between different occupations would breed neither jealousy (the porter does not appear to envy the philosopher, whose role he could so easily have played) nor frustration (the porter does not appear disgruntled at being unable to 'fulfil' himself, or at least to find a less boring job). If there is malaise, it can only come from the vertical division of labour (between employee and employer), and is not a problem of the division of employments and character-patterns so much as a problem of the division of monetary rewards. We will return to this question in Chapter 6, Section III.
22. *LJ*, p. 255.
23. *WN*, II, p. 308.
24. *LJ*, p. 255.
25. *LJ*, p. 258.
26. *WN*, II, p. 220.
27. *WN*, II, p. 151. See also p. 223.
28. *WN*, II, p. 103.
29. *MS*, p. 297.
30. *MS*, p. 297.
31. *WN*, II, p. 251.
32. *MS*, p. 305.
33. *MS*, p. 305.
34. *MS*, p. 298.
35. *MS*, p. 502
36. *MS*, p. 215.
37. *LJ*, p. 80.
38. *MS*, p. 302. In other words, man being a social animal, the savage denies his nature, he does not express it.
39. *WN*, I, p. 468. See also I, p. 178; II p. 188.
40. *WN*, I, p. 410. See also I, p. 433.
41. *WN*, II, p. 442.
42. *WN*, I, p. 277. See also I, p. 484.
43. *MS*, p. 78. See also p. 87.
44. *MS*, p. 264.
45. *MS*, p. 78.

46. *WN*, I, p. 433.
47. *WN*, p. 127.
48. *WN*, I, p. 519.
49. *WN*, II, p. 232. See also I, pp. 278, 440.
50. *MS*, p. 77
51. *MS*, p. 77. Thus, while 'people of fashion' can with propriety indulge in the 'loose system' of morality (for example, vanity, luxury and dissipation), other classes should confine themselves to the more appropriate 'austere system' (for example, industry, prudence, and temperance). See *WN*, II, pp. 315-6; *MS*, pp. 86-8.
52. *MS*, p. 313.
53. *MS*, p. 315.
54. *LRBL*, p. 186.
55. *MS*, p. 316.
56. *MS*, p. 315.
57. *MS*, p. 434.
58. *WN*, I, p. 351. See also I, pp. 294, 301, 353, 362-3.
59. *WN*, I, p. 362.
60. *WN*, I, pp. 362-3.
61. *MS*, p. 311.
62. *LJ*, p. 254. See also *MS*, p. 86.
63. *LJ*, p. 254.
64. *LJ*, p. 253. Smith's student, John Millar, describes the situation as follows: 'According as the intercourse of society is extended, it requires more and more a mutual trust and confidence, which cannot be maintained without the uniform profession and rigid practice of honesty and fair-dealing. Whoever is unable in this respect, to maintain a fair character, finds himself universally reprobated, is of course disqualified for the exercise of any lucrative profession, and becomes a sort of outcast, who, like the stricken deer, is carefully avoided by the whole herd.' (*An Historical View of the English Government*, vol. IV, quoted in Lehmann, *John Millar of Glasgow*, p. 384.)
65. A, Ferguson, *An Essay on the History of Civil Society* (1767), ed. D. Forbes (Edinburgh: The University Press, 1966), p. 143.
66. See M. Weber, *The Theory of Social and Economic Organization,* pp. 158-323, and *The Protestant Ethic and the Spirit of Capitalism*, trans. T. Parsons (London: George Allen and Unwin, 1971).
67. Marshall, *op. cit.*, p. 1. Marshall expected the challenge of free enterprise capitalism to generate virtues of energy, initiative, rationality, frugality, industry, honesty, ambition, efficiency, reliability, which would thus not be found in either primitive or socialist societies (or, for that matter, in highly-bureaucratised corporations.)
68. *MS*, p. 314.
69. *MS*, p. 272. Perseverence and application cause the spectator to regard our activity 'with a considerable degree of wonder and admiration', although he realises it is 'directed to no other purpose than the acquisition of fortune' (*MS*, p. 273).
70. *MS*, p. 246. See also p. 77; *WN*, I, p. 433.
71. *WN*, I, p. 412.
72. *LJ*, p. 96. As, for example, in the case of slavery.
73. *WN*, II, pp. 127-8.
74. *MS*, p. 291.
75. *WN*, I, pp. 77, 96, 101.
76. For example: 'The price of monopoly is upon every occasion the highest which can be got. The natural price, or the price of free competition, on the contrary, is the lowest which can be taken, not upon every occasion indeed, but for any considerable time altogether. The one is upon every occasion the

highest which can be squeezed out of the buyers, or which, it is supposed, they will consent to give: the other is the lowest which the sellers can commonly afford to take, and at the same time continue their business.' (*WN*, I, p. 69.)

77. *WN*, I, p. 432.
78. *WN*, II, p. 338.
79. *WN*, I, p. 440.
80. *WN*, II, p. 455.
81. *LJ*, p. 255.
82. *WN*, I, p. 108.
83. *LJ*, p. 252. Smith ignores (here and elsewhere) the effect of climate on character, a topic much discussed in the work of Montesquieu, Hume, and other eighteenth-century authors. Thus Ferguson, for example, while agreeing that the Dutch were industrious because of their economic situation, felt this would only be true in a cool climate: 'Fire and exercise are the remedies of cold; repose and shade the securities from heat. The Hollander is laborious and industrious in Europe; he becomes more languid and slothful in India.' (A. Ferguson, *Essay*, p. 118.) And John Millar, relating climate to character *through* the work-function, wrote: 'In warm countries, the earth is often extremely fertile, and with little culture is capable of producing whatever is necessary for substance. To labour under the extreme heat of the sun is, at the same time, exceedingly troublesome and oppressive. The inhabitants, therefore, of such countries, while they enjoy a degree of affluence, and, while by the mildness of the climate they are exempted from many inconveniencies and wants, are seldom disposed to any laborious exertion, and thus, acquiring habits of indolence, become addicted to sensual pleasure, and liable to all those infirmities which are nourished by idleness and sloth.' (J. Millar, 'The Origin of the Distinction of Ranks', (3rd edn, 1779), in Lehmann, *John Millar of Glasgow*, p. 178.)
84. *WN*, I, p. 356.
85. *WN*, I, p. 357.
86. *WN*, II, p. 128.
87. *MS*, p. 124.
88. *MS*, p. 124. See also p. 325. In a commercial society characterised by sub-division of function, it is impossible to avoid a market mentality. The fact is that 'every man . . . lives by exchanging, or becomes in some measure a merchant.' (*WN*, I, p. 26).
89. *MS*, p. 124.
90. *WN*, I, p. 371. See also I, pp. 437, 440.
91. *MS*, p. 124.
92. *WN*, II, p. 188. John Millar took a similar view: in polished nations, people are 'constantly engaged in the pursuit of gain, and immersed in the cares of business', and have as result 'contracted habits of industry, avarice, and selfishness' (J. Millar, 'The Origin of the Distinction of Ranks', in Lehmann, *op. cit.*, p. 207).
93. *WN*, I, p. 384.
94. *WN*, I, p. 384.
95. See Chapter 6, Section IV.
96. *WN*, I, p. 10.
97. *WN*, II, p. 148.
98. *WN*, I, p. 404, II, p. 191.
99. *WN*, II, p. 207. See also I, p. 401 and S. Hollander, *The Economics of Adam Smith* (London: Heinemann, 1973), ch. 10.
100. Ferguson, *Essay*, p. 19.

CHAPTER 4. CONSUMER BEHAVIOUR

Introduction

1. *WN*, II, p. 179. Elsewhere he says: 'The riches of a country consist in the plenty and cheapness of provisions.' (*LJ*, p. 130.) See also *WN*, I, pp. 34, 69, 451-66; II, p. 199.
2. *WN*, I, p. 368.
3. *WN*, I, p. 437.
4. This, along with the provision of revenue for the state, is one of the twin goals of political economy that Smith specified. See *WN*, I, p. 449.
5. K. Polanyi, *The Great Transformation* (Boston: Beacon Press, 1957), p. 46.
6. *WN*, II, p. 308.
7. *MS*, p. 259.
8. *MS*, p. 86.
9. *MS*, p. 70.
10. *WN*, I, p. 210.
11. *MS*, p. 332.
12. *MS*, p. 89.
13. Montesquieu, *op. cit.*, p. 195.
14. Berger, *op cit.*, p. 73.
15. Just as a progressive income tax or discriminatory purchase tax penalises some sectors and favours others, so in a growing economy some groups and trades benefit more than others. For example, *WN*, I, pp. 195, 210, 242-3.
16. Durkheim, *The Division of Labor in Society*, p. 235.
17. *ibid.*, p. 244.
18. Quoted in Scott, *Adam Smith as Student and Professor*, p. 311.
19. Dr Mishan, following Galbraith,has expressed his regret that politicians are compelled by public opinion 'to keep their eyes glued to the speedometer without regard to the direction taken' (E.J. Mishan, *The Costs of Economic Growth*, p. 32). Adam Smith would have been the first to share this view that there may be other indices of the national interest besides the GNP; but he welcomed economic change because of the desirable if unintended social changes it brought in its wake.

I. Consumption and Social Status

1. *WN*, II, p. 284.
2. *LJ*, p. 199.
3. *WN*, II, p. 179. See also p. 272.
4. *WN*, I, p. 137. Italics mine.
5. *WN*, p. 183.
6. *WN*, I, p. 183. See also p. 440; *MS*, pp. 263-4.
7. *WN*, I, p. 439.
8. *MS*, p. 259. See also p. 453.
9. *MS*, p. 262.
10. *WN*, I, p. 439.
11. *MS*, p. 263.
12. *MS*, p. 259.
13. *MS*, p. 263.
14. *MS*, p. 70.
15. *WN*, I, p. 180. He elsewhere adds heating by coal to the list of necessities. Where coal is expensive, wages are high; and thus industry tends to be located near the coalfields, to minimise the cost of fuel to the consumer and thereby keep wages down. See *WN*, II, p. 404.
16. *MS*, p. 310. Reference should also be made to J.S. Davis, 'Adam Smith and the Human Stomach', *Quarterly Journal of Economics*, May 1954.

17. *LJ*, p. 158. See also *WN*, I, p. 182.
18. *LJ*, p. 160.
19. *'IA'*, *p. 148*,
20. See B. Malinowski, *A Scientific Theory of Culture* (London: Oxford University Press, 1960), ch. 9-11 for a functionalist theory of needs very similar to that of Smith. Marshall makes a similar disaggregation of wants into wants related to biological needs, 'artificial wants', and wants 'adjusted to activities' (Marshall, *op. cit.*, pp. 87-9). See also the discussion of Marshall in Parsons, *The Structure of Social Action*, ch. 4.
21. *LJ*, p. 160. Even the lower classes consume some luxuries, since wages are above subsistence: see, for example, *WN*, I, pp. 82-3, 223; II, p. 418.
22. Galbraith, *The Affluent Society*, p. 32
23. *WN*, I, p. 383.
24. *MS*, pp. 261-2. See also pp. 162-3, 170-2, 202, 236, 436-7; *WN*, I, p. 119
25. Durkheim, *The Rules of Sociological Method*, pp. 2-3, 11. A similarly relativistic, sociological view of men's needs and wants is taken, from a different ideological universe, by Karl Marx: 'A house may be large or small; as long as the surrounding houses are equally small it satisfies all social demands for a dwelling. But if a palace arises beside the little house, the little house shrinks into a hut . . . Our needs and enjoyments spring from society; we measure them, therefore, by society and not by the objects of their satisfaction. Because they are of a social nature, they are of a relative nature.' (K. Marx, 'Wage-Labour and Capital', in *Selected Works* (London: Lawrence and Wishart Ltd, 1942), vol. I, pp. 268-9.) See also the views of Max Weber in H.H. Gerth and C.W. Mills (eds.), *From Max Weber: Essays in Sociology* (London: Routledge and Kegan Paul Ltd, 1948), pp. 187-93. It is interesting that Weber (like Veblen and Galbraith) is here referring to the United States, a society with more insecurity concerning the proof of status than, say, Scotland in the eighteenth century.
26. *WN*, II, p. 400.
27. *WN*, II, p. 399.
28. *WN*, II, p. 405. See also I, pp. 208-9.
29. *WN*, I, p. 183.
30. *WN*, II, p. 405.
31. *MS*, p. 281.
32. *WN*, II, p. 400.
33. *WN*, II, p. 405.
34. Ferguson, *Essay* p. 246. Similar views can be found in Montesquieu, *op cit.*, letters 30, 78, 82, 99, 106, 110, 142.
35. *WN*, I, p. 132.
36. *WN*, I, p. 132.
37. *WN*, II, p. 399.
38. Professor Macfie nonetheless insists on forcing Smith into the utilitarian strait-jacket: 'Utility is his inevitable starting point in the *Wealth of Nations* . . . inevitable because economics is the science of scarce means and their most useful application.' (A.L. Macfie, *The Individual in Society* (London: George Allen and Unwin Ltd, 1967), p. 45.) Our argument has been that this sort of view, while not wrong in itself, neglects Smith's unique contribution of tracing even the perception of scarcity back to its social origins, and thus showing its relativity and contingency.
39. *MS*, p. 284.
40. *WN*, I, p. 307. Italics mine.
41. *MS*, p. 284.
42. *MS*, p. 311.
43 *MS*, pp. 70-1. Italics mine. See also pp. 79, 81, 89, 310-11.

44. *WN*, I, p. 362.
45. *MS*, p. 236.
46. *MS*, p. 46.
47. *MS*, pp. 331-2. See also p. 85; *LRBL*, p. 120.
48. *MS*, p. 73.
49. *MS*, p. 71. See also pp. 202, 291, 332.
50. *WN*, I, p. 192.
51. *MS*, p. 71.
52. *WN*, II, p. 207.
53. T. Veblen, *The Theory of the Leisure Class* (London: George Allen and Unwin Ltd, 1970), p. 111.
54. *ibid.*, p. 109.
55. *ibid*, p. 42. A similar view of the relationship between wealth, consumption, and social status was taken by Adam Ferguson in 1767: 'The sovereign himself owes great part of his authority to the sounding titles and the dazzling equipage which he exhibits in public. The subordinate ranks lay claim to importance by a like exhibition, and for that purpose carry in every instant the ensigns of their birth, or the ornaments of their fortune. What else could mark out to the individual the relation in which he stands to his fellow-subjects, or distinguish the numberless ranks that fill up the interval between the state of the sovereign and that of the peasant? . . . Every condition is possessed of peculiar dignity, and points out a propriety of conduct, which men of station are obliged to maintain.' (Ferguson, *Essay*, pp. 69-70. See also pp. 161-2.)
56. *WN*, I, p. 192.
57. 'IA', p. 145.
58. 'IA', p. 145.
59. 'IA', p. 145.
60. Veblen, *op. cit.*, p. 95.
61. *ibid.*, p. 98.
62. *LJ*, p. 178.
63. *LJ*, p. 177.
64. *MS*, p. 282. See also pp. 87-8.
65. *MS*, p. 282.
66. *MS*, p. 282. See also p. 281.
67. Veblen, *op. cit.*, p. 86.
68. *MS*, p. 381.
69. *WN*, II, p. 338.
70. *MS*, p. 375.
71. *MS*, p. 380.
72. *MS*, p. 88.
73. *MS*, p. 166.
74. *MS*, p. 262.
75. *MS*, pp. 73-4.
76. *MS*, p. 333. See also pp. 72, 188, 291.
77. *MS*, p. 85.
78. *WN*, II, p. 236; *LJ*, p. 15.
79. *MS*, pp. 76, 84, 318, 331-2.
80. *MS*, p. 75.
81. *LRBL*, p. 152.
82. *MS*, p. 87.
83. *LJ*, p. 42.
84. *LJ*, p. 9.
85. *MS*, p. 80. And elsewhere he writes: 'Though it is in order to supply the necessities and conveniences of the body that the advantage of external

fortune are originally recommended to us, yet we cannot live long in the
world without perceiving that the respect of our equals, our credit and rank
in the society we live in, depend very much upon the degree in which we
possess, or are supposed to possess, those advantages. The desire of
becoming the proper objects of this respect, of deserving and obtaining this
credit and rank among our equals, is perhaps the strongest of all our desires;
and our anxiety to obtain the advantages of fortune is, accordingly, much
more excited and irritated by this desire than by that of supplying all the
necessities and conveniences of the body, which are always very easily
supplied.' (*MS*, pp. 310-1.)

86. *WN*, II, p. 240.
87. *LJ*, p. 175. However, by the time he came to write *The Wealth of Nations*,
    Smith had apparently decided that men flood into the legal profession not
    only because of its prestige but because of their conceit: each mistakenly
    thinks he will succeed, where most of his predecessors have failed, in making
    a fortune (*WN*, I, p. 119.)
88. *WN*, II, p. 442.
89. *WN*, I, p. 418.
90. *MS*, p. 495.
91. *WN*, II, pp. 136-8.
92. Berger, *op. cit.*, p. 157.
93. J.K. Galbraith, *The New Industrial State* (Harmondsworth: Penguin Books,
    1969), p. 77.

II. Tranquility, Ambition and Progress

 1. *MS*, p. 360.
 2. *MS*, pp. 265, 209, 211.
 3. *MS*, p. 49.
 4. *MS*, p. 213. See also p. 371.
 5. *MS*, p. 260.
 6. *MS*, p. 260.
 7. *WN*, II, p. 234.
 8. *MS*, p. 55.
 9. *MS*, p. 259.
10. *WN*, I, p. 363.
11. *MS*, pp. 62-3, 262.
12. *MS*, p. 258.
13. *MS*, p. 63.
14. *MS*, p. 262.
15. *MS*, p. 261.
16. *MS*, pp. 219-20. See also pp. 221-3.
17. *MS*, p. 215
18. *MS*, p. 339. See also pp. 210, 340.
19. This 'deception . . . rouses and keeps in continual motion the industry of
    mankind. It is this which first prompted them to cultivate the ground, to
    build houses, to found cities and commonwealths, and to invent and
    improve all the sciences and arts, which ennoble and embellish human life.'
    (*MS*, pp. 263-4.)
20. *MS*, p. 449. See also pp. 31, 350-1, 400, 448. Dr West points out ('Adam
    Smith's Philosophy of Riches', *Philosophy*, April 1969, p. 115) that in the
    often-quoted passage: 'Every man . . . lives by exchanging, or becomes in
    some measure a merchant' (*WN*, I, p. 26), Smith qualifies his view with the
    words 'in some measure'. In other words, a balance of virtues is still needed.
21. *MS*, p. 446.
22. *MS*, p. 56.

23. D. Hume, 'Of Refinement in the Arts', in Rotwein, *op. cit.*, p. 21.
24. D. Hume, 'Of Interest', *ibid.*, p. 53. See also 'Of Commerce', *ibid.*, pp. 17-18.
25. Hume, *Treatise*, pp. 497-8; Ferguson, *Essay*, p. 50.
26. Hume, *Treatise*, p. 498; Ferguson, *Essay*, pp. 42-3.
27. D. Hume, *Treatise*, pp. 402, 498; Ferguson, *Essay*, pp. 42-3.
28. Ferguson, *Essay*, p. 49. See also p. 45.
29. An example we have already considered is that of the businessman, whose normal patterns of behaviour (involving virtues such as frugality and self-command) make him the main source of economic and social change.
30. Ferguson, *Essay*, p. 24.
31. E. Durkheim, *Moral Education*, p. 40. A similar view of the threat of infinite aspirations is expressed by Lord Kames: 'An infallible way of rendering a child unhappy is to indulge it in all its demands. Its desires multiply by gratification, without ever resting satisfied; it is lucky for the indulgent parents if it demand not the moon for a plaything.' Quoted in Lehmann, *Henry Home, Lord Kames*, p. 173.
32. Durkheim, *Suicide*, trans. J.A. Spaulding and G. Simpson (London: Routledge and Kegan Paul Ltd, 1952), p. 249.
33. *WN*, I, p. 437.
34. *WN*, I, p. 238.
35. *WN*, I, p. 212.
36. *WN*, II, p. 367. Italics mine. See also *MS*, p. 70.
37. *WN*, II, p. 368.
38. *WN*, I, p. 492.
39. *WN*, II, p. 104.
40. *WN*, II, p. 443.
41. *WN*, I, p. 352.
42. *WN*, I, p. 352.
43. *WN*, I, p. 368.
44. *WN*, I, p. 297. See also pp. 369-70, 384-5; *MS*, p. 283. The problem of Smith's views on consumer durables has been studied by Professor Rosenberg, who concludes: 'If we look upon economic growth as a matter of accumulating things which will provide a flow of useful services in the future, then it is clear that the greater the durability of an item, the more it approximates the characteristics of an investment good. A growing taste for durables is, therefore, favorable to economic growth.' (N. Rosenberg, 'Adam Smith, Consumer Tastes, and Economic Growth', *Journal of Political Economy*, June 1968, p. 372.)
45. *WN*, I, p. 228. See also pp. 240, 242, 264.
46. *WN*, I, p. 402.
47. *MS*, p. 263. The most famous examples of Smith's propensity to divorce satisfaction from market price is his distinction between 'value in use' and 'value in exchange' (as in the case of the diamonds/water paradox). See *WN*, I, pp. 32-3, where Smith makes the explicit value judgement that diamonds (despite their high exchange value) are less 'useful' than water, at least in his opinion.
48. *WN*, I, p. 437.

CHAPTER 5. THE UPPER CLASSES

Introduction

1. *WN*, I, p. 440.

I. Aristocracy, Clergy and Feudalism

1. *WN*, I, p. 408.

2. *WN*, I, p. 409.
3. *WN*, I, p. 408.
4. 'He is at all times, therefore, surrounded with a multitude of retainers and dependents, who having no equivalent to give in return for their maintenance, but being fed entirely by his bounty, must obey him, for the same reason that soldiers must obey the prince who pays them.' (*WN*, I, pp. 433-4.)
5. *WN*, I, p. 181. Hospitality was thus not a benevolent act.
6. *MS*, p. 264.
7. *WN*, II, p. 408.
8. *WN*, I, p. 435. See also I, pp. 264, 426; II, p. 445.
9. *WN*, I, p. 426.
10. *WN*, II, p. 125. See also I, pp. 205-6.
11. *WN*, I, p. 437. See also I, p. 355.
12. *LJ*, p. 234.
13. *WN*, I, p. 301.
14. *WN*, I, p. 301.
15. *WN*, I, p. 359. See also I, pp. 312, 370-1; II, pp. 195-6.
16. *WN*, I, p. 362. For references to the prodigality of the clergy, see *WN*, II, pp. 86, 338.
17. *WN*, I, p. 360.
18. *WN*, II, p. 302.
19. *LJ*, p. 233.
20. *WN*, I, p. 277.
21. *WN*, I, pp. 409-10.
22. *WN*, I, p. 436. Human laws reflect the 'interests, prejudices, and temper of the times'. (II, p. 52.) For this reason it is necessary continually to revise them, as otherwise the statute-books may get out of touch with reality: 'Laws frequently continue in force long after the circumstances, which first gave occasion to them, and which could alone render them reasonable, are no more.' (*WN*, I, p. 408.) Smith believed that, in his own time, the law relating to entailing land was a mere survival of past social conditions, a vestige of an era when land was the unique source of power, a social institution with no present-day function.
23. *WN*, I, p. 357.
24. *WN*, I, p. 357.
25. *WN*, I, p. 358.
26. *WN*, II, p. 323.
27. *WN*, II, p. 322.
28. *WN*, II, p. 319.
29. *WN*, II, p. 325.
30. *WN*, II, p. 319.
31. *WN*, II, p. 325.
32. *WN*, II, p. 319.
33. *WN*, II, p. 325.
34. 'HA', p. 49.
35. *LJ*, p. 95.
36. *WN*, II, p. 290.
37. *WN*, II, p. 293.
38. *MS*, p. 203.
39. *MS*, p. 469.
40. *WN*, II, p. 293; *MS*, p. 251.
41. For example, *MS*, p. 190.
42. It is surprising that Smith did not have more to say about superstition as an ideological brake on capitalism. John Millar, for example, offers this account of how the 'ignorance and superstition' of the Roman Catholic Church

became increasingly incompatible with the new commercial ethos, a contradiction which ultimately forced an ideological reformation: 'Independent of accidental circumstances, it was to be expected that those countries which made the quickest progress in trade and manufactures, would be the first to reject and dispute the papal authority. The improvement of arts, and the consequent diffusion of knowledge, contributed, on the one hand, to dispel the mist of superstition, and, on the other, to place the bulk of a people in situations which inspired them with sentiments of liberty . . . This alone will account for the banishment of the Romish religion from the independent towns of Germany, from the Dutch provinces, and from England; those parts of Europe which were soon possessed of an extensive commerce.' (J. Millar, *Historical View*, vol. II, quoted in Lehmann, *John Millar of Glasgow*, pp. 364-5.)

43. *MS*, p. 251.
44. *MS*, p. 252.
45. *MS*, p. 242. See also p. 491.
46. *MS*, pp. 219-20.
47. *WN*, II, p. 313.
48. *WN*, II, p. 313. See also pp. 310, 331-3.
49. *WN*, II, p. 328.
50, *WN*, II, p. 310.
51. *MS*, p. 253.
52. *WN*, II, p. 483.
53. *WN*, II, p. 483.

II. Historical Evolution

1. *LJ*, P. 107. The economic factor is not the *sole* explanation of the historical process. He considers other theories too, such as cultural interaction and transfer. See *WN*, II, pp. 76, 202. Usually, however, the economic factor is implicit. See for example *MS*, pp. 263-4.
2. *WN*, II, p. 214.
3. *WN*, II, p. 233.
4. *WN*, II, p. 234.
5. *WN*, II, p. 232.
6. *LJ*, p. 262. Less division of labour means less distinction of rank. In primitive society 'every man does, or is capable of doing, almost every thing which any other man does, or is capable of doing'. (*WN*, II, p. 304.) In other words, there was less differentiation of work-function and, as result, a greater concentration of intelligence around the mean.
7. *WN*, II, p. 232. Thus, the Hobbesian *bellum omnium contra omnes* does not date from a mythical state of nature, nor even from the first observed stage in historical evolution. Its appearance coincides with the appearance, and unequal distribution, of private property.
8. *WN*, II, pp. 233-4.
9. *LJ*, p. 16.
10. *WN*, II, p. 236.
11. 'The most barbarous nations either of Africa or of the East Indies were shepherds . . . Those nations were by no means so weak and defenceless as the miserable and helpless Americans . . . In Africa and the East Indies, therefore, it was more difficult to displace the natives'. (*WN*, II, pp. 150-1.) And: 'If the hunting nations of America should ever become shepherds, their neighbourhood would be much more dangerous to the European colonies than it is at present.' (*WN*, II, p. 215.)
12. *WN*, II, pp. 214-15.
13. *WN*, II, p. 226. See also pp. 213-4, 223.

14. *WN*, II, p. 223.
15. *WN*, II, p. 214.
16. *MS*, p. 264.
17. *LJ*, p. 108.
18. *WN*, I, p. 420.
19. *WN*, I, p. 424.
20. *WN*, I, p. 422.
21. *WN*, I, p. 423.
22. *WN*, I, p. 428.
23. *WN*, I, p. 437. See also *LJ*, pp. 35-6, *WN*, II; pp. 441-3.
24. *WN*, I, p. 439. See also pp. 18, 35, 275, 438.
25. Slavery was abolished, not because it was inhumane (*WN*, I, p. 412) but because it was 'inconvenient' (*WN*, I, p. 413): slaves 'have no motive to industry' (*LJ*, p. 225) and do not produce the greatest possible output per unit of input. Clearly there is no conflict between pecuniary self-interest and humanity when it comes to a discussion of abolition.
26. *WN*, I, p. 439.
27. *LJ*, pp. 44-5. See also *WN*, II, pp. 445-6. David Hume too related security of life and fortune to 'progress in the arts'. In a static agricultural society, he argued, the people are divided into two classes, the proprietors of the land and their tenants (the former tyrannical, the latter dependent). But, 'where luxury nourishes commerce and industry, the peasants, by a proper cultivation of the land, become rich and independent; while the tradesmen and merchants acquire a share of the property, and draw authority and consideration to that middling rank of men, who are the best and firmest basis of public liberty . . . They covet equal laws, which may secure their property, and preserve them from monarchical, as well as aristocratical tyranny.' The result is a balance of political power: 'The lower house is the support of our popular government; and all the world acknowledges, that it owed its chief influence and consideration to the encrease of commerce, which threw such a balance of property into the hands of the commons.' (D. Hume, 'Of Refinement in the Arts', in Rotwein, *op. cit.*, pp. 28-9.)
28. *WN*, I, p. 438.
29. *LJ*, p. 10.
30. *LJ*, p. 223.
31. *LJ*, p. 220.
32. *WN*, I, p. 426.
33. *WN*, I, p. 439.
34. *LJ*, p. 233.
35. *WN*, I, p. 439.
36. *WN*, I, p. 433.
37. *WN*, II, p. 246.
38. *WN*, II, p. 250.
39. *WN*, I, p. 439.
40. *WN*, II, p. 318.
41. *WN*, I, p. 25.
42. *WN*, I, p. 80.
43. Stewart, in Smith, *op. cit.*, p. xlvi.
44. *WN*, I, p. 82.
45. *LJ*, p. 32. Italics mine.
46. *WN*, I, p. 443. Italics mine.
47. Ferguson, *Essay*, pp. 109-10.
48. For example, *WN*, I, p. 295.
49. For example, *WN*, I, p. 74.
50. See Chapter 6, Section III.

51. *WN*, II, p. 234. See also *LJ*, p. 10.
52. See T. Parsons, *Societies: Evolutionary and Comparative Perspectives* (Englewood Cliffs: Prentice-Hall, 1966), and *The System of Modern Societies* (Englewood Cliffs: Prentice-Hall, 1971).
53. *WN*, II, p. 308. See below Chapter 6, Section I.
54. *WN*, I, p. 106. See below, Chapter 6, Section II.
55. W. Bagehot, *Biographical Studies,* 2nd edn, (London: Longmans, Green, and Co., 1889), p. 255.

III. Clergy and Commerce

1. *WN*, II, p. 326.
2. *WN*, II, p. 325.
3. *WN*, II, p. 330.
4. *WN*, II, p. 330. In Catholic countries the effect would be to reduce the influence of the Pope. See *WN*, II, p. 327.
5. *WN*, II, p. 331.
6. *WN*, II, p. 72.
7. *WN*, II, p. 74.
8. *WN*, II, p. 251.
9. *WN*, II, p. 50.
10. *WN*, I, p. 412.
11. *LJ*, p. 101.
12. *LJ*, p. 272.
13. *WN*, II, p. 306.
14. *LJ*, p. 256.
15. See, for example, Book 24.
16. *WN*, II, p. 314.
17. *WN*, II, p. 312.
18. *WN*, II, p. 314.
19. *WN*, II, p. 301.
20. *WN*, II, p. 315.
21. *WN*, II, p. 315.
22. *WN*, II, p. 317.
23. *WN*, I, p. 93. See also *MS*, p. 329.
24. *WN*, II, p. 317.
25. *WN*, II, p. 311.
26. *WN*, II, p. 311.
27. *WN*, II, p. 334.
28. *WN*, II, p. 333. See also pp. 337-8.
29. *WN*, II, pp. 127-8, 337-8.

CHAPTER 6. THE LOWER CLASSES

Introduction

1. *LJ*, p. 161.
2. *WN*, I, p. 16.
3. *LJ*, p. 256.
4. *WN*, II, p. 302. See also *MS*, pp. 19-20
5. See R.L. Meek, 'Adam Smith and the Classical Theory of Profit', in *Economics and Ideology* (London: Chapman and Hall Ltd, 1967), pp. 32-3.
6. *WN*, I, p. 74.
7. *WN*, II, p. 234. See also *LJ*, p. 10.
8. See J. Robinson, 'Euler's Theorem and the Problem of Distribution' (1934), in *Collected Economic Papers* (Oxford: Blackwell, 1951), vol. I.

9. For example, E. Halevy, *The Growth of Philosophic Radicalism* (London: Faber and Faber Ltd, 1972), pp. 16, 89, 107, 238, 247, 338-9; J. Plamenatz, *The English Utilitarians*, 2nd edn. (Oxford: Blackwell, 1966), pp. 111-14.
10. Gerth and Mills. *op. cit.,* p. 186.
11. See Montesquieu, *Persian Letter,* letters 112-22, and *The Spirit of the Laws,* Book 23, ch. 17-29.
12. See Lehmann, *Henry Home, Lord Kames,* pp. 113, 127, 263.
13. D. Hume, 'Of Money', in Rotwein, *op. cit.,* p. 38.
14. *WN,* II, pp. 114-6. See also, I, p. 151.
15. D. Hume, 'Of Commerce', in Rotwein, *op. cit.,* p. 15.
16. *MS,* p. 110.
17. *WN,* I, p. 35. See also pp. 178, 275.
18. T. Hobbes, *Leviathan* (Harmondsworth: Penguin Books, 1968), pp. 151-2.
19. C.B. Macpherson, *The Political Theory of Possessive Individualism* (London: Oxford University Press, 1962), Part Two.

I. The Division of Labour

1. *WN,* I, p. 7. See also p. 226.
2. Schumpeter, *History of Economic Analysis,* p. 187.
3. See below, Section IV.
4. *LJ,* p. 161.
5. *LJ,* p. 162.
6. *WN,* I, p. 15. The gains from trade are 'mutual and reciprocal, and the division of labour is . . . advantageous to all the different persons employed in the various occupations into which it is sub-divided'. (*WN,* I, p. 401.) See also *LJ,* pp. 178-9, 204-7, 232-3.
7. *WN,* II, p. 303; *WN,* II, p. 308.
8. *WN,* I, p. 12.
9. *LJ,* p. 166.
10. *WN,* I, p. 12.
11. *LJ,* p. 166.
12. *WN,* I, p. 13.
13. *LJ,* p. 167, *WN,* I, p. 13.
14. *LJ,* p. 158.
15. *LJ,* p. 167. In *The Wealth of Nations,* however, he argues that slaves do not after all invent. See *WN,* II, p. 205; *LJ,* p. 231.
16. *WN,* I, pp. 13-14.
17. *LJ,* p. 167.
18. See below, Section II.
19. *WN,* I, p. 14.
20. 'Early Draft', p. 337.
21. *WN,* I, p. 14.
22. *WN,* II, p. 304.
23. 'Early Draft', p. 344.
24. *WN,* II, p. 304.
25. *LJ,* p. 168.
26. *WN,* II, p. 304. It is clear that, at least in *The Wealth of Nations,* Smith believed that in the separation of persons as well as of functions, and that the following comment in the 'Early Draft' is not typical of his (later) view: 'When an artist makes any (major) discovery he showes himself to be, not a meer artist, but a real philosopher, whatever may be his nominal profession.' ('Early Draft', p. 338.)
27. 'Early Draft', p. 338.
28. 'Early Draft', p. 338.

29. *WN*, I, p. 13.
30. 'Early Draft', p. 338.
31. *WN*, p. 13. However, as many writers have pointed out, Smith does tend to play down major inventions and technological breakthroughs, and to emphasise instead the gradual and cumulative progress of discovery. To a considerable extent this was because industrial improvement meant for him not a 'scientific revolution' in the application of machinery but greater opportunities for division of labour and organisation of work that would result once the domestic system was superseded by men collected in 'the same workhouse'. (*WN*, I, p. 8.) He also believed that the greatest advances in the use of machinery were to be found in the Birmingham and Sheffield cutlery and metal trades, not in textiles. (*WN*, I, p. 270). He thus failed to foresee two important aspects of the Industrial Revolution: the central role of sophisticated power-driven machinery and the rise of the cotton-textiles industry. But Professor Hollander offers the following defence: 'We cannot conclude that he failed to anticipate the industrial revolution. To have paid the degree of attention we find in the *Wealth of Nations* to the determinants of plant and industry organization, to fixed capital and its maintenance, to the differential factor-saving effects of technical change, to the contributions to knowledge of specialist inventors and machine makers, at a time when the changes usually associated with the industrial revolution had not yet occurred, or were only just occurring, shows remarkable insight.' (Hollander, *op. cit.*, p. 241.)
32. *WN*, I, pp. 302-3. See also N. Rosenberg, 'Adam Smith on the Division of Labour: Two Views or One?' *Economica*, 1965.
33. Quoted in Lehmann, *Henry Home, Lord Kames*, pp. 188-9.
34. *ibid.*, p. 189.
35. Ferguson, *Essay*, p. 183.
36. *ibid.*, pp. 182-3. The comparison with Ferguson is particularly significant as Smith (whose views on the division of labour are not always interpreted as pessimistically as I have chosen to do in this book) accused Ferguson of plagiarising some of his ideas on this subject. See R. Hamowy, 'Adam Smith, Adam Ferguson, and the Division of Labour', *Economica*, 1968.
37. J. Millar, *Historical View*, vol. IV, quoted in Lehmann, *John Millar of Glasgow*, p. 380. Karl Marx, as is well known, was an avid student of the Scottish Enlightenment, and passages such as the following can perhaps be traced back to its influence: 'The habit of doing only one thing converts (the labourer) into a never-failing instrument, while his connexion with the whole mechanism compels him to work with the regularity of the parts of a machine.' (K. Marx, *Capital*, vol. I (Moscow: Foreign Languages Publishing House, 1961), p. 349. Ferguson and Smith are quoted at length on pp. 361-2.)
38. *WN*, I, p. 141.
39. *LJ*, p. 255.
40. 'HA', p. 35.
41. *WN*, I, p. 142. Note that this example of the unfavourable effects of the industrial division of labour is found in Book I, and that such examples are not confined to Book V.
42. *MS*, p. 289.
43. *LJ*, p. 159.
44. *WN*, I, p. 142. Durkheim appears to have taken the opposite view: he felt that the industrial division of labour had a favourable intellectual effect on the worker, and that the absence of it meant intellectual stagnation for the farmer. In a dynamic economy, the worker continually has to exercise his intelligence in learning new operations and adjusting to changed conditions: 'Cerebral life develops, then, at the same time as competition becomes

keener, and to the same degree. These advances are observed not only among the elite, but in all classes of society. On this point, it is only necessary to compare the worker with the farmer. It is a known fact that the first is a great deal more intelligent in spite of the mechanical nature of the tasks to which he is often subject.' (*The Division of Labor in Society*, p. 273.)

45. *WN*, II, p. 305.
46. *WN*, II, p. 304.
47. *WN*, II, p. 305.
48. *WN*, II, p. 303.
49. *WN*, II, p. 308.
50. *WN*, II, p. 303.
51. J. Mill, 'On Education' (1818), *Encyclopedia Brittanica*, 5th edn, reprinted in F.A. Cavenagh (ed.), *James and John Stuart Mill on Education* (Cambridge: the University Press, 1931), p. 46. This view is also expressed in E.G. West, 'Adam Smith's Two Views on the Division of Labour', *Economica*, 1964.
52. *WN*, II, p. 308.
53. *LJ*, p. 257. The economic implications of this passage for the supply curve of labour (that high wages lead to voluntary unemployment) are not typical of Smith, at least not of his views in *The Wealth of Nations*. See below, Section IV.
54. *WN*, II, p. 306.
55. *WN*, I, p. 298.
56. *WN*, II, p. 305.
57. *WN*, II, *p. 295.*
58. *WN*, II, p. 302. Here Smith shows the influence of Locke who pioneered the utilitarian approach to education. Consider, for example, the following passage: 'Can there be any thing more ridiculous, than that a Father should waste his own Money, and his Son's time, in setting him to learn the *Roman Language,* when at the same time he designs him for a Trade, wherein he having no use of *Latin* fails not to forget that little, which he brought from School?' (J. Locke, *Some Thoughts Concerning Education* (1693), para. 164.)
59. *WN*, II, p. 302.
60. Locke, *op. cit.,* para. 216.
61. *ibid.,* para. 1.
62. *WN*, II, p. 309.
63. *LJ*, p. 256.
64. *WN*, I, p. 433.
65. *MS*, pp. 72-5, 371.
66. *MS*, p. 230.
67. *MS*, p. 380.
68. i.e. Scotland.
69. *LJ*, p. 256. Paradoxically, by setting their children so soon to work, parents give them a bracing sense of financial independence which weakens the authority of the family: 'Besides this want of education, there is another great loss which attends the putting boys too soon to work. The boy begins to find that his father is obliged to him, and therefore throws off his authority.' (*LJ*, pp. 256-7.) Thus, the division of labour carries on the work of undermining the family that was begun by the commercial revolution itself: 'It is not many years ago that, in the Highlands of Scotland, the chieftain used to consider the poorest man of his clan as his cousin and relation', since they were of importance to one another for their common defence. In 'commercial countries', however, 'where the authority of law is always perfectly sufficient to protect the meanest man in the state, the descendants of the same family, having no such motive for keeping together,

naturally separate and disperse, as interest or inclination may direct.' (*MS*, p. 327.) In other words, the division of labour threatens the nuclear family in the same way as the rule of law threatened the extended family and the web of tribal loyalties.
70. *WN*, I, p. 113.
71. *WN*, I, pp. 19-20.
72. *WN*, I, p. 53.
73. *WN*, II, p. 305. Naturally, on-the-job training in that trade can make the worker the proprietor of a human capital without having to surmount the entry barriers associated with full-time schooling. This was the case with grocers, whose qualifications were not only book-learning (the ability to 'read, write, and account'), but the need to be 'a tolerable judge too of, perhaps, fifty or sixty different sorts of goods, their prices, qualities, and the markets where they are to be had cheapest.' (*WN*, I, p. 125.) Such practical expertise can be acquired without extensive schooling.
74. There is evidence, however, that he may have considered this latter possibility. For example: 'For a very small expence the public can facilitate, can encourage, and *can even impose* upon almost the whole body of the people, the necessity of acquiring those most essential parts of education.' (*WN*, II, p. 305. Italics mine.)

II. Value, Distribution and Solidarity

1. M. Myers, 'Division of Labour as a Principle of Social Cohesion', *Canadian Journal of Economics and Political Science*, 1967, p. 439.
2. E.G. West, 'The Political Economy of Alienation: Karl Marx and Adam Smith', *Oxford Economic Papers*, 1969, p. 7.
3. *WN*, I, p. 519.
4. *WN*, II, p. 141. See also I, pp. 395, 514.
5. *WN*, I, pp. 401-3, 469-70.
6. *WN*, I, pp. 395, 480, 514.
7. *WN*, II, pp. 47-8.
8. *WN*, I, pp. 486, 520-2; *MS*, p. 336. See also the 'Early Draft', p. 350, where he writes: 'A free trade to France would tend infinitely more to enrich Great Britain than a free trade to Portugal, because, France, on account of its superior opulence having more to give could take more from us, and exchanging to a much greater value and in a much greater variety of ways, would encourage more industry in Great Britain and give occasion to more subdivisions of labour.'
9. *WN*, I, p. 471. As David Hume somewhat histrionically put it, 'Not only as a man, but as a British subject, I pray for the flourishing commerce of Germany, Spain, Italy, and even France itself.' The view that trading partners are to be looked on with suspicion is a 'narrow and malignant opinion': in truth, 'the encrease of riches and commerce in any one nation, instead of hurting, commonly promotes the riches and commerce of all its neighbours ... A state can scarcely carry its trade and industry very far, where all the surrounding states are buried in ignorance, sloth, and barbarism.' The gains from trade arises through the stimulation to industry and trade of wider markets, through mutual emulation of new products, and through the ability to produce goods based on particular factor-endowments (countries have different 'geniuses, climates, and soils') and to export them: clearly, 'if our neighbours have no art or cultivation, they cannot take them; because they will have nothing to given in exchange. In this respect states are in the same condition as individuals. A single man can scarcely be industrious, where all his fellow-citizens are idle.' (D. Hume, Of the Jealousy of Trade' (1758), in Rotwein, *op. cit.*, pp. 82, 78-9. See also 'Of Commerce', *ibid.*, p. 14.)

10. *WN*, II, p. 28.
11. *WN*, II, p. 141. Moreover, as we saw in Chapter 3, a mercantile nation is likely to develop habits of honesty and probity rather than dupery and injustice, and this too is likely to foster good international relations.
12. *WN*, I, p. 20.
13. *WN*, I, p. 403. See also p. 18.
14. *WN*, I, p. 17.
15. *WN*, I, p. 15. See also p. 9, and 'Early Draft', p. 324.
16. *WN*, I, p. 17.
17. *LJ*, p. 171.
18. *WN*, I, p. 16.
19. S. Andreski (ed.), *Herbert Spencer: Structure, Function and Evolution* (London: Thomas Nelson and Sons, Ltd, 1972), p. 139.
20. *WN*, I, p. 438.
21. *WN*, I, p. 15.
22. *WN*, I, p. 36.
23. *WN*, I, p. 37.
24. *WN*, I, p. 37. See also *LJ*, p. 190.
25. *WN*, I, p. 37. See also pp. 35-6, 41-3, 207-9.
26. *WN*, I, p. 56. This passage reminds us that Smith's two approaches to the labour theory of value need not be mutually exclusive: labour-embodied might explain the source of value and labour-commanded still provide a constant measuring rod to use in explaining changes in value over time. In such a case the two approaches are not substitutes but complements and refer to different sorts of problems.
27. *WN*, I, p. 34.
28. *WN*, I, p. 34.
29. *WN*, I, p. 34.
30. R.L. Meek, *Studies in the Labour Theory of Value*, 2nd edn. (London: Lawrence and Wishart, 1973), p. 62.
31. *WN*, I, p. 35.
32. P.H. Douglas, 'Smith's Theory of Value and Distribution', in J.M. Clark and others, *Adam Smith 1776-1926* (1928) (New York: Augustus M. Kelley, 1966), p. 87.
33. *WN*, I, p. 62.
34. *WN*, I, p. 117.
35. *WN*, I, p. 84.
36. *WN*, I, p. 37
37. *WN*, I, p. 223.
38. W.J. Barber, *A History of Economic Thought* (Harmondsworth: Penguin Books, 1967), pp. 34-5. Smith admits that in 'an opulent and commercial society, labour becomes dear and work cheap', and finds the coincidence of these two events perfectly natural. ('Early Draft', p. 332.) Natural it may be, but it creates enormous problems for the statistician seeking to use the labour theory of value to calculate changes in the national income.
39. *WN*, I, pp. 19-20.
40. See above, Section I.
41. *WN*, I, p. 118. Smith made a similar point concerning the functional necessity of stratification of incomes (even where there is no stratification of abilities) when, as Commissioner of Customs in Edinburgh in 1782, he opposed reduction of fees paid to customs-inspectors: if they were, 'the income of many officers may be so far reduced as to make it difficult for them to subsist in the society which, in reason, ought to belong to them.' Quoted in Scott, *op. cit.*, p. 17. Smith seems completely unaware of the possibility of a contradiction between the level of income set by supply and demand and the

level of income prescribed by social status and convention. To make matters still more confusing, it is difficult to reconcile his 'equality-of-sacrifice' approach to the pay-structure with passages such as the following, which suggest he at least on occasion felt the 'sweets of labour' to be unfairly distributed: 'Those who labour most get least. The opulent merchant, who spends a great part of his time in luxury and entertainments, enjoys a much greater proportion of the profits of his traffic, than all the Clerks and Accountants who do the business. These last, again, enjoying a great deal of leisure, and suffering scarce any other hardship besides the confinement of attendance, enjoy a much greater share of the produce, than three times an equal number of artizans, who, under their direction, labour much more severely and assiduously.' As for the 'poor labourer' at the bottom of the pyramid, who bears 'upon his shoulders the whole fabric of human society', he 'seems himself to be pressed down below ground by the weight, and to be buried out of sight in the lowest foundations of the building.' ('Early Draft', pp. 327-8.) See also *LJ*, pp. 162-3 for a similar view on the price and distribution of affluence.

42. J. Robinson, *Economic Philosophy* (Harmondsworth: Penguin Books, 1962), p. 47.
43. *WN*, I. p. 53. See also p. 72. If it is assumed implicitly that disutility per hour of beaver-hunting is the same as the disutility of deer-hunting, then labour-time may be taken as the index of labour-embodied in such a pre-market economy. As Professor Hollander points out, however, Smith recognised that exchange ratios even in a primitive economy would be influenced by differential amounts of 'hardship . . . dexterity and ingenuity' associated with different occupations. (Hollander, *op. cit.*, pp. 116-17.)
44. See for example, E.G. West, *Adam Smith* (New Rochelle: Arlington House, 1969), pp. 169-70; H.J. Bittermann, *loc. cit.*, p. 706; J.A. Schumpeter, *op. cit.*, pp. 188-9.
    op. cit., pp. 188-9.
45. *WN*, I, p. 59.
46. *WN*, I, p. 61.
47. *WN*, I, p. 54.
48. *WN*, I, p. 55. Italics mine.
49. *WN*, I, p. 351. See also II, p. 19. Note that Smith is clearly thinking of industrial profit, which is qualitatively as well as quantitatively different from mercantile profit: the latter is merely 'the gain from buying cheap and selling dear', while the former appears to be a clear deduction from the value added by labour. That surplus bears some proportion to the stock accumulated beforehand by the capitalist, who is thus more than a mere entrepreneur: he possesses the factor of capital and makes use of it. See R. Meek. 'Adam Smith and the Classical Theory of Profit', *loc. cit.* This does not, of course, mean that Smith ignored mercantile profit: see, for example, *WN*, I, pp. 294-5.
50. *WN*, I. p. 54. Nor are the workers unaware of 'the great profit which the masters make by *their* work'. (*WN*, I, p. 75. Italics mine.) See also I, pp. 60, 164; and the example in 'Early Draft', p. 331.
51. *WN*, I, p. 353.
52. *WN*, I, p. 73. See also pp. 88, 364.
53. Perhaps this is what Smith, ever practical and pragmatic, had in mind when he wrote: 'This original state of things, in which the labourer enjoyed the whole produce of his own labour, could not last beyond the first introduction of the appropriation of land and the accumulation of stock. It was at an end, therefore, long before the most considerable improvements were made in the productive powers of labour, and it would be to no purpose to trace further what might have been its effects upon the recompence or wages of

labour.' (*WN*, I, p. 73.)
54. *WN*, I, p. 276.
55. The Earl of Lauderdale, *An Inquiry into the Nature and Origin of Public Wealth* (Edinburgh: Arch. Constable and Co., and T.N. Longman and O. Rees, 1804), p. 155. See also pp. 117-9, 169-70; and the views of John Millar, in *Historical View*, vol. IV, quoted in Lehmann, *John Millar of Glasgow*, pp. 333-4.
56. P. Douglas, *op. cit.*, pp. 98, 77.
57. i.e. accumulated labour.
58. M. Bowley, *Nassau Senior and Classical Economics* (London: Allen and Unwin, 1937), p. 138.
59. See Section IV of this chapter.
60. *WN*, I, p. 292. See also pp. 96-7, 269.
61. *WN*, II, p. 272.
62. *WN*, I, p. 170. See also p. 298.
63. See Chapter 7, Section II.
64. *WN*, I, p. 55.
65. *WN*, I, p. 54.
66. *WN*, I, p. 54.
67. *WN*, I, p. 54.
68. *WN*, I, p. 123.
69. *WN*, I, p. 120.
70. *WN*, II, p. 374.
71. *WN*, I, p. 124. See also p. 171.
72. *WN*, II, pp. 358, 363.
73. *WN*, I. p. 128. See also p. 189; II, pp. 34, 73, 148, 277.
74. *WN*, I, pp. 62-3, 67, 111, 150, 224, 252; II, pp. 185, 366.
75. *WN*, I, p. 161.
76. *WN*, I, pp. 63-4. This passage suggests Smith was aware both of price-elasticity and income-elasticity of demand.
77. *WN*, I, p. 67. See also pp. 51, 214; II, p. 32.
78. *LJ*, p. 157. See also pp. 176-7.
79. *WN*, I. p. 193. See also pp. 209-10; II, p. 476.
80. *WN*, II, p. 31.
81. *WN*, I, p. 186.
82. *WN*, II, p. 401.
83. *WN*, I, p. 69.
84. *WN*, I, p. 65.
85. *WN*, I, p. 65.
86. *LJ* p. 180. There is no contradiction between the approach to utility in the *Lectures* and in *The Wealth of Nations*. There is, however, a difference in emphasis. In the latter book, Smith is more concerned with the long-run concept of national wealth and its rate of growth (as measured by the constant standard of labour-value), and thus with the underlying trend in the supply of goods rather than with short-run, transient, subjective, purely allocative fluctuations in price around that trend. Smith never denies the role of utility in influencing exchange-values in the market-place (indeed, his whole theory of the market mechanism presupposes flexible prices and a downward-sloping demand curve), but often his analysis is telescoped so as to concentrate on long-run static positions of equilibrium where market price and natural price coincide, i.e. where exchange-values are equal to the total cost of production of commodities. For an important exposition of this argument, see H.M. Robertson and W.L. Taylor, 'Adam Smith's Approach to the Theory of Value', *Economic Journal*, 1957.
87. Even though profits (and rents) are included in Smith's estimates of the national income, while the pay of non-productive labourers is not.

88. *WN*, II, p. 113. See also I, pp. 109-10; II, pp. 374-5.
89. *WN*, I, p. 54.
90. *WN*, II, p. 375.
91. *WN*, I, p. 102.
92. *WN*, II, pp. 127-8.
93. *WN*, I, p. 384.
94. *WN*, I, p. 385.
95. *WN*, I, p. 385.
96. *WN*, I, p. 407.
97. *WN*, I, p. 56.
98. Locke, *Second Treatise,* para. 27.
99. *WN*, I, p. 73. In the 'Early Draft', he expresses his view of rent as a transfer
    with particular clarity: 'In a Civilized Society the poor provide both for
    themselves and for the enormous luxury of their Superiors. The rent, which
    goes to support the vanity of the slothful Landlord, is all *earned* by the
    industry of the peasant. The monied man indulges himself in every sort of
    ignoble and sordid sensuality, at the expence of the merchant and the
    Tradesman, to whom he lends out his stock at interest. All the indolent and
    frivolous retainers upon a Court, are, in the same manner, fed, cloathed and
    lodged by the labour of those who pay the taxes which support them. Among
    savages, on the contrary, every individual enjoys the whole produce of his
    own industry. There are among them, no Landlords, no usurers, no tax-
    gathers.' ('Early Draft', p. 326.) Labour is not in itself an automatic claim to
    property: there are some 'who don't labour at all' and who still claim a huge
    share of the national product 'either by violence, or by the more orderly
    oppression of law' ('Early Draft', p. 327).
100. *WN*, I, p. 298.
101. *WN*, I, p. 184. See also II, p. 77.
102. *WN*, I, pp. 276-7.
103. *WN*, I, p. 56.
104. *WN*, I, p. 277.
105. *WN*, I, p. 132. See also II, p. 370.
106. For example, *WN*, I, p. 165.
107. *WN*, I, p. 162. Note Smith's tendency to personalise: he speaks of 'the farmer'
    and 'the landlord' rather than treating them merely as inanimate owners of
    inanimate inputs.
108. *WN*, II, p. 370.
109. *WN*, II, p. 370.
110. *WN*, I, p. 163.
111. *WN*, I, pp. 108, 180-6, 237.
112. *WN*, I, pp. 161-3, 193, 275.
113. *WN*, I, p. 164. See also II, pp. 85, 186.
114. *WN*, I, p. 276. See also pp. 275, 356.
115. *WN*, I, pp. 98. 105, 128; II, pp. 112-3, 383; See also G.S.L. Tucker, *Progress
    and Profits in British Economic Thought 1650-1850* (Cambridge: the
    University Press, 1960), ch. 4.
116. *WN*, I, p. 96. See also II, pp. 400-2, where he explains that if there is an
    uncompensated rise in the price of necessities, the rate of growth of the
    population will be retarded, i.e. there will be a conflict between the policy-
    aim of public revenue and the goal of a rising population.
117. *WN*, I, p. 96.
118. *WN*, I, p. 186.
119. *WN*, I, p. 402. See also p. 419.
120. *WN*, II, pp. 402-3. In passages such as this Smith appears to foreshadow Henry
    George and the Single Tax Movement.

121. *WN*, I, p. 375.
122. *WN*, I, p. 104.
123. *WN*, I, p. 106.
124. *WN*, I, p. 106.

III. The Sense of Exploitation

1. Durkheim, *The Division of Labor in Society*, p. 228.
2. Durkheim, *Moral Education*, p. 246.
3. *WN*, I, p. 36. See also pp. 65, 67, 366-7.
4. *WN*, II, p. 278. See also I, p. 489; II, pp. 108-9.
5. *WN*, I, p. 74.
6. *WN*, I, p. 75.
7. *WN*, I, p. 144.
8. *WN*, II, p. 32. See also I, pp. 140-1, 483-4; II, pp. 88, 152, 259.
9. *WN*, II, p. 173.
10. *WN*, I, p. 74.
11. *WN*, I, pp. 74-5.
12. *WN*, I, p. 154.
13. 'Early Draft', p. 335.
14. *WN*, I, p. 75.
15. *WN*, I, p. 483. See also II, pp. 31-2, 380, 411.
16. *WN*, I, p. 77. See also pp. 96, 101
17. *WN*, I, p. 93.
18. *WN*, II, p. 76. See also p. 358.
19. *WN*, I. p. 411.
20. *WN*, I. p. 414.
21. *WN*, I, p. 441.
22. *WN*, II, p. 67.
23. *WN*, I, p. 404.
24. *WN*, II, p. 232.
25. *WN*, I, p. 190.
26. *WN*, II, p. 232.
27. *WN*, II, p. 232.

IV. Employment and Standards of Living

1. *WN*, I, p. 54. See also p. 384; II, p. 186.
2. *WN*, I, p. 291.
3. *WN*, I, p. 74. See also pp. 60, 73.
4. *WN*, I, p. 127
5. *MS*, p. 236. The passage continues: 'What is the reward most proper for
   encouraging industry, prudence, and circumspection? – Success in every sort
   of business. And is it possible that in the whole of life these virtues should
   fail of attaining it? – Wealth and external honours are their proper recompence,
   and the recompence which they can seldom fail of acquiring.' A similar view
   is found in *MS*, p. 86.
6. *WN*, I, p. 397.
7. *WN*, I, p. 294. See also p. 354; II, p. 67.
8. *WN*, I, p. 136.
9. *WN*, I, pp. 77-8.
10. *WN*, I, pp. 92-3.
11. *WN*, I, pp. 297-8.
12. *WN*, I, p. 295. See also II, p. 94.
13. *WN*, I, p. 326.
14. *WN*, I, p. 494.
15. *WN*, I, p. 8.

16. *WN*, I, p. 13.
17. *WN*, II, p. 159.
18. *WN*, I, p. 326. See also II, p. 464. The distinction between circulating and fixed capital appears to be an artificial one, however, since the latter is the resultant of the former: 'All useful machines and instruments of trade are originally derived from a circulating capital, which furnishes the materials of which they are made, and the maintenance of the workmen who make them.' (*WN*, I, p. 299.) This implies that Smith believed machinery simply to be past, embodied, stored-up labour.
19. *WN*, II, p. 43.
20. *WN*, I, p. 318. See also pp. 309, 313, 459.
21. *WN*, I, p. 364. See also pp. 77, 384-5; II, pp. 197-8.
22. *WN*, I, p. 78. See also p. 475.
23. *WN*, I, p. 516. See also p. 390; II, pp. 57, 116, 118, 122-4, 126, 144.
24. *WN*, I, p. 462.
25. *WN*, II, p. 351.
26. *WN*, I, p. 479; II, p. 123.
27. *WN*, I, p. 480.
28. *WN*, I, p. 367.
29. *WN*, I, p. 165.
30. *WN*, II, pp. 127-8.
31. *WN*, I, p. 352. See also pp. 354-5, 370.
32. *WN*, I, p. 359.
33. *WN*, II, p. 198.
34. *WN*, II, p. 376.
35. *WN*, I, p. 96. See also pp. 77, 101.
36. *WN*, I, p. 277.
37. *WN*, I, p. 82.
38. *WN*, I, p. 81. See also p. 76; II, p. 402.
39. *WN*, I, pp. 80-1. See also p. 211.
40. *WN*, I, p. 264.
41. *WN*, I, pp. 228-9.
42. *WN*, I, p. 93.
43. *WN*, II, p. 76.
44. *WN*, II, p. 76.
45. *WN*, I, pp. 106-7. See also II, p. 201.
46. *WN*, I, p. 78.
47. *WN*, II, p. 77.
48. *WN*, I, p. 79.
49. *WN*, I, p. 223.
50. *WN*, I, p. 223.
51. *WN*, I, pp. 82-3.
52. *WN*, I, p. 157. Such restrictions meant that there was no national labour market and hence great fluctuation in wages and employment from parish to parish.
53. *WN*, I, pp. 137-8, 150. Long apprenticeships are unnecessary to learn requisite skills and extend the period of frictional unemployment by preventing a man displaced in one trade from moving easily into another. Similarly, the lack of education can be an obstacle to full employment, since it means that an industrial worker specialised in one trade may be incapable of exercising 'any other employment than that to which he has been bred'. (*WN*, II, p. 303.)
54. *WN*, I, pp. 90-1.
55. See E.S. Furniss, *The Position of the Laborer in a System of Nationalism* (Boston: Houghton Miflin Co., 1920).
56. *WN*, I, p. 88.

57. *WN*, I, p. 456.
58. *WN*, I, p. 89.
59. *WN*, I, p. 78. See also pp. 40, 211.
60. *WN*, I, p. 90. Note the general equilibrium formulation 'necessary effect and cause'.
61. Smith's principal concern was with *per capita* standards of living, not aggregate levels of national income, as he makes clear on the first page of *The Wealth of Nations*.
62. *WN*, II, p. 418.
63. *WN*, I, p. 359.
64. *WN*, I, p. 91. See also p. 92.
65. *WN*, I, p. 91.
66. *WN*, I, p. 91. That goal is thus more than simple adaptation to a traditional standard of living. See Weber, *The Protestant Ethic and the Spirit of Capitalism*, pp. 59-60.
67. *WN*, I, p. 91.
68. 'IA', p. 148.
69. *WN*, II, p. 105. See also pp. 29, 106, 171.
70. *WN*, I, p. 37.
71. *WN*, I, p. 113.
72. *WN*, II, p. 283.
73. See, for example, *WN*, II, pp. 265-9.
74. *WN*, II, p. 284.
75. *WN*, II, p. 232.
76. *WN*, I, pp. 251-2. This was not, however, the case with English wool because of counteracting forces. (*WN*, II, p. 171.)
77. *WN*, I, p. 269. See also p. 97.
78. *WN*, I, p. 492. Hume was equally optimistic on the question of displacement and reabsorption of labour: 'If the spirit of industry be preserved, it may easily be diverted from one branch to another; and the manufacturers of wool, for instance, be employed in linen, silk, iron, or any other commodities, for which there appears to be a demand.' (Hume, 'Of the Jealousy of Trade', in Rotwein, *op. cit.*, p. 80.)
79. *WN*, I, p. 303.
80. *WN*, I, p. 364.
81. *WN*, I, p. 304.
82. *WN*, I, p. 273.
83. *WN*, I, p. 298.
84. *WN*, I, p. 292. As is well known, Ricardo took a more pessimistic view of mechanisation and displacement of labour in the famous Chapter 31 of his *Principles of Political Economy*.
85. Hollander, *op. cit.*, Ch. 7, esp. pp. 219-26.
86. *WN*, I, p. 292. See also II, pp. 271-2.
87. *WN*, I, p. 269. See also pp. 250, 273.

CHAPTER 7. THE STATE

Introduction

1. *WN*, II, pp. 49-50. See also pp. 194-5.
2. *WN*, I, p. 475,
3. Montesquieu, *Persian Letters*, p. 57.
4. A. Pope, *An Essay on Man*, Epistle Three, lines 317-8.
5. *WN*, I, p. 402. See also p. 157.
6. *WN*, II, p. 208. See also p. 121.

7. 'Early Draft', p. 346.
8. *MS*, p. 126. See also p. 235.
9. *MS*, p. 239.
10. *MS*, p. 240. See also pp. 187-8.
11. *MS*, p. 238.

I. Balance of Interest and Balance of Power

1. *WN*, II, p. 171.
2. *WN*, II, p. 236. See also *LJ*, p. 15.
3. *WN*, I, p. 190.
4. *WN*, I, p. 136.
5. 'Though the earth and all inferior creatures be common to all men, yet every man has a *property* in his own *person*. This nobody has any right to but himself. The *labour* of his body and the *work* of his hands, we may say, are properly his. Whatsoever, then, he removes out of the state that nature hath provided and left it in, he hath mixed his labour with it, and joined to it something that is his own, and thereby makes it his property.' (Locke, *Second Treatise*, para. 27.)
6. *LJ*, pp. 107, 108.
7. *LJ*, p. 107.
8. See *MS*, pp. 260-5, 331-2.
9. *WN*, I, p. 219.
10. For example, *WN*, I, pp. 276, 410; II, pp. 338, 356.
11. *WN*, II, p. 22.
12. *WN*, I, p. 278.
13. *WN*, II, p. 180.
14. *WN*, II, p. 129. See also I, p. 493; II, p. 160.
15. 'Early Draft', p. 352.
16. *WN*, II, p. 159.
17. *WN*, II, p. 161.
18. *WN*, I, pp. 158-9.
19. *WN*, I, p. 110.
20. *WN*, I, pp. 489-90. He attacks Colbert's belief in the virtues of direction and organisation in *WN*, II, p. 183.
21. *WN*, II, pp. 160, 165.
22. *WN*, II, p. 165. See also pp. 179-80.
23. *WN*, II, p. 417.
24. *WN*, I, p. 258.
25. *WN*, II, p. 62.
26. *WN*, II, p. 251.
27. *WN*, I, pp. 139-40.
28. *WN*, I, p. 140.
29. *MS*, p. 502.
30. *WN*, I, p. 522.
31. *LJ*, p. 15.
32. *WN*, II, p. 140.
33. Locke, *Second Treatise*, para. 143.
34. See *The Spirit of the Laws*, Book 11, ch. 6.
35. Montesquieu, *The Spirit of the Laws*, trans. T. Nugent and ed. by F. Neumann (New York: Hafner Publishing Company, 1966), vol. I, pp. 150, 152.
36. *WN*, II, p. 244; *LJ*, p. 45.
37. *LJ*, p. 46.
38. *LJ*, p. 51.
39. *LJ*, p. 45.

40. *WN*, II, p. 98.
41. *WN*, II, p. 97. See also p. 471.
42. *WN*, II, pp. 97-8.
43. *WN*, II, p. 98.
44. *WN*, II, p. 98.
45. *WN*, II, pp. 83, 98-9.
46. *WN*, II, p. 439.
47. *WN*, II, 439-40. See also I, p. 418.
48. *WN*, II, p. 141.
49. *MS*, p. 338.
50. *MS*, p. 358.
51. *MS*, pp. 338-9. See also *WN*, II, pp. 136-7, 259.
52. *MS*, p. 339.
53. *MS*, p. 341.
54. *MS*, p. 343.
55. *WN*, I, p. 518.
56. *WN*, I, p. 519.
57. *WN*, I, p. 519.
58. *WN*, I, p. 278.
59. *WN*, I, p. 278.
60. *WN*, II, p. 343. See also pp. 81, 88, 154.
61. See Chapter 5.
62. *WN*, II, p. 342.
63. *WN*, II, p. 137; *MS*, p. 78.
64. *WN*, II, p. 342.
65. *LJ*, p. 54.
66. *WN*, I, p. 277.
67. *WN*, II, p. 299.
68. *WN*, II, p. 331.
69. *LJ*, p. 28. See also p. 262.
70. *WN*, I, p. 157.
71. *MS*, p. 372. See also *WN*, II, pp. 232-3, 235.
72. *MS*, p. 367.
73. *MS*, p. 371. See also *MS*, pp. 65, 381.
74. *WN*, I, p. 277. Or elsewhere: 'The servant who shapes his work according to the pattern which his master prescribes to him, will shape his life too according to the example he sets him.' (*WN*, II, p. 128.) See also I, p. 494.
75. *WN*, II, p. 303.
76. *WN*, II, p. 303. If the minds of the masses have decayed so far as to make political democracy undesirable, it is hard to see why Smith still insists on the possibility of moral democracy and the universal diffusion of moral values throughout the populace. As we pointed out in Chapter 3, insensitivity can be a serious threat to sympathy and propriety.
77. *LJ*, pp. 20, 261-2.
78. A view of degeneration and mental decay also shared by Adam Ferguson. See the *Essay*, p. 186.
79. *MS*, p. 371.
80. See W.L. Taylor, *Francis Hucheson and David Hume as Predecessors of Adam Smith* (Durham, North Carolina: Duke University Press, 1965), ch. 7.
81. For example: 'To expect, indeed, that the freedom of trade should ever be entirely restored in Great Britain, is as absurd as to expect that an Oceana or Utopia should ever be established in it.' (*WN*, I, p. 493.) See also *WN*, II, p. 472.
82. *WN*, I, p. 408.
83. *MS*, p. 266.

84. *LJ*, pp. 70, 72.
85. *MS*, p. 340.
86. *LJ*, p. 69.
87. *WN*, II, p. 78.
88. *WN*, II, p. 229.
89. *WN*, II, p. 229.
90. Elsewhere, as we saw in Chapter 5, Smith gives a similar account of the banding together of different classes with common interests. In pastoral society, the owners of small flocks are eager to defend magnates with large flocks: 'Men of inferior wealth combine to defend those of superior wealth in the possession of their property, in order that men of superior wealth may combine to defend them in the possession of theirs.' (*WN*, II, p. 236.) See also II, p. 252.
91. *MS*, p. 219.
92. *WN*, I, p. 490.
93. *WN*, II, p. 137. See also pp. 143-4.
94. *WN*, II, p. 136.
95. *WN*, II, p. 138
96. *MS*, p. 341.
97. *WN*, II, p. 131. It is easy to forget how much bribery, corruption, nepotism and patronage there was in British political life at the time Smith was writing. His contemporary, Lord Kames, gives this account of how some constituencies selected their member of parliament: 'The greatest evil of all respects the choice of their representatives in parliament. A habit of riot and intemperance, makes them fit subjects to be corrupted by every adventurer who is willing to lay out money for purchasing a seat in parliament. Hence the infamous practice of bribery at elections, which tends not only to corrupt the whole mass of the people, but, which is still more dreadful, tends to fill the House of Commons with men of dissolute manners, void of probity and honour.' Quoted in Lehmann, *Henry Home, Lord Kames*, p. 120.
98. *WN*, II, p. 484. See also p. 297. In a letter to Lord Fitzmaurice dated 21 February 1759 Smith wrote: 'I hear there is no faction in parliament, which I am glad of. For tho' a little faction now and then gives spirit to the nation the continuance of it obstructs all public business and puts it out of the power of the best Minister to do much good.' Quoted in Scott, *Adam Smith as Student and Professor*, p. 241.
99. *MS*, p. 73.
100. *WN*, II, p. 155.
101. *WN*, II, p. 234. The Earl of Buchan, said that Smith 'approached to republicanism in his political principles . . . hereditary succession in the chief magistrate being necessary only to prevent the commonwealth from being shaken by ambition, or absolute dominion introduced by the consequences of contending factions.' Quoted in Rae, *op. cit.*, p. 124.
102. *MS*, p. 331. See also *LJ*, p. 69.
103. *MS*, p. 342. In any case, the monarchy already existed, and it would have been seditious to advocate revolution to overthrow it. Smith may have disguised his true feelings on this (as possibly his true view on the existence of God) for the sake of convenience, but it is in our view extremely unlikely that he was a radical (as some writers, immediately after 1789, seemed to think). Nor is there any reason to think liberalism in economics always leads to philosophical radicalism in politics, as the example of Bentham's early writings shows.
104. *MS*, p. 340.
105. *WN*, II, p. 321.

106. *WN*, II, p. 238.
107. *LJ*, p. 69.

II. The Case Against the State

1. *WN*, I, p. 455.
2. *WN*, II, p. 11. See also pp. 3, 21.
3. *LJ*, p. 181.
4. *WN*, II, p. 11. Compare this with the effects in France of a tax levied directly on the farmer's capital: I, p. 417.
5. *WN*, II, p. 14.
6. *WN*, II, p. 19.
7. *WN*, II, p. 27.
8. *WN*, II, p. 25.
9. *WN*, II, p. 38.
10. *WN*, II, p. 33.
11. *WN*, I, p. 313. See also pp. 306, 308, 389, 451, 454, 466, 473.
12. *WN*, II, p. 109. Trade treaties have been used to give foreign merchants the same right to demand monopoly prices from the British consumer: *WN*, I, pp. 53-4.
13. *WN*, II, p. 259. See also pp. 180, 394, 401-3, 401-3, 429; 476, I, pp. 172, 176-7.
14. *WN*, II, p. 278.
15. *WN*, II, pp. 112-13, *LJ*, p. 246.
16. *WN*, II, p. 116.
17. *WN*, I, p. 87. See also pp. 136, 144, 493.
18. *WN*, I, p. 138. See also p. 259.
19. *WN*, II, p. 285.
20. *WN*, I, p. 136.
21. See West, *Adam Smith*, pp. 159-62.
22. *WN*, I, p. 519.
23. *WN*, II, p. 119.
24. For example, English woollens manufacturers secured an export prohibition on raw wool from England. The result was catastrophic: the price of English wool fell with the limitation of the market and the wool trade was harmed. Such 'violence and artifice' victimises one trade for the benefit of another. (*WN*, I, p. 256, II, pp. 165-72.) Another example is the diversion of capital by monopolies to trades where profits are maintained artificially high. Interest rates are kept unnaturally high, and, as rent is inversely related to the rate of interest, rents and land prices are kept unnaturally low. The capitalist gains and the landlord loses. (*WN*, II, p. 127.) Yet all men have equal rights to happiness.
25. *WN*, II, p. 86.
26. *WN*, I, p. 468.
27. *WN*, II, p. 443.
28. *WN*, I, p. 363.
29. *WN*, I, p. 367.
30. *WN*, I, p. 358.
31. *MS*, p. 46.
32. *WN*, I, p. 367.
33. *WN*, I, p. 352.
34. *WN*, I, p. 352. See also *LJ*, p. 208.
35. *WN*, I, p. 352.
36. *WN*, II, p. 343. See also p. 247.
37. *WN*, II, p. 241.
38. *WN*, II, p. 347.
39. *WN*, II, p. 357.

40. *WN*, II, p. 347.
41. *WN*, II, p. 364.
42. 'Whatever keeps down the produce of the land below what it would otherwise rise to, keeps down the revenue of the great body of the people, still more than it does that of the proprietors of land.' (*WN*, II, p. 348.)
43. *WN*, II, p. 364.
44. *WN*, II, p. 349.
45. *WN*, II, p. 269.
46. *WN*, II, p. 267.
47. *WN*, II, p. 264.
48. *WN*, II, p. 268.
49. *WN*, II, pp. 276-8. See also pp. 147, 274-5, 365-6.
50. *WN*, II, pp. 264-5.
51. *WN*, II, p. 158.
52. *WN*, II, p. 157. Hume makes a similar point in a letter to Montesquieu dated 10 April 1749, where he praises tax-farmers since such men experience no conflict between duty and interest: 'There are a hundred thousand tricks and devices for dealing with fraud on the part of individuals, and which are suggested to the *fermiers* by self-interest, and which the government collectors would never have dreamed of.' Reprinted in Rotwein, *op. cit.*, p. 187.
53. *WN*, II, p. 278.
54. *WN*, II, p. 265. See also pp. 269-70.
55. *WN*, II, p. 98.
56. *WN*, II, p. 99.
57. *WN*, II, pp. 154-8.
58. *WN*, II, p. 351. See also I, p. 422, and 'Early Draft', p. 332, where he complains that the 'licensed insolence of the officers of revenue' is 'frequently more vexatious than all the taxes which they levey'.
59. *WN*, II, p. 285.
60. *WN*, II, p. 396. Such a tax thus contravenes Smith's second maxim of taxation, which states that taxes should be of certain value and not arbitrary in their incidence. See *WN*, II, p. 350.
61. *WN*, II, p. 285.
62. *WN*, II, p. 285.
63. *WN*, II, p. 285.
64. *WN*, I, p. 497.
65. *WN*, II, p. 172. See also p. 176.
66. *WN*, II, p. 429.
67. *WN*, II, p. 60. Other examples of evasion are of the law prohibiting interest (I, p. 107) or laws to prevent restrictive practices by employers (I, p. 144).
68. *WN*, II, p. 375. See also I, pp. 444-5.
69. *MS*, p. 343. See also p. 239; *WN*, I, p. 457.
70. *WN*, II, p. 208.
71. *WN*, II, p. 3.
72. *WN*, II, p. 146.
73. *WN*, II, p. 18.
74. *WN*, II, p. 208.
75. *WN*, II, p. 38. See also I, pp. 144-5, 157, 167.
76. *WN*, I, p. 396.
77. *WN*, I, p. 396.
78. *WN*, I, pp. 477-8.
79. *WN*, I, p. 394.
80. *WN*, II, p. 146.
81. *WN*, II, pp. 145-6.
82. *WN*, II, pp. 271-2.

83. *WN*, II, pp. 30-3.
84. *WN*, II, p. 41.
85. *WN*, I, p. 475.
86. *WN*, I, pp. 90-1.
87. *WN*, II, p. 183.
88. *WN*, II, p. 190. See also I, pp. 63, 70, 111, 150.
89. *WN*, II, p. 190. Dugald Stewart quotes Smith as having written in 1755 that 'Projectors disturb nature in the course of her operations in human affairs; and it requires no more than to let her alone and give her fair play in the pursuit of her ends, that she may establish her own designs . . . Little else is requisite to carry a state to the highest degree of opulence from the lowest barbarism, but peace, easy taxes, and a tolerable administration of justice.' (Stewart, in Smith, *op. cit.*, p. lxxxi.) Smith also recommended, however, that the process of liberalisation should be gradual: the sudden institution of free trade at a stroke would be inhumane, since it would cause upset and dislocation in many sectors of the economy. (*WN*, I, p. 491.)
90. *WN*, II, p. 32. See also I, p. 383.
91. See, for example, *WN*, I, pp. 74-5, 140-1, 483-4; *WN*, II, pp. 88, 173.
92. *WN*, II, p. 22.
93. *WN*, I, p. 246.
94. See *WN*, I, pp. 161. 410.
95. *WN*, I, p. 439.
96. *WN*, I, p. 298; II, p. 357.
97. *WN*, II, p. 284.
98. *WN*, II, p. 283.

III. The Scope for Intervention

1. *WN*, II, pp. 208-9.
2. *WN*, I, p. 462.
3. *WN*, I, p. 487.
4. *WN*, I, p. 487.
5. *WN*, II, p. 28.
6. *WN*, II, p. 220. See also p. 231.
7. *WN*, II, pp. 214, 219, 227, 307.
8. *LJ*, p. 257; *WN*, II, p. 219.
9. *WN*, II, p. 221.
10. *LJ*, p. 258.
11. *LJ*, p. 258.
12. *WN*, II, p. 209.
13. *WN*, II, p. 49. See also I, pp. 264, 328; II, pp. 178, 445; *MS*, p. 502.
14. *WN*, I, p. 31; II, pp. 125, 467; *LJ*, p. 189.
15. *WN*, II, p. 125.
16. *WN*, II, p. 244. It is worthwhile noting that Smith does not include poor-relief among the activities in which the state ought to indulge: there would simply not be much need for poor-relief in a fully-employed economy with minimal restrictions on geographical and occupational mobility. In other words, the invisible hand of self-interest automatically causes the rich to extend charity to the poor by giving them employment, if only the state does not prevent them from dispensing such charity. See *MS*, pp. 264-5.
17. *WN*, II, p. 340.
18. *WN*, II, p. 304.
19. *WN*, I, p. 150.
20. For example, *WN*, I, pp. 148-9; II, pp. 283, 306. Smith was thus a forerunner of present-day schemes for education vouchers.
21. *WN*, II, p. 246.

22. *WN*, II, p. 339.
23. *WN*, II, p. 246.
24. *WN*, II, pp. 252-3.
25. *WN*, II, p. 350.
26. *WN*, II, p. 247. See also p.251.
27. *WN*, II, pp. 247-8. The implication seems to be that, at least in the operation of turnpikes, the state bureaucrat is marginally less inefficient than the corporate bureaucrat or even the private entrepreneur.
28. *WN*, II, p. 248. Clearly, even the 'prudent man' can yield to temptation in a non-competitive situation, and behave in a manner that the impartial spectator might find reprehensible.
29. This is brought out particularly clearly in the following: J. Viner, 'Adam Smith and Laissez-Faire', in J.M. Clark *et. al., Adam Smith 1776-1926;* and L. Robbins, *The Theory of Economic Policy in English Classical Political Economy* (London: Macmillan & Co. Ltd, 1953).
30. *WN*, I, pp. 344-5.
31. *WN*, I, pp. 320, 350.
32. *WN*, I, p. 379.
33. *WN*, II, p. 357.
34. *WN*, II, p. 356.
35. *WN*, II, p. 357.
36. *WN*, II, p. 368.
37. *WN*, II, p. 368.
38. *WN*, II, p. 246. See also p. 250.
39. *WN*, II, pp. 342-3. See also p. 246.
40. *WN*, II, p. 377.
41. *WN*, II, pp, 342, 344.
42. *WN*, II, p. 342.

ABBREVIATIONS OF WORKS BY ADAM SMITH

WN I, II	*The Wealth of Nations* (1776), ed. by Edwin Cannan (London. Methuen, 1961), Volumes I and II.
MS	*The Theory of Moral Sentiments* (1759) (New York: Augustuc M. Kelley, 1966).
LJ	*Lectures on Justice, Police, Revenue and Arms* (lectures given in 1763), ed. by Edwin Cannan Oxford: Clarendon Press, 1896).
LRBL	*Lectures on Rhetoric and Belles Lettres* (lectures given in 1762-3), ed. by John M. Lothian London: Thomas Nelson and Sons Ltd, 1963).
'HA'	'The History of Astronomy', in *Essays on Philosophical Subjects* (1795), reprinted in J. Ralph Lindgren (ed.), *The Early Writings of Adam Smith* (New York: Augustus M. Kelley, 1967).
'HAP'	'The History of the Ancient Physics', *ibid.*
'ALM'	'The History of the Ancient Logics and Metaphysics', *ibid.*
'IA'	'The Imitative Arts', *ibid.*
'AEIV'	'Of the Affinity Between Certain English and Italian Verses', *ibid.*
'ES'	'Of the External Senses', *ibid.*
'Considerations'	'Considerations Concerning the First Formation of Languages', *ibid.*
'A Letter'	'A Letter to the Authors of the *Edinburgh Review*', *ibid.*
'Early Draft'	'An Early Draft of Part of *The Wealth of Nations*' (probably written about 1763), in W.R. Scott, *Adam Smith as Student and Professor* (Glasgow: University of Glasgow, 1937).

FURTHER READING

The secondary literature on Adam Smith is vast and not always illuminating. The following, however, while no substitute for reading the originals, are particularly helpful:

T.D. Campbell, *Adam Smith's Science of Morals* (London: George Allen and Unwin Ltd, 1971).

S. Hollander, *The Economics of Adam Smith* (London: Heinemann, 1973).

J.R. Lindgren, *The Social Philosophy of Adam Smith* (The Hague: Martinus Nijhoff, 1973).

R.L. Meek, 'Adam Smith and the Classical Theory of Profit', in *Economics and Ideology* (London: Chapman and Hall Ltd, 1967).

G.R. Morrow, *The Ethical and Economic Theories of Adam Smith* (1923) (New York: Augustus M. Kelley, 1969).

H.M. Robertson and W.L. Taylor, 'Adam Smith's Approach to the Theory of Value', *Economic Journal*, June, 1957.

N. Rosenberg, 'Some Institutional Aspects of the *Wealth of Nations*', *Journal of Political Economy*, December 1960.

———, 'Adam Smith on the Division of Labour: Two Views or One?' *Economica*, May 1965.

E.G. West, 'Adam Smith's Two Views of the Division of Labour', *Economica*, February 1964.

———, 'The Political Economy of Alienation: Karl Marx and Adam Smith', *Oxford Economic Papers*, March 1969.

INDEX

Admiration, 31, 65
Ambition, 110-11, 116-20
America, 17, 101, 162, 181, 187, 209, 218, 250
Aristotle, 42

Bagehot, W., 138
Balance of powers, 162-3, 194, 198-211
Bank of England, 200
Barber, W.J., 166
Benevolence, 70-1, 80-5
Bengal, 136, 186
Bentham, J., 17-18, 227
Berger, P.L., 73, 104
Bergson, H., 21, 54
Berkeley, G., 23-4
Bowley, M., 169
Buffier, Father, 49
Bureaucracy, 89-90, 195, 216-19, 226
Burrow, J., 11
Businessmen, 72-3, 93-8, 205, 210

Campbell, T.D., 85
Capital, 100-1, 146-7, 182-93
China, 84, 121, 136, 186-7
Cicero, 55, 59
Colbert, M., 200, 264
Commons, House of, 14, 134, 202
Comte, A., 11, 20

Defence, 223-4
Demosthenes, 55, 59
Descartes, R., 22, 24, 32, 69
Distribution, 168-78
Division of labour, 90-1, 143, 148-56, 206-7
Douglas, P., 165, 169
Durkheim, E., 11, 66, 69-70, 86-7, 105, 107-8, 119-20, 141, 145, 178, 240-1, 254-5

Education, 135, 155-61, 256, 269
External phenomena, 22-8

Ferguson, A., 71, 77, 95, 101, 108-9, 119, 136, 153, 243, 246, 254
Feudalism, 92-3, 100, 114-15, 124-7, 131-3

Galbraith, J.K., 12, 14, 34, 106, 116, 245

Glasgow, 12, 16, 36

Hampson, N., 12, 72
Hegel, G.W.F., 65, 136
Helvetius, C.A., 158
Herodotus, 46
Historicism, 12, 135-6, 229
Hobbes, T., 67, 147-8, 179, 250
Holland, 98-100, 143, 173, 202-3, 205-6, 212, 224, 243
Hollander, S., 192, 254
Hume, D., 22-3, 26, 59, 61-3, 118-19, 146-7, 207, 236, 243, 251, 256, 263, 268
Hunting, 91, 129-30
Hutcheson, F., 45, 48, 71, 77, 81, 207

Invention, 31-2, 150-3, 253-4
Ireland, 129

Justice, 80-1, 134, 224, 249

Kames, Lord (Henry Home), 146, 153, 236, 248, 266
Kepler, J., 33, 44-5
Keynes, J.M. 96-7, 184
Kirkcaldy, 16, 36
Kolakowski, L., 15

Laissez-faire, 51, 115, 135, 194-5, 219-23, 269
Language, 33, 39, 47, 50, 56-7
Lauderdale, Earl of, 169
Law, 60-1, 90
Locke, J., 22-4, 40, 62, 158, 174, 198, 201-2, 208, 255, 264
Lukács, G., 17

Macfie, A.L., 245
Machiavelli, 58, 136
Macpherson, C.B., 148
Malinowski, B., 245
Mandeville, B., 40, 81, 195
Marshall, A., 9, 95, 242, 245
Marx, K., 17, 96-7, 148, 169, 245, 254
Meek, R., 165
Mercantilism, 17, 55, 102, 146, 184, 188, 194-5, 199-200, 211-14
Mill, J., 156
Mill, J.S., 9, 20

273